Yachtsn

GW00786648

ACKNOWLEDGEMENTS

So many people, firms and Government departments have helped me to compile this dictionary that it is impossible to mention them all. My especial thanks go to the people who have worked on the other seven languages:

French: Mme L. van de Wiele
German: Herr Otto Albrecht Ernst and Herr Ludwig Dinklage
Dutch: Ir. M. F. Gunning
Danish: Redaktør G. Strømberg
Italian: Signor Adolfo Grill
Spanish: Contralmirante Julio Guillen and Duque de Arion
Portuguese: Antonio and Patricia Potier

In addition the Hydrographic and Meteorological Departments of the United Kingdom, France, Belgium, Germany, Holland, Denmark, Norway, Sweden, Italy and Spain have provided me with information about buoyage and meteorology. My thanks go, too, to the British Motor Corporation, Messrs International Paints, Volvo, C.A.V. and Solex, and the very many others who have given advice, information and encouragement. Last, but not least, I would like to acknowledge my debt of gratitude to my mother, Helen Tobin, who introduced me to the fun of 'messing about in boats'.

Published by Adlard Coles Nautical
an imprint of A & C Black (Publishers) Ltd
35 Bedford Row, London WC1R 4JH

©Barbara Webb 1965, 1977, 1983
First edition 1965, Reprinted 1969
Second edition 1977, Reprinted 1978
Third edition 1983
Reprinted 1985, 1988, 1989, 1991, 1994

ISBN 0 7136 3480 4

Apart from any fair dealing for the purposes of research or private study, or criticism or review, as permitted under the Copyright, Designs and Patents Act, 1988, this publication may be reproduced, stored or transmitted, in any forms or by any means, only with the prior permission in writing of the publishers, or in the case of reprographic reproduction in accordance with the terms of licences issued by the Copyright Licensing Agency. Inquiries concerning reproduction outside those terms should be sent to the publishers at the address above.

A CIP catalogue record for this book is available from the British Library.

Printed in Great Britain by
The Cromwell Press, Melksham, Wiltshire.

Barbara Webb

Yachtsman's 8 Language Dictionary

Third Edition

English
French
German
Dutch
Danish
Italian
Spanish
Portuguese

ADLARD COLES NAUTICAL
London

INTRODUCTION   ENGLISH

The same order of arrangement of the languages has been used throughout: English, French, German, Dutch, Danish, Italian, Spanish and Portuguese. All the words that are illustrated are printed in italics.

The aim has been to translate a noun by a noun, a verb by a verb, etc, but this has not always proved possible. Whilst every care has been taken to ensure the accuracy of the equivalents given, yachting is a live sport and the language grows and changes rapidly. The author would be very pleased to receive comments, criticisms and suggestions.

The reader's attention is drawn to the fact that, as shown on pp. 86 and 144, the German and Dutch definitions of port and starboard tack are the opposite to those of every other country.

EINLEITUNG   DEUTSCH

In diesem Wörterbuch sind die acht Sprachen Englisch, Französisch, Deutsch, Holländisch, Dänisch, Italienisch, Spanisch und Portugiesisch der Reihenfolge nach zusammengestellt. Die in einer Zeichnung verdeutlichten Begriffe sind kursiv gedruckt.

Es war nicht immer möglich, ein Substantiv in ein Substantiv, ein Verb in ein Verb usw. zu übersetzen. Die Verfasserin war jedoch bemüht, eine genaue Übersetzung zu erzielen oder zumindest ein Äquivalent zu finden. Der Wassersport ist jedoch ein lebender Sport, dessen Fachsprache sich ständig weiterentwickelt. Kommentare, Kritik und Vorschläge des Lesers sind deshalb willkommen.

Der Leser sei besonders darauf hingewiesen, daß die deutsche und holländische Bezeichnung für Steuerbordbug und Backbordbug das Gegenteil von jener in den anderen Ländern bedeutet (siehe Seite 86 und 144).

INTRODUCTION   FRANÇAIS

Dans tout le texte, nous avons pris soin de respecter l'ordre des langages: anglais, français, allemand, néerlandais, danois, italien espagnol, portugais. Tous les mots illustrés sont en italique.

Notre but a été de traduire partout où c'était possible un substantif par un substantif, un verbe par un verbe, etc. La plus grande attention a été accordée à l'exactitude des traductions ou équivalents. Mais le yachting est un sport vivant dont le jargon spécialisé évolue constamment. Tous commentaires, critiques ou suggestions seront donc reçus avec reconnaissance.

Nous attirons l'attention du lecteur sur le fait que l'acception néerlandaise et allemande de 'tribord et bâbord amures' est à l'opposé de celle de tous les autres pays (voir pp. 86 et 144).

INLEIDING   NEDERLANDS

Bij het samenstellen van dit woordenboek is de hand gehouden aan de identieke wijze van rangschikking met betrekking tot Engels, Frans, Duits, Nederlands, Deens, Italiaans, Spaans en Portugees In deze volgorde. Die woorden die schuingedrukt zijn, zijn geïllustreerd.

Zoveel mogelijk is getracht om een naamwoord met een naamwoord te vertalen, en een werkwoord met een werkwoord enz.: het bleek echter dat dit niet altijd mogelijk was. Ofschoon alle voorzorgen zijn genomen om de juistheid van de gegeven vertalingen te verzekeren, moet men er rekening mee houden dat de zeilsport een levende sport is én dat de taal snel groeit en verandert. Het zou de schrijfster genoegen doen opmerkingen, kritiek en ideeën te ontvangen.

De aandacht van de lezer is erop gevestigd dat de Duitse en Nederlandse definities van bak- en stuurboordsboeg de tegenovergestelde zijn van die van elk ander land (zie pagina 86 en 144).

FORORD DANSK

De forskellige sprog er placeret i samme rækkefølge: engelsk, fransk, tysk, hollandsk, dansk, italiensk, spansk, portugisisk. Teksten under alle illustrerede ord er kursiveret.

Hensigten har været, at oversætte et navneord til et navneord, og et verbum til et verbum, hvilket ikke altid kunne gennemføres. Trods den største omhu har det været umuligt at give alle ord den nøjagtigste betydning. Yachting er en levende sport, sproget vokser og veksler hurtigt.

Læsernes opmærksomhed henledes på den kendsgerning, at de tyske og hollandske definitioner af styrbord- og bagbord-halse, side 86 og 144, er den modsatte af de seks andre landes.

Kommentarer, kritik, råd og vink er meget velkommen.

PREFAZIONE ITALIANO

In tutto il testo è stato seguito lo stesso ordine di successione delle lingue e cioè: Inglese, francese, tedesco, olandese, danese, italiano, spagnolo e portoghese. Tutte le parole che hanno riferimento nelle illustrazioni sono stampate in corsivo.

Lo scopo era quello di tradurre letteralmente i sostantivi con i sostantivi, i verbi con i verbi e così via, purtroppo, però, si è visto che questo non lo si è potato sempre ottenere perchè, anche se si è posta ogni cura nella traduzione, lo yachting è uno sport vivo ed il relativo linguaggio è in continua evoluzione. L'autore sarà quindi ben felice di ricevere osservazioni, critiche e consigli.

Il lettore noti come le definizioni in tedesco e olandese di mure a sinistra e a dritta (vedi pag. 86 e 144) sono il contrario di quelle di tutti gli altri paesi.

INTRODUCCIÓN ESPAÑOL

En toda la obra hemos seguido el mismo orden de idiomas, a decir: Inglés, Francés, Alemán, Holandes, Danés, Italiano, Español y Portugués.

Todas las palabras a las que corresponde una ilustración, están impresas en letra bastardilla.

Hemos intentado traducir un adjetivo por un adjetivo, un verbo por un verbo, pero esto no siempre ha sido posible.

Aunque hemos tomado todas las precauciones posibles para asegurar la exactitud de los términos equivalentes dados, hay que tener en cuenta que la navegación es un deporte vivo y que la lengua crece y cambia con rapidez.

El autor agradecería mucho recibir comentarios, críticas y sugerencias. Llamamos especialmente la atención al lector del hecho, como puede verse en las pgs. 86 y 144, que las definiciones alemana y holandesa de amurado a babor y a estribor son las totalmente opuestas a todos los demás idiomas.

INTRODUÇÃO PORTUGUÊS

Utilizou-se a mesma ordenação de línguas em todo o livro: Inglês, Francês, Alemão, Holandês, Dinamarquês, Italiano, Espanhol e Português. Todas as palavras acompanhados de figura estão impressas em itálico.

O fim em vista foi de traduzir um nome próprio por um nome próprio, um verbo por um verbo etc:, mas nem sempre foi possível. Apesar de ter havido o máximo cuidado quanto à exactidão dos equivalentes dados, sendo o Yachting um desporto em evolução a sua linguagem aumenta e modifica-se rápidamente. O Autor estará sempre pronto a aceitar comentários, críticas e sugestões.

Chama-se a atenção dos leitores para o facto, como está indicado nas páginas 86 e 144, das definições de bombordo e estibordo em Alemão e Holandês serem contrárias às dos outros Países.

LIST OF CONTENTS

TABLE DES MATIERES

INHALTSVERZEICHNIS

INHOUDSOPGAVE

INDHOLDSFORTEGNELSE DANSK

INDICE DELLA MATERIA

ITALIANO

11

LISTA DE MATERIAS

CONTEÚDO

ENGLISH
Yachts and rigs
A masthead cutter
B bermudian sloop
C gaff cutter
D bermudian yawl
E bermudian ketch
F staysail schooner

1 mainsail
2 topsail
3 mizzen
4 main staysail
5 fisherman staysail
6 mizzen staysail
7 jib
8 genoa

9 staysail
10 genoa staysail
11 brig
12 barque
13 cruiser
14 racer
15 ocean racer
16 racing dinghy

FRANÇAIS
Yachts et leur gréement
A cotre en tête de mât
B sloop bermudien
C cotre franc, aurique
D yawl bermudien
E ketch bermudien
F goélette à voile d'étai
1 grand'voile
2 flèche
3 (E) artimon
3 (D) tape-cul
4 grand'voile d'étai
5 voile d'étai de flèche
6 foc ou voile d'étai
   d'artimon
7 foc
8 génois
9 trinquette
10 foc ballon
11 brick
12 barque
13 bateau de croisière
14 bateau de course
15 bateau de course-
   croisière
16 dériveur de course

DEUTSCH
Yachten und Takelagen
A Kutter mit Hochtakelung
B Slup
C Gaffelkutter
D Yawl
E Ketsch
F Stagsegelschoner
1 Großsegel
2 Toppsegel
3 (E) Besan
3 (D) Treiber
4 Großstagsegel
5 Fischermann-Stagsegel
6 Besanstagsegel
7 Fock
7 (A & C) Klüver
8 Genua, Kreuzballon
9 Stagsegel
10 Raumballon
11 Brigg
12 Bark
13 Fahrtenyacht
14 Rennyacht
15 Hochseerennyacht
16 Rennjolle

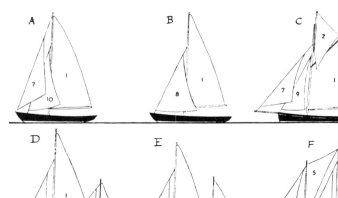

NEDERLANDS	DANSK	ITALIANO	ESPAÑOL	PORTUGUÊS
Jachten en tuigen	**Yachts og rigning**	**Yachts e attrezzature**	**Yates y aparejos**	**Iates de recreio e suas armações**
A masttop getuigde kotter	A mastetop-rig	A cutter con fiocco in testa d'albero	A balandra de mastelero	A cuter
B torengetuigde sloep	B Bermuda slup	B sloop a vela Marconi	B balandro de Bermudas	B sloop
C gaffelgetuigde kotter	C kutter, gaffelrigget	C cutter con randa e picco	C cachemarin	C cuter de Carangueja
D torengetuigde yawl	D Bermuda yawl	D yawl a vela Marconi	D balandro de batículo	D yawl Marconi
E torengetuigde kits	E Bermuda ketch	E ketch a vela Marconi	E queche bermudo	E ketch Marconi
F stagzeil schoener	F stagsejls skonnert	F schooner a vele di taglio	F goleta a la americana	F palhabote
1 grootzeil	1 storsejl	1 randa	1 vela mayor	1 vela grande
2 topzeil	2 topsejl	2 controranda	2 escandalosa	2 gave-tope
3 druil of bezaan	3 mesan	3 mezzana	3 mesana	3 mezena
4 schoenerzeil	4 store mellem stagsejl	4 strallo di maestra	4 vela de estay mayor	4 traquete
5 grootstengestagzeil	5 top mellem stagsejl	5 vela di strallo "Fisherman"	5 vela alta de estay	5 extênsola
6 aap, bezaanstagzeil	6 mesan stagsejl	6 v. di s. di mezzana	6 entrepalos	6 estai entre mastros
7 fok	7 fok	7 fiocco	7 foque	7 bujarrona
7 (A & C) kluiver	7 (A & C) klyver			
8 genua	8 genua	8 genova	8 génova	8 genoa
9 fok	9 fok	9 vela di taglio, vela di strallo	9 vela de estay	9 estai
10 botterfok	10 genua-fok	10 trinchettina	10 foque balón	10 estai de genoa
11 brik	11 brig	11 brigantino	11 bergantín	11 brigue
12 bark	12 bark	12 brigantino a palo	12 barca	12 barca
13 toerjacht	13 lystfartøj	13 barca da crociera	13 yate crucero	13 barco de cruzeiro
14 wedstrijdjacht	14 kapsejlads-fartøj	14 barca da regata	14 yate de regatas	14 barco de regata
15 zeewedstrijdjacht	15 ocean-kapsejler	15 barca da regata oceanica	15 yate de regatas oceánica	15 barco de regatas oceânicas
16 jol	16 kapsejlads-jolle	16 dinghy da regata	16 barco de regatas	16 dinghy de regata

ENGLISH	FRANÇAIS	DEUTSCH	NEDERLANDS
Vessel	**Vaisseau**	**Fahrzeug**	**Vaartuig**
1 motor boat	1 bateau à moteur	1 Motoryacht	1 motorboot
2 motor sailer	2 bateau mixte, motor-sailer	2 Motorsegler	2 motorzeiljacht
3 dinghy	3 youyou, dinghy, canot	3 Beiboot, Dingi	3 bijboot
4 launch	4 vedette	4 Barkasse	4 barkas
5 rescue launch	5 ⎱ ⎰bateau ou	5 Bergungsfahrzeug	5 reddingsbarkas
6 life boat	6 ⎰ ⎱canot de sauvetage	6 Rettungsboot	6 reddingsboot
7 pilot cutter	7 bateau pilote	7 Lotsenfahrzeug	7 loodskotter
8 ship	8 navire	8 Schiff	8 schip
9 tug	9 remorqueur	9 Schlepper	9 sleepboot
Materials	**Matériaux**	**Materialien**	**Materialen**
1 cotton	1 coton	1 Baumwolle	1 katoen
2 Italian hemp	2 chanvre d'Italie	2 Hanf	2 hennep
3 sisal	3 sisal	3 Sisal	3 sisal
4 coir	4 coco	4 Kokos	4 kokostouw
5 manilla	5 manille, abaca	5 Manila	5 manillatouw
6 leather	6 cuir	6 Leder	6 leer
7 nylon	7 nylon	7 Nylon, Perlon	7 nylon
8 Terylene, Dacron	8 Tergal	8 Diolen	8 Dacron
9 plastic	9 plastique	9 Kunststoff	9 plastic
10 laminated plastic, Tufnol	10 plastique stratifié, Céloron	10 laminierter Kunststoff	10 gelamineerd plastic
11 fibreglass	11 fibre de verre	11 Glasfaser	11 fiberglas
12 glass cloth	12 tissu de verre	12 Glasfasermatte	12 glasmat, glasweefsel
13 resin	13 résine	13 Harz	13 hars
14 catalyst	14 catalyseur	14 Katalysator	14 catalysator
15 polyester	15 polyester	15 Polyester	15 polyester

DANSK	ITALIANO	ESPAÑOL	PORTUGUÊS
Fartøjer	**Imbarcazione**	**Barco**	**Navio**
1 motorbåd	1 barca a motore	1 motora	1 barco a motor
2 motor-fartøj med sejl	2 motor-sailer	2 moto-velero	2 barco a motor e à vela
3 jolle	3 dinghy	3 bote, chinchorro	3 escaler
4 challup	4 lancia	4 lancha	4 lancha
5 følgebåd ved jolle-kapsejladser	5 lancia di salvataggio	5 bote de salvamento	5 barco de socorro
6 redningsbåd	6 scialuppa di salvataggio	6 bote salvavidas	6 barco salva vidas
7 lodsbåd	7 pilotina, barca del pilota	7 bote del práctico	7 embarcação dos pilôtos
8 skib, fregat	8 nave	8 buque	8 navio
9 bugserbåd	9 rimorchiatore	9 remolcador	9 rebocador
Materiale	**Materiali**	**Materiales**	**Materiais**
1 bomuld	1 cotone	1 algodón	1 algodão
2 Italiensk hamp	2 canapa	2 cáñamo	2 linho italiano
3 sisal	3 canapa sisal	3 sisal	3 sisal
4 kokus	4 fibra di cocco	4 estopa	4 cairo
5 manilla-hamp	5 manila	5 abacá, manila	5 cabo de manila
6 læder	6 cuojo	6 cuero	6 coiro
7 nylon	7 nylon	7 nilon	7 nylon
8 Terylene, Dacron	8 Terylene, Dacron	8 terilene, dacron	8 Terylene, Dacron
9 plastic	9 plastica	9 plástico	9 plástico
10 lamineret plastic	10 plastica laminata	10 plástico laminado	10 plástico laminado
11 fiberglas	11 lana di vetro	11 fibra de vidrio	11 fibra de vidro
12 glas klæde	12 panno di vetro	12 tejído de vidrio	12 tecido de vidro
13 harpiks	13 resina	13 resina	13 resina
14 catalyst	14 catalizzatore	14 catalizado	14 catalizador
15 polyester	15 poliestere	15 poliester	15 polyester

ENGLISH	FRANÇAIS	DEUTSCH	NEDERLANDS
Timber	**Bois**	**Holz**	**Timmerhout**
1 oak	1 chêne	1 Eiche	1 eikenhout
2 teak	2 teck	2 Teak	2 teakhout
3 mahogany	3 acajou	3 Mahagoni	3 mahoniehout
4 elm	4 orme	4 Ulme	4 iepenhout
5 spruce	5 spruce	5 Fichte	5 spruce
6 cedar	6 cèdre	6 Zeder	6 ceder
7 pitch pine	7 pitchpin	7 Pitchpine, Pechkiefer	7 amerikaans grenenhout
8 ash	8 frêne	8 Esche	8 essenhout
9 larch	9 mélèze	9 Lärche	9 lorkehout
10 lignum vitæ	10 gaïac	10 Pockholz	10 pokhout
11 seasoned timber	11 bois sec, bois séché	11 abgelagertes Holz	11 droog, uitgewerkt hout
12 rot	12 pourriture	12 Fäulnis	12 vuur, rotting
13 dry rot	13 pourriture sèche	13 Trockenfäule	13 droog vuur
14 steamed	14 ployé à la vapeur	14 dampfgeformt	14 gestoomd
15 laminated	15 contré, laminé	15 laminiert	15 gelamineerd
16 grain	16 fil ou grain du bois	16 Faser	16 draad
Joints	**Joints**	**Verbände**	**Verbindingen**
1 scarf	1 écart	1 Laschung	1 lassing
2 rabbet	2 râblure	2 Sponung	2 sponning
3 mortise and tenon	3 mortaise et tenon	3 Nut und Zapfen	3 pen en gat
4 butted	4 bout à bout	4 Stoß	4 gestuikt
5 dovetail	5 en queue d'aronde	5 verzahnen, Schwalben-schwanz	5 zwaluwstaart
6 faired	6 caréné, poncé	6 geglättet	6 gestroomlijnd

DANSK	ITALIANO	ESPAÑOL	PORTUGUÊS
Træsorter	**Legnami**	**Maderas**	**Madeira**
1 eg	1 quercia	1 roble	1 carvalho
2 teak	2 tek	2 teca	2 teca
3 mahogni	3 mogano	3 caoba	3 mogno
4 elm	4 olmo	4 olmo	4 ulmo
5 gran	5 abete	5 abeto	5 spruce
6 ceder	6 cedro	6 cedro	6 cedro
7 pitch pine	7 pitch pine	7 pino	7 pitch pine
8 ask	8 frassino	8 fresno	8 freixo
9 lærk	9 larice	9 alerce	9 larico
10 pokkenholt	10 legno santo	10 palo santo	10 lignum vitæ, gaiaco
11 lagret træ	11 legname stagionato	11 madera seca	11 sêca
12 råd	12 marcito, cariato	12 putrición	12 carruncho
13 tør råd	13 carie secca	13 hongo de madera	13 carruncho, está podre
14 kogt-dampet	14 trattato con vapore	14 al vapor	14 de estufa a vapor
15 lamelleret	15 laminato	15 laminado	15 laminado
16 årer i træet	16 venatura	16 veta	16 grainha
Samlinger	**Giunti**	**Juntas, costuras**	**Juntas de carpintaria**
1 lask	1 ammorsatura	1 empalme	1 escarva
2 spunding	2 incavo	2 rebajo	2 rebaixo
3 notgang og tap af træ, taphul og sportap	3 tenone o mortasa	3 encaje y mecha	3 fêmea e espiga
4 stød-plankeender	4 giunto di testa	4 unido a tope	4 topado
5 sammensænke	5 palella, incastro a coda di rondine	5 cola de milano	5 emalhetado
6 slette efter med skarøkse	6 spianato	6 encajar	6 desempolado

ENGLISH
Metals
From electro positive to electro negative
1 copper
2 brass
3 bronze
4 lead
5 tin
6 nickel
7 iron
8 cast iron
9 steel
10 chromium
11 zinc
12 aluminium
13 alloy
14 gunmetal
15 stainless steel
16 galvanise
17 corrosion

Fastenings
1 bolt
2 nail
3 screw
4 rivet
5 metal dowel
6 weld
7 wooden dowel

FRANÇAIS
Métaux
La série galvanique d'anodique à cathodique
1 cuivre
2 laiton
3 bronze
4 plomb
5 étain
6 nickel
7 fer
8 fonte
9 acier
10 chrome
11 zinc
12 aluminium
13 alliage
14 bronze de canon
15 acier inoxydable, inox
16 zinguer, chouper
17 corrosion

Chevillage
1 boulon
2 clou
3 vis
4 rivet
5 goujon
6 souder
7 cheville

DEUTSCH
Metalle
Vom positiven zum negativen Pol
1 Kupfer
2 Messing
3 Bronze
4 Blei
5 Zinn
6 Nickel
7 Eisen
8 Gußeisen
9 Stahl
10 Chrom
11 Zink
12 Aluminium
13 Legierung
14 Geschützbronze
15 rostfreier Stahl
16 galvanisieren, verzinken
17 Korrosion

Befestigungen
1 Bolzen
2 Nagel
3 Schraube
4 Niet
5 Metalldübel
6 schweißen
7 Holzdübel, Holzpropfen

NEDERLANDS
Metalen
Van elektro positief naar elektro negatief
1 koper
2 messing
3 brons
4 lood
5 tin
6 nikkel
7 ijzer
8 gietijzer
9 staal
10 chroom
11 zink
12 aluminium
13 legering
14 geschutsbrons
15 roestvrij staal
16 galvaniseren
17 corrosie

Bevestigingsmiddelen
1 bout
2 nagel
3 schroef
4 klinknagel
5 metalen pen
6 lassen
7 houten plug

DANSK	ITALIANO	ESPAÑOL	PORTUGUÊS
Metaller	**Metalli**	**Metales**	**Metáis**
kan skifte fra positiv til negativ	dall'elettrodo positivo all'elettrodo negativo	electro positivo a electro negativo	electro positivo a electro negativo
1 kobber	1 rame	1 cobre	1 cobre
2 messing	2 ottone	2 latón	2 latão
3 bronze	3 bronzo	3 bronce	3 bronze
4 bly	4 piombo	4 plomo	4 chumbo
5 tin	5 stagno	5 estaño	5 estanho
6 nikkel	6 nichel	6 níquel	6 níquel
7 jern	7 ferro	7 hierro	7 ferro
8 støbe-jern	8 ghisa	8 hierro calado	8 ferro fundido
9 stål	9 acciaio	9 acero	9 aço
10 krom	10 cromo	10 cromo	10 cromo
11 zink	11 zinco	11 cinc	11 zinco
12 aluminium	12 allumino	12 aluminio	12 aluminio
13 legering	13 lega	13 aleación	13 liga
14 kanon-metal	14 bronzo duro	14 bronce de cañón	14 liga de cobre e zinco ou estanho
15 rustfri stål	15 acciaio inossidabile	15 acero inoxidable	15 aço inoxidável
16 galvaniseret	16 zincare	16 galvanizar	16 galvanisar
17 rust-tæring	17 corrosione	17 corrosión	17 corrosão
Befæstninger	**Elementi di fissaggio**	**Perneria, clavazon**	**Ferragem de ligação**
1 bolt	1 bullone	1 perno	1 cavilha
2 søm	2 chiodo	2 clavo	2 prego
3 træskrue	3 vite	3 tornillo	3 parafuso
4 nagle	4 chiodo	4 remache	4 rebite
5 metal låseprop	5 caviglia di ferro	5 espiga de metal	5 rôlha metálica
6 svejse	6 saldare	6 soldar	6 soldar
7 låseprop	7 tassello di legno	7 espiga de madera	7 rôlha

ENGLISH	FRANÇAIS	DEUTSCH	NEDERLANDS
Naval architect	**Architecte naval**	**Schiffbauingenieur**	**Scheepsbouwkundige**
1 designer	1 architecte naval	1 Konstrukteur	1 ontwerper
2 surveyor	2 expert maritime	2 Gutachter	2 opzichter
3 builder	3 constructeur	3 Bootsbauer	3 bouwmeester
4 light displacement	4 déplacement léger	4 Leichtdeplacement	4 met kleine waterverplaatsing, licht
5 heavy displacement	5 déplacement lourd	5 Schwerdeplacement	5 met grote waterverplaatsing, zwaar
6 clinker	6 à clins	6 klinker	6 overnaadse bouw, klinker
7 carvel	7 à franc-bord	7 karweel oder kraweel	7 karweelbouw
8 moulded plywood	8 contreplaqué moulé	8 formverleimtes Sperrholz	8 gevormd plakhout
9 open	9 non ponté	9 offen	9 open
10 half-decked	10 semi-ponté	10 halbgedeckt	10 halfgedekt
11 cabin yacht	11 cabinier, ponté	11 Kajütyacht	11 kajuitjacht
12 round bilged	12 en forme	12 Rundspant	12 rondspantig
13 hard chine	13 à bouchain vif	13 Knickspant	13 knikspant
14 overhang	14 élancement	14 Überhang	14 overhang
15 sheer	15 tonture	15 Sprung	15 deksprong, zeeg
16 transom stern	16 arrière à tableau	16 Plattgattheck, Spiegelheck	16 platte spiegel
17 canoe stern	17 arrière canoë	17 Kanuheck	17 kano-achtersteven
18 counter stern	18 arrière à voûte	18 Yachtheck	18 overhang met kleine spiegel
19 spoon bow	19 étrave en cuiller	19 Löffelbug	19 lepelboeg
20 fin keel	20 fin keel	20 Flossenkiel	20 vinkiel
21 trim	21 assiette	21 Trimm, Trimmlage	21 ligging
22 mast rake	22 quête, inclinaison	22 Fall des Mastes	22 valling
23 sail area	23 surface de voilure	23 Segelfläche	23 zeiloppervlak
24 sail plan	24 plan de voilure	24 Segelriß	24 zeilplan
25 scantlings	25 échantillonnage	25 Materialstärke, Profil	25 afmeting van constructiedelen

DANSK	ITALIANO	ESPAÑOL	PORTUGUÊS
Yachtkonstruktør	**Architetto navale**	**Ingeniero naval**	**Engenheiro Construtor Naval**
1 konstruktør	1 progettista	1 proyectista	1 projectista
2 synsmand	2 perito navale	2 inspector	2 inspector
3 skibsbygmester	3 costruttore navale	3 constructor	3 construtor
4 lille deplacement	4 piccolo dislocamento	4 pequeño desplazamiento	4 deslocamento pequeno
5 stort deplacement	5 grosso dislocamento	5 gran desplazamiento	5 deslocamento grande
6 klinkbygget	6 a fasciame sovrapposto	6 tingladillo	6 tabuado trincado
7 kravel	7 a paro, fasciame a comenti appaiati	7 unión a tope	7 tabuado liso
8 formet finer	8 legno compensato modanato	8 contrachapado moldado	8 contraplacado moldado
9 åben	9 aperto, spontato	9 abierto	9 aberto
10 halvdæk	10 semiappontato	10 con media cubierta, tillado	10 meio convez
11 kahyt	11 cabina	11 yate con camara	11 iate de cabine
12 rundbundet	12 carena curva, tonda	12 pantoque redondo	12 fundo redondo
13 V-bund	13 carena a spigolo	13 chine	13 hidrocónico
14 overhang	14 slancio	14 sobresalir	14 lançamento
15 konveks, spring	15 cavallino	15 arrufo	15 tosado
16 agterspejl	16 poppa a specchio	16 popa de yugo	16 pôpa arrasada
17 kano-agterende	17 poppa tipo canoa	17 popa de canoa	17 pôpa de canoa
18 gilling	18 poppa a volta	18 revés	18 pôpa de painel
19 ske bov	19 prora tondeggiante, a cucchiaio	19 proa de cuchara	19 proa de colher ou de iate
20 finnekøl	20 deriva	20 quilla de aleta	20 quilha em forma de barbatana
21 styrlastighed	21 assetto	21 estiba	21 caimento
22 mastens hældningsvinkel	22 inclinazione dell'albero	22 inclinación del palo	22 inclinação do mastro
23 sejlareal	23 superfice velica	23 superficie vélica	23 área de vela
24 sejlplan	24 piano velico	24 plano de velámen	24 plano vélico
25 scantling, materiale dimensioner	25 dimensioni	25 escantillón	25 dimensões dos materiais

ENGLISH

Accommodation plan

1 fo'c's'le
2 forepeak
3 chain locker
4 cabin, saloon
5 berth
6 pipe cot
7 quarter berth
8 galley
9 table
10 locker,
   stowage space
11 bosun's locker
12 bulkhead
13 bridgedeck
14 companion way
15 engine compartment
16 freshwater tank
17 hatch,
   sliding hatch
18 cockpit,
   a self-draining
   b watertight
19 sail locker
20 bow; forward
21 stern; aft
22 beam
23 port
24 starboard

FRANÇAIS

Plan d'aménagements

1 poste avant
2 pic avant
3 puits à chaîne
4 carré, cabine
5 couchette
6 cadre
7 couchette de quart
8 cuisine
9 table
10 coffre, placard, sur-
   face de rangement
11 coffre à outils, cambuse
12 cloison
13 bridge-deck
14 descente
15 chambre du moteur
16 réservoir d'eau douce
17 écoutille,
   capot coulissant
18 baignoire, cockpit
   a auto-videur
   b étanche
19 soute à voiles
20 étrave ; avant
21 poupe ; arrière
22 largeur, bau
23 bâbord
24 tribord

DEUTSCH

Einrichtungsplan

1 Vorschiff
2 Vorpiek
3 Kettenkasten
4 Kajüte, Messe
5 Koje
6 Gasrohrkoje, Klappkoje
7 Hundekoje
8 Kombüse
9 Tisch
10 Schrank,
   Stauraum
11 Hellegat
12 Schott
13 Brückendeck
14 Niedergang
15 Motorenraum
16 Frischwassertank
17 Luk,
   Schiebeluk
18 Plicht,
   a selbstlenzend
   b wasserdicht
19 Segelkoje
20 Bug ; vorn
21 Heck ; achtern
22 Breite
23 Backbord
24 Steuerbord

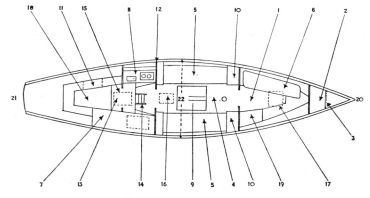

NEDERLANDS	DANSK	ITALIANO	ESPAÑOL	PORTUGUÊS
Inrichtingsplan	Apterings-plan	Pianta delle sistema-zioni di bordo	Acondicionamiento interior	Plano de alojamentos
1 vooronder	1 mandskabslukaf	1 castello di prora	1 castillo proa	1 castelo de proa
2 voorpiek	2 forpeak	2 gavone di prora	2 tilla	2 pique de vante
3 kettingbak	3 kædekasse	3 pozzo delle catene	3 pañol de cadenas	3 paiol da amarra
4 kajuit	4 kahyt, salon	4 cabina, locale	4 camarote	4 cabine, salão
5 kooi, slaapplaats	5 køje	5 cuccetta	5 litera	5 beliche
6 pijpkooi	6 klapkøje	6 branda in ferro	6 catre	6 beliche em tubo desmontável
7 hondenkooi	7 hundekøje	7 impavesata, bastingaggio	7 litera del tambucho	7 beliche de quarto
8 kombuis	8 kabys	8 cucina	8 fogón	8 cozinha
9 tafel	9 bord	9 tavolo	9 mesa	9 mesa
10 kastje, bergruimte	10 kistebænk stuverum	10 stipetti, scansie per stivaggio	10 pañol, caja	10 paióis, armários, arrumação
11 kabelgat	11 bådsmandens stuverum	11 cala del nostromo	11 pañol contramaestre	11 paiol do mestre
12 schot	12 skot	12 paratia	12 mampara	12 antepara
13 brugdek	13 brodæk	13 plancia comando	13 puente, toldilla	13 pavimento da ponte
14 kajuitstrap	14 kahytstrappe	14 scaletta	14 escalera de la cámara	14 escotilha de passagem
15 motorruim	15 maskinrum	15 locale motore	15 cuarto de máquinas	15 casa do motor
16 drinkwatertank	16 ferskvandstank	16 cassa d'acqua dolce	16 tanque de agua potable	16 tanque de aguada
17 luik, schuifkap	17 luge, skydekappe	17 boccaporto,—con portella scorrevole	17 escotilla, escotilla de corredera	17 alboi, tampa de escotilha de correr
18 kuip,	18 cockpit	18 pozzetto	18 bañera	18 poço
a zelflozende	a selvlænsende	a con ombrinale	a de imbornales	a com esgoto para o mar
b waterdichte	b vandtæt	b stagno	b estanca	b estanque
19 zeilkooi	19 sejlkøje	19 stipetto delle vele	19 pañol de velas	19 paiol das velas
20 boeg ; vooruit	20 bov ; forude	20 prora ; proravia	20 proa ; a proa	20 proa ; avante
21 achtersteven ; achteruit	21 agterende ; agter	21 poppa ; poppavia	21 popa ; a popa	21 pôpa ; aré
22 breedte	22 bredde	22 traverso	22 manga	22 bocadura, bôca
23 bakboord	23 bagbord	23 sinistra	23 babor	23 bombordo
24 stuurboord	24 styrbord	24 dritta	24 estribor	24 estibordo

ENGLISH

Sheer plan

1 stem
2 breasthook
3 apron
4 wood keel
5 keelson
6 ballast keel
7 keel bolts
8 sternpost
9 horn timber
10 stern knee
11 deadwood
12 rudder trunk
13 rudder
14 tiller
15 deck
16 beam
17 shelf
18 rib
19 bilge stringer
20 length overall LOA
21 load waterline LWL
22 bilges
23 hull
24 net registered
   tonnage

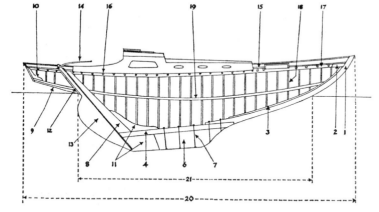

FRANÇAIS

Plan longitudinal

1 étrave
2 guirlande
3 contre-étrave
4 quille de bois
5 carlingue
6 lest
7 boulons de quille
8 étambot
9 allonge de voûte
10 marsouin, courbe de
   poupe
11 massif
12 jaumière
13 gouvernail, safran
14 barre
15 pont
16 barrot
17 bauquière
18 membrure, couple
19 serre de bouchain
20 longueur hors-tout
21 ligne de flottaison
22 bouchain, fonds
23 coque
24 tonnage net officiel,
   enregistré

DEUTSCH

Längsriß

1 Vorsteven
2 Bugband
3 Binnenvorsteven
4 Holzkiel
5 Kielschwein
6 Ballastkiel
7 Kielbolzen
8 Achtersteven
9 Heckbalken
10 Achterstevenknie
11 Totholz
12 Ruderkoker
13 Ruder
14 Ruderpinne
15 Deck
16 Decksbalken
17 Balkweger
18 Spant
19 Stringer, Kimmweger
20 Länge uber Alles,
   Lüa
21 Konstruktionswasser-
   linie (KWL, CWL)
22 Bilge
23 Rumpf
24 Netto-Registertonne,
   NRT

NEDERLANDS	DANSK	ITALIANO	ESPAÑOL	PORTUGUÊS
De tekening der verticalen	**Opstalt**	**Sezione longitudinale**	**Planos del casco**	**Plano de ferros**
1 voorsteven	1 forstævn	1 ruota di prora	1 roda	1 roda de proa
2 dekknie	2 bovbånd	2 gola, ghirlanda	2 buzarda	2 buçarda
3 stevenknie	3 inderstævn	3 controruota	3 contrarroda	3 contra-roda
4 houtenkiel	4 trækøl	4 chiglia di legno	4 quilla de madera	4 quilha
5 kielbalk	5 kølsvin	5 paramezzale	5 sobrequilla	5 sobreçame
6 ballast kiel	6 ballastkøl	6 chiglia zavorrata	6 quilla lastrada	6 patilhão
7 kielbouten	7 kølbolte	7 bulloni di chiglia	7 pernos de quilla	7 cavilhas do patilhão
8 achtersteven	8 agterstævn	8 dritto di poppa	8 codaste	8 cadaste
9 hekbalk	9 hækbjælke	9 puntale, volta di poppa	9 gambota de la limera	9 cambota
10 hekknie	10 hæk-knæ	10 bracciolo della controruota di poppa	10 curva coral	10 curva do painel
11 doodhout	11 opklodsning	11 massiccio di poppa	11 macizo	11 coral
12 hennegatskoker	12 rorbrønd	12 losca del timone	12 limera de timon	12 caixão do leme
13 roer	13 ror	13 timone	13 timón	13 leme
14 helmstok	14 rorpind	14 barra del timone	14 caña	14 cana de leme
15 dek	15 dæk	15 ponte	15 cubierta	15 convez
16 dekbalk	16 bjælke	16 baglio	16 bao	16 vau
17 balkweger	17 bjælkevæger	17 dormiente	17 durmiente	17 dormente
18 spant	18 spanter	18 ordinata	18 cuaderna	18 caverna
19 kimweger	19 langsskibsvæger	19 corrente	19 vagra	19 escôa
20 lengte over alles	20 længde o.a.	20 lunghezza fuori tutto, L.F.T.	20 eslora total	20 comprimento fora a fora
21 lengte in de waterlijn	21 længde vandlinie	21 lunghezza al galleggiamento	21 eslora en el plano de flotación	21 comprimento na linha de água
22 kim	22 kimingen	22 sentina	22 sentina	22 entre fundo
23 romp	23 skrog	23 scafo	23 casco	23 casco
24 netto tonnage	24 netto tonnage	24 stazza netta	24 tonelaje de registro	24 tonelagem de registo líquida

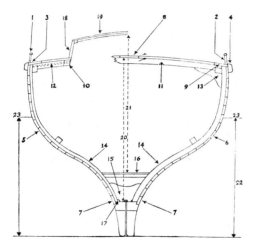

ENGLISH	FRANÇAIS	DEUTSCH
Half-sections	**Sections**	**Spantenriß**
1 rail	1 liston	1 Reling
2 bulwark	2 pavois	2 Schanzkleid
3 scupper	3 dalot	3 Speigatt
4 rubbing strake	4 bourrelet, ceinture	4 Scheuerleiste
5 planking	5 bordage	5 Beplankung
6 skin	6 bordé	6 Außenhaut
7 garboard strake	7 virure de galbord	7 Kielgang
8 king plank	8 faux étambrai,	8 Fischplanke
9 covering board	virure d'axe	9 Schandeck
10 carline	9 plat-bord	10 Schlinge
11 beam	10 élongis	11 Decksbalken
12 tie-rod	11 barrot	12 Stehbolzen
13 knee	12 tirant	13 Knie
14 timber, frame	13 courbe	14 Spant
15 floor	14 membrure	15 Bodenwrange
16 cabin sole	15 varangue	16 Bodenbrett
17 limber holes	16 plancher	17 Wasserlauflöcher
18 coaming	17 anguillers	18 Süll
19 coachroof	18 hiloire	19 Kajütsdach
20 depth	19 rouf	20 Raumtiefe
21 headroom	20 creux	21 Stehhöhe
22 draught	21 hauteur sous	22 Tiefgang
23 waterline	barrots	23 Wasserlinie
24 topsides	22 tirant d'eau	24 Überwasserschiff
25 bottom	23 ligne de flottaison	25 Schiffsboden
26 freeboard	24 œuvres-mortes	26 Freibord
	25 œuvres-vives,	
	carène	
	26 franc-bord	

NEDERLANDS	DANSK	ITALIANO	ESPAÑOL	PORTUGUÊS
De tekening der spantdoorsneden	**Halve sektioner**	**Sezione maestra**	**Sección**	**½ Cortes transversais**
1 reling	1 ræling	1 capo di banda	1 tapa de regala	1 talabardão
2 verschansing	2 skanseklædning	orlo di murata	2 borda, regala	2 borda falsa
3 spuigat	3 spygatter	2 parapetto	3 imbornal	3 embornais, portas
4 berghout	4 fenderlist	3 ombrinale	4 cintón	de mar
5 beplanking	5 rangene	4 righello, bottazzo	5 tablazón del casco	4 cinta, verdugo
6 huid, beplating	6 klædning	5 fasciame	6 forro	5 tabuado
7 zandstrook	7 kølplanke	6 rivestimento	7 aparadura	6 querena
8 vissingstuk	8 midter fisk	7 torello	8 tabla de crujía	7 tábua de resbôrdo
schaarstokplank	9 skandæk	8 tavolato di coperta	9 trancanil	8 tábua da mediania
9 lijfhout, potdeksel	10 kraveller	9 trincarino	10 gualdera	9 tabica
10 langsligger	11 bjælke	10 corrente, anguilla	11 bao	10 longarina da cabine
11 dekbalk	12 spænde-bolt	11 baglio	12 tiranta	11 vau
12 trekstang	13 knæ	12 tirante	13 curva, curvatón	12 tirante de ligação
13 knie	14 svøb, fast spant	13 bracciolo	14 madero, pieza	13 curva de reforço
14 spant	15 bundstokke	14 ordinata, costola	15 varenga	14 caverna
15 wrang	16 kahytsdørk	15 madiere	16 plan de la cámara	15 reforços do pé da
16 vloer	17 sandspor	16 piano di calpestio	17 imbornales de la	caverna
17 waterloopgaten	18 lugekarm	17 fori degli ombrinali	varenga	16 paneiros
18 opstaande rand	19 ruftag	18 mastra	18 brazola	17 boeiras
19 kajuitdek	20 dybde indvendig	19 tetto della tuga	19 tambucho	18 braçola
20 holte	21 højde i kahytten	20 altezza, puntale	20 puntal	19 teto da cabine
21 stahoogte	22 dybgående	21 altezza libera di	21 altura de techo	20 pontal
22 diepgang	23 vandlinie	passaggio	22 calado	21 pé direito
23 waterlijn	24 højde over vand-	22 pescaggio	23 linea de flotación	22 calado
24 bovenschip	linien	23 linea di galleggiamento	24 obra muerta	23 linha de água
25 onderwaterschip,	25 bund	24 opera morta	25 fondo, carena	24 costado, obras mortas
bodem, vlak	26 fribord	25 carena, opera viva	26 franco bordo	25 fundo, obras vivas
26 vrijboord		26 bordo libero		26 altura do bordo livre

ENGLISH

Mast and boom

1 mast
2 truck
3 hounds
4 partners
5 step and heel
6 wedges
7 collar
8 crosstrees
9 jumper struts
10 pin rail
11 crutch, gallows
12 boom
13 boom claw

Standing rigging

14 topmast stay
15 forestay, jib stay
16 preventer backstay
17 runner and lever
18 jumper stay
19 shroud
20 chain plate
21 bottle screw, turnbuckle
22 ratlines
23 diamonds

FRANÇAIS

Mât et bôme

1 mât
2 pomme
3 jottereaux, capelage
4 étambrai
5 emplanture et pied
6 cales
7 jupe
8 barres de flèche
9 guignol
10 râtelier
11 support de bôme, portique
12 bôme
13 croissant

Gréement dormant

14 grand étai, étai de flèche
15 étai avant ou de trinquette, draille
16 pataras, étai arrière
17 bastaque et levier
18 étai de guignol
19 hauban
20 cadène
21 ridoir
22 enfléchures
23 losanges

DEUTSCH

Mast und Baum

1 Mast
2 Masttopp, Mastspitze
3 Mastbacken
4 Mastfischung
5 Mastspur und Mastfuß
6 Mastkeile
7 Mastkragen
8 Saling
9 Jumpstagspreize
10 Nagelbank
11 Baumbock Baumstütze
12 Baum
13 Baumklaue

Stehendes Gut

14 Toppstag
15 Vorstag, Fockstag
16 Achterstag
17 Backstag und Strecker
18 Jumpstag
19 Want
20 Rüsteisen, Pütting
21 Wantenspanner
22 Webeleine
23 Diamantwanten

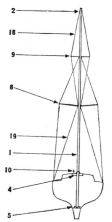

NEDERLANDS	DANSK	ITALIANO	ESPAÑOL	PORTUGUÊS
Mast en giek	**Mast og bom**	**Albero e boma**	**Palo y botavara**	**Mastro e retranca**
1 mast	1 mast	1 albero	1 palo	1 mastro
2 top	2 fløjknap	2 formaggetta	2 tope	2 galope, topo do mastro
3 kroos	3 kindbakker	3 intelaiature di	3 cacholas de un	3 calcês
4 mastknie	4 mastefisk	supporto	palo	4 enora do mastro
5 mastspoor en	5 mastespor og hæl	4 mastra d'albero	4 fogonadura	5 carlinga e pé
mastvoet	6 kiler	5 scassa e piede	5 carlinga y coz	6 cunhas
6 keggen	7 mastekrave	6 cunei	o mecha	7 colar
7 mastbroeking	8 spredere til riggen,	7 collare	6 cuñas	8 vaus
8 dwarszaling	salingshorn	8 crocette basse	7 encapilladura	9 diamante
9 knikzalingen	9 strut til violinstaget	9 crocette alte	8 crucetas	10 mesa das malagetas
10 nagelbank	10 naglebænk	10 pazienza	9 contrete	11 descanço da retranca
11 schaar, vang	11 bomstol, permanent	11 sostegno boma, for-	10 cabillero	12 retranca
12 giek	12 bom	cola, forcaccia	11 posa botavara	13 colar de fixação da
13 schootring	13 bomklo, lyre	12 boma	12 botavara	escota á retranca
		13 trozza, gola di boma	13 media-luna	
Staand want	**Stående rig**	**Manovre fisse o dormienti**	**Maniobra**	**Aparelho fixo**
14 topstag	14 topstag	14 strallo d'alberetto	14 estay de tope,	14 estai do galope
15 voorstag, fokkestag	15 fokkestag	15 strallo di prora	estay de galope	15 estai real
16 achterstag	16 fast bagstag	16 strallo di poppa	15 estay de proa	16 brandal fixo da pôpa
17 backstag en hefboom	17 bagstag med løfte	17 sartia volante	16 poparrás	17 brandal volante e
18 knikstag	stangudløsning	18 strallingaggi	17 burda volante y palanca	alavanca
19 want	18 violinstag	19 sartia	18 estay de boza	18 estai de diamante
20 putting	19 vant	20 landa	19 obenque	19 enxárcia
21 wantspanner,	20 røstjern	21 arridatoio, tendi-	20 cadenote	20 chapa de fixação do
spanschroef	21 vantskrue	sartie	21 tensor	olhal das enxárcias
22 weeflijnen	22 vævlinger	22 griselle	22 flechadura,	21 esticador
23 diamantstagen	23 diamant-stag	23 strallingaggi	flechates	22 enfrechates
			23 losange	23 diamante

ENGLISH

1 **Gooseneck**
2 track
3 slide
4 gate
5 roller reefing
6 ratchet and pawl
7 worm gear

9 **Bowsprit**
10 dolphin striker
11 bobstay
12 cranze iron
13 gammon iron
14 traveller

Spars
15 solid

16 hollow
17 bumpkin
18 jib boom
19 spinnaker boom
20 jury mast
21 yard
22 gaff and jaws
23 topmast
24 tabernacle

FRANÇAIS

1 **Vit-de-mulet**

2 rail
3 coulisseau
4 verrou
5 bôme à rouleau
6 rochet à linguet
7 vis sans fin

9 **Beaupré**
10 martingale
11 sous-barbe
12 collier à pitons
13 liure
14 rocambeau

Espars
15 massif, plein
16 creux
17 queue-de-mallet
18 bôme de foc ou de trinquette
19 tangon de spi
20 mât de fortune
21 vergue
22 corne et mâchoires
23 mât de flèche
24 tabernacle

DEUTSCH

1 **Lümmelbeschlag des Baumes**
2 Mastschiene
3 Rutscher, Reiter
4 Gatchen
5 Patentreffer
6 Pallkranz und Pall
7 Schneckenreff

9 **Bugspriet**
10 Stampfstock
11 Wasserstag
12 Bugsprietnockband
13 Bugsprietzurring
14 Bugsprietausholring

Spieren, Rundhölzer
15 voll
16 hohl
17 Heckausleger
18 Fock-, Klüverbaum
19 Spinnakerbaum
20 Notmast
21 Rah
22 Gaffel und Gaffelklau
23 Toppstenge
24 Mastkoker

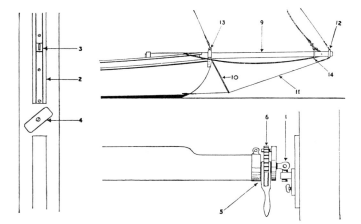

NEDERLANDS	DANSK	ITALIANO	ESPAÑOL	PORTUGUÊS
1 **Zwanehals, lummel**	*1* **Svanehals**	*1* **Snodo e attacco della boma**	*1* **Pescante arbotante,**	*1* **Mangual**
2 mastrail	*2* skinne	*2* colisse, fighera	*2* guía, carril	*2* calha
3 sleetjes	*3* slæde	*3* garroccio scorrevole	*3* corredera	*3* corrediça
4 wissel	*4* åbning, kulisse	*4* scambio	*4* boca del esnón	*4* abertura da calha
5 patentrif	*5* rulle-rebning	*5* molinello per terzaruolare	*5* rizo de catalina	*5* sistema de rizar por enrolamento da retranca
6 palrad en pal	*6* rebeapparat med skralle	*6* dente d'arresto	*6* catalina y pal	
7 worm en wormwiel		*7* ingranaggio elicoidale	*7* husillo	*6* roquete
9 **Boegspriet**	*7* rebeapparat med snekke		*9* **Botalón, baupré**	*7* sem-fim
10 stampstok, spaanse ruiter	*9* **Spryd**	*9* **Bompresso**	*10* moco	*9* **Pau da bujarrona**
11 waterstag	*10* pyntenetstok	*10* pennaccino	*11* barbiquejo	*10* pau de pica peixe
12 boegspriet nokring	*11* vaterstag	*11* briglia	*12* raca	*11* cabresto
13 boegspriet stevenring	*12* sprydring med øjer	*12* collare d'incappellaggio dello strallo	*13* zuncho de botalón	*12* braçadeira do pau
14 traveller	*13* sprydring	*13* trinca di bompresso	*14* racamento	*13* braçadeira da prôa
Rondhouten	*14* udhalerring til klyver	*14* collare scorrevole	**Arboladura**	*14* urraca
15 massief	**Rundholter**	**Antenne**	*15* macizo	**Mastreação**
16 hol	*15* massiv	*15* pieno	*16* hueco	*15* maciço
17 papegaaistok	*16* hul	*16* cavo, vuoto	*17* arbotante	*16* ôco
18 kluiverboom	*17* buttelur, udligger	*17* buttafuori	*18* tangoncillo de foque	*17* pau da pôpa
19 jager- of spinnakerboom	*18* klyverbom	*18* asta di fiocco	*19* tangón del espinaquer	*18* retranca do estai
20 noodmast	*19* spilerstage	*19* asta dello spinnaker, tangone	*20* palo del jurado	*19* pau de spinnaker
21 ra	*20* nød-mast	*20* albero di fortuna	*21* verga	*20* mastro de recurso
22 gaffel en klauw	*21* rå	*21* pennola	*22* pico y boca de cangrejo	*21* verga
23 steng	*22* gaffel og klo	*22* picco e gola	*23* mastelero	*22* carangueja e bôca
24 mastkoker	*23* topmast	*23* alberetto	*24* carlinga de charnela	*23* mastaréu
	24 tabernakel	*24* supporto d'albero a cerniera		*24* carlinga superior no convez, para um mastro basculante

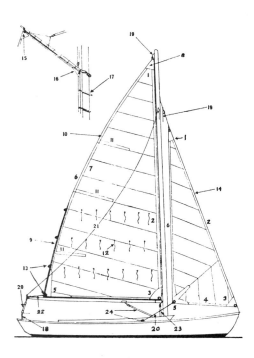

ENGLISH	FRANÇAIS	DEUTSCH
Sails	**Voiles**	**Segel**
1 head	1 point de drisse	1 Kopf
2 luff	2 guindant, envergure	2 Vorliek
3 tack	3 point d'amure	3 Hals
4 foot	4 bordure	4 Unterliek
5 clew	5 point d'écoute	5 Schothorn
6 leech	6 chute	6 Achterliek
leechline	hale-bas de chute	Regulierleine
7 roach	7 rond, arrondi	7 Rundung des Achterlieks
8 headboard	8 planche de tête	8 Kopfbrett
9 bolt rope	9 ralingue	9 Liektau
10 tabling	10 doublage, gaine	10 Doppelung
11 batten pocket	11 étui ou gaine de latte	11 Lattentasche
12 reef point	12 garcette	12 Reffbändsel
13 cringle	13 anneau, patte	13 Legel
14 luff wire	14 ralingue d'acier	14 Drahtvorliek
15 peak	15 pic, empointure	15 Piek
16 throat	16 gorge	16 Klau
17 mast hoop	17 cercle de mât	17 Mastring, Legel
18 horse	18 barre d'écoute	18 Leitwagen
Running rigging	**Gréement courant**	**Laufendes Gut**
19 halyard	19 drisse	19 Fall
20 sheet	20 écoute	20 Schot
21 topping lift	21 balancine	21 Dirk
22 outhaul	22 hale-dehors, étarqueur	22 Ausholer
23 downhaul	23 hale-bas	23 Halsstreckertalje
24 kicking strap, vang	24 hale-bas de bôme	24 Baumniederholer

NEDERLANDS	DANSK	ITALIANO	ESPAÑOL	PORTUGUÊS
Zeilen	**Sejl**	**Vele**	**Velas**	**Velas**
1 top	1 top	1 antennale	1 puño de driza	1 punho da pena
2 voorlijk	2 mastelig	2 lato d'inferitura	2 gratil	2 testa
3 hals	3 hals	3 angolo di mura	3 puño de amura	3 punho da amura
4 voetlijk, onderlijk	4 underlig	4 base o piede	4 pujamen	4 esteira
5 schoothoorn, -hoek	5 skødebarm	5 bugna	5 puño de escota	5 punho da escota
6 achterlijk	6 agterlig, agterline	6 balumina e tirante	6 baluma	6 valuma, linha da valuma
reguleerlijntje	i storsejlet	della balumina	ánima	7 curvatura convexa
7 gilling	7 bugt på storsejlets	7 lunata	7 alunamiento	da valuma
8 zeilplankje	agterlig	8 tavoletta	8 tabla de gratll	8 refôrço triangular
9 lijkentouw	8 flynderen	9 gratile	9 relinga	do punho da pena
10 dubbeling	9 liget	10 vaina	10 vaina	9 tralha
11 zeillatzak	10 forstærkning	11 guaina per stecca	11 bolsa del sable	10 forras de refôrço
12 knuttel	11 lommer til sejl-pinde	12 matafione di	12 tomadores de rizo	11 bôlsa da régua
13 grommer, kousje	12 rebknyttelser	terzaruolo	13 garrucho de cabo	12 rizes
14 staaldraad voorlijk	13 kovs	13 brancarella	14 relinga de envergue	13 olhal
15 piek	14 wire-forlig	14 tirante della ralinga	15 pico	14 cabo da testa
16 klauw	15 pikken (gaffelrig)	15 angolo di penna	16 puño de driza	15 pique
17 hoepel	16 kværken	16 gola	17 zuncho	16 bôca
18 overloop	17 mastering	17 canestrello	18 pie de gallo	17 aro
	18 løjboom	18 barra o ferroguida		18 varão de escota
Lopend want		di scotta	**Jarcias de labor**	
19 val	**Løbende rig**		19 driza	**Aparelho de laborar**
20 schoot	19 fald	**Manovre correnti**	20 escota	19 adriça
21 kraanlijn, dirk	20 skøde	19 drizza	21 amantillo	20 escota
22 uithaler	21 bomdirk	20 scotta	22 envergue de puño	21 amantilho
23 neerhaler	22 udhaler	21 mantiglio	23 cargadera	22 talha do punho da escota
24 neerhouder	23 nedhaler	22 fuetto	24 trapa	23 teque do peão de
	24 kicking strap	23 carica-basso		retranca
		24 ostino, ritenuta		24 kicking strap

35

ENGLISH	FRANÇAIS	DEUTSCH	NEDERLANDS
Sails (contd)	**Voile** (suite)	**Segel** (Fortsetzung)	**Zeilen** (vervolg)
1 yankee	1 yankee	1 grosser Klüver	1 grote kluiver
2 trysail	2 voile de cape	2 Trysegel	2 stormzeil, drentse fok
3 spitfire, storm jib	3 tourmentin	3 Sturmfock	3 stormfok
4 spritsail	4 livarde	4 Sprietsegel	4 sprietzeil
5 wishbone staysail	5 wishbone	5 Spreizgaffel-Stagsegel	5 wishbone-stagzeil
6 headsail	6 voile d'avant	6 Vorsegel	6 voorzeil
7 spinnaker	7 spinnaker	7 Spinnaker	7 spinnaker
8 lugsail	8 voile à bourcet, au tiers	8 Luggersegel	8 loggerzeil, emmerzeil
9 gunter	9 houari	9 Huari-, Steilgaffeltakelung	9 houari
10 fore and aft sail	10 voile longitudinale	10 Schratsegel	10 langsscheeps tuig
11 square sail	11 voile carrée	11 Rahsegel	11 razeil
Sailmaker	**Voilier**	**Segelmacher**	**Zeilmaker**
12 weight of canvas	12 poids de la toile	12 Tuchstärke	12 gewicht van canvas
13 area	13 surface	13 Segelfläche	13 oppervlak
14 flat	14 plate	14 flach geschnitten	14 vlak
15 full, belly	15 creuse, le creux	15 bauchig geschnitten, Bauch	15 bol, buikig
16 stretch a sail	16 roder, faire une voile	16 ein Segel ausstraken	16 een zeil rekken
17 chafe	17 ragage, usure	17 schamfilen	17 schavielen
18 mildew	18 moisissure	18 Stockflecke	18 weer in de zeilen
19 seam	19 couture, lé	19 Naht	19 naad
20 patch	20 rapiécer	20 flicken	20 lappen
21 restitch	21 recoudre	21 Nähte nachnähen	21 opnieuw naaien
22 mend	22 réparer	22 ausbessern, reparieren	22 stoppen, repareren
23 baggywrinkle	23 fourrage, gaine de hauban	23 Tausendfuß	23 lusplatting
24 sail tiers, gaskets	24 rabans	24 Zeisinge	24 zeilbanden
25 sailbag	25 sac à voile	25 Segelsack	25 zeilzak

DANSK	ITALIANO	ESPAÑOL	PORTUGUÊS
Seji (forts.)	**Vele**	**Velas** (cont.)	**Velas** (cont. ção)
1 yankee	1 fiocco	1 trinquetilla	1 giba
2 stormsejl	2 vela di cappa	2 vela de capa	2 cachapana
3 stormklyver	3 fiocco di cappa	3 foque de capa	3 estai de tempo
4 sprydsejl	4 vela a tarchia	4 vela tarquina, abaníco	4 vela de espicha
5 wishbone staysail	5 vela di strallo ''wishbone''	5 vela de pico vacio	5 traquete especial ''wishbone''
6 forsejl	6 vela di prora	6 foque, vela de proa	6 pano de proa
7 spiler	7 spinnaker	7 espinaquer	7 spinnaker, balão
8 luggersejl	8 vela al quarto o al terzo	8 vela cangreja, al tercio	8 vela de pendão
9 gunterrig	9 vela alla portoghese	9 vela de cortina, guaira	9 vela de baioneta
10 for og agter sejl	10 vela di taglio	10 vela cuchillo	10 vela latina
11 bredfok	11 vela quadra	11 vela cuadra, redonda	11 pano redondo
Sejlmager	**Velaio**	**Velero**	**Veleira, fabricante de velas**
12 dugens vægt	12 peso della tela	12 peso de la lona	12 espessura da lona
13 areal	13 superfice velica	13 area	13 área
14 flad	14 piatta	14 vela plana	14 plana, sem saco
15 stor bugt, pose	15 grassa, pancia	15 bolso, papo	15 vela cheia, com saco
16 strække et sejl	16 stendere una vela	16 estirar una vela	16 esticar uma vela
17 skamfiling	17 usura da sfregamento	17 rozar	17 desgaste do velame
18 jordslået	18 muffa	18 moho	18 carruncho
19 søm, nåd	19 cucitura	19 costura	19 baínha
20 lappe	20 rattoppare	20 reforzar	20 remendar
21 sy efter	21 ricucire	21 recoser	21 recoser
22 reparere	22 riparare	22 reparar	22 consertar
23 skamfilings-gods	23 guarnitura contro l'usura	23 pallete	23 coxim de enxárcia
24 sejsinger (til at beslå sejlet med)	24 gerlo di vela	24 tomadores	24 bichas
25 sejlpose	25 sacco per vele	25 saco de vela	25 saco das velas

ENGLISH	FRANÇAIS	DEUTSCH	NEDERLANDS
Wire rope	**Fil, câble d'acier**	**Drahttauwerk**	**Staaldraadtouw**
1 strand	1 toron	1 Kardeel, Ducht	1 streng, kardeel
2 core	2 âme	2 Seele	2 hart, kern
3 flexible	3 souple	3 biegsam	3 buigzaam, soepel
4 stretch	4 élasticité	4 recken, Reck	4 rekken
5 shrink	5 rétrécissement	5 einlaufen	5 krimpen
6 breaking strain	6 charge de rupture	6 Bruchlast	6 breekspanning
7 the coil	7 glène	7 Tauwerksrolle	7 rol
8 kink	8 coque	8 Kink	8 kink, slag
9 circumference	9 circonférence	9 Umfang	9 omtrek
10 diameter	10 diamètre	10 Durchmesser	10 diameter
11 swaged fittings	11 embout serti	11 Endbeschlag	11 aangerolde fitting
Rope	**Cordage**	**Tauwerk**	**Touw**
12 pennant, pendant	12 itague, pantoire	12 Schmeerreep	12 smeerreep
13 lacing	13 transfilage	13 Reihleine	13 marllijn
14 warp	14 amarre, grelin, aussière, haussière	14 Festmacher	14 landvast, meertouw, tros
15 spring	15 garde montante	15 Spring	15 scheertouw, spring
16 painter	16 bosse de canot	16 Fangleine	16 vanglijn
17 guy	17 retenue	17 Bullentalje	17 bulletalje
18 spinnaker guy	18 bras de spi	18 Spinnaker-Achterholer	18 buitenschoot
19 marline	19 merlin	19 Marlleine	19 marllijn
20 cod line	20 quarantenier, ligne	20 Hüsing	20 dunne lijn
21 braided cotton	21 coton tressé	21 geflochtenes Baumwolltauwerk	21 gevlochter katoentouw
22 whipping twine	22 fil à surlier	22 Takelgarn	22 garen, huizing
23 yarn	23 lusin, fil	23 Garn	23 garen
24 tarred	24 goudronné	24 geteert	24 geteerd

DANSK	ITALIANO	ESPAÑOL	PORTUGUÊS
Stål-wire	**Cavi d'acciaio o metallici**	**Cable**	**Cabo de aço**
1 kordel	1 trefolo	1 cordón	1 cordão
2 hjerte	2 anima centrale	2 alma	2 madre
3 bøjelig	3 flessibile	3 flexible	3 flexível
4 strække	4 stiramento	4 estirar	4 alongamento, esticar
5 krympe	5 restringersi	5 encoger	5 encolher
6 brudgrænse	6 carico di rottura	6 carga de rotura	6 carga de rotura
7 kvejl	7 rotolo	7 muela de cabo	7 pandeiro
8 kinke, tørn	8 cocca, volta	8 coca	8 coca
9 omkreds	9 circonferenza	9 mena	9 perímetro
10 diameter	10 diametro	10 diámetro	10 diâmetro
11 endebeslag presset på	11 ——	11 efectos estampados	11 ferragem especial para ligar os cabos de aço sem costura
Tovværk	**Cavi, cordami**	**Cabulleria**	**Cordame**
12 vimpel	12 penzolo	12 amante	12 chicote
13 lidseline	13 sagola	13 envergue	13 armarilho
14 varpetrosse	14 cavo da tonneggio	14 estacha, amarra	14 espia
15 spring	15 spring	15 esprín	15 regeiras, espringues
16 fangeline	16 barbetta	16 boza	16 boça
17 bomnedhaler	17 bozza	17 retenida	17 gaio
18 agterhaler	18 tirante dello spinnaker	18 guía	18 gaio de spinnaker
19 merling	19 merlino	19 merlín	19 merlim
20 stikline	20 lezzino o lusino	20 piola	20 linha de pesca
21 flettet bomuldsline	21 sagola trefolo	21 algodón trenzado	21 trançado de algodão
22 taklegarn	22 spago	22 piolilla	22 cordame de pequena bitola
23 kabelgarn	23 filo	23 meollar	23 fibra
24 tjæret	24 catramato	24 alquitranado	24 alcatroado

ENGLISH	FRANÇAIS	DEUTSCH	NEDERLANDS
Splicing	**Episser**	**Spleiße**	**Splitsen**
1 eye splice	1 œil épissé	1 Augspleiß	1 oogsplits
2 long splice	2 épissure longue	2 Langspleiß	2 lange splits
3 short splice	3 épissure courte, carrée	3 Kurzspleiß	3 korte splits
4 parcel	4 limander	4 schmarten	4 smarten
5 serve	5 fourrer	5 kleeden, bekleiden	5 kleden
6 whip	6 surlier	6 takeln	6 takelen
7 lashing	7 saisine	7 Lasching	7 seizing, bindsel
Knots and hitches	**Nœuds**	**Knoten und Steke**	**Knopen en steken**
8 reef knot	8 nœud plat	8 Kreuzknoten, Reffknoten	8 platte knoop
9 figure of eight	9 nœud en huit, —en lacs	9 Achtknoten	9 achtknoop
10 bowline	10 nœud de chaise	10 Palstek	10 paalsteek
11 fisherman's bend	11 nœud de grappin	11 Roringstek	11 werpankersteek
12 double sheet bend	12 nœud d'écoute double	12 doppelter Schotstek	12 dubbele schootsteek
13 clove hitch	13 demi-clés à capeler	13 Webeleinstek	13 mastworp, weeflijnsteek
14 rolling hitch	14 nœud de bois, —de fouet	14 Stopperstek	14 mastworp met voorslag
15 round turn and two half hitches	15 tour mort et deux demi-clés	15 Rundtörn mit zwei halben Schlägen	15 rondtorn en twee halve steken
Bosun's locker	**Cambuse**	**Hellegat**	**Kabelgat**
1 serving mallet	1 mailloche à fourrer	1 Kleedkeule	1 kleedkuil
2 marline spike	2 épissoir	2 Marlspieker	2 marlspijker
3 caulking iron	3 fer ou ciseau de calfat	3 Kalfateisen	3 breeuw-, kalefaatijzer
4 bosun's chair	4 chaise de gabier	4 Bootsmannsstuhl	4 bootsmansstoel
5 sailmaker's palm	5 paumelle	5 Segelhandschuh	5 zeilplaat
6 needle and thread	6 aiguille et fil à voile	6 Nadel und Garn	6 zeilnaald en zeilgaren
7 funnel with filter	7 entonnoir à filtre	7 Trichter mit Filter	7 trechter met filter
8 adhesive	8 colle	8 Leim, Klebstoff	8 lijm
9 insulating tape	9 ruban isolant, Chatterton	9 Isolierband	9 isolatieband

DANSK	ITALIANO	ESPAÑOL	PORTUGUÊS
Splejse	**Impiombature**	**Costuras**	**Costuras**
1 øjesplejsning	1 impiombatura di gassa	1 gaza	1 mãozinha, costura de mão
2 langsplejsning	2 impiombatura lunga	2 costura larga	2 costura de laborar
3 kortsplejsning	3 impiombatura corta	3 costura redonda	3 costura redonda
4 smerting	4 bendaggio	4 precintar	4 percintar
5 klæ	5 fasciatura	5 aforrar	5 forrar
6 takle	6 ghia semplice	6 falcacear	6 falcassar
7 bændsel	7 legature, minutenze	7 ligada	7 amarrar
Knob	**Nodi e colli**	**Nudos y vueltas**	**Nós**
8 råbåndsknob	8 nodo piano	8 nudo llano o de rizo	8 nó direito
9 flamsk knob	9 nodo di savoia	9 nudo de 8	9 nó de trempe
10 pælestik	10 gassa d'amante	10 as de guía	10 lais de guia pelo chicote
11 baghånds knob	11 gruppo di ancorotto	11 cote y ballestrinque	11 volta de anête
12 dobbelt flagstik	12 gruppo doppio di bandiera	12 vuelta de escota doble	12 nó de escota dobrado
13 dobbelt halvstik	13 nodo parlato semplice	13 ballestrinque, cote doble	13 volta de fiél
14 stopperstik	14 nodo parlato doppio	14 doble vuelta mordida	14 volta de tomadouro
15 rundtørn med to halvstik	15 doppio nodo di bitta e due mezzi colli	15 vuelta redonda y dos cotes	15 volta redonda e cotes
Bådsmandens værktøjsskab	**Cala del nostromo**	**Pañol de contramaestre**	**Paiol do mestre**
1 klæ-kølle	1 maglietto per fasciare	1 maceta de aforrar	1 macete de forrar
2 merlespiger	2 caviglia per impiombatura	2 pasador	2 espicha
3 kalfatrejern	3 presello per calafatare	3 hierro de calafatear	3 ferro de calafate
4 bådsmandsstol	4 balzo, banzíco	4 guindola	4 balso de carpinteiro
5 sejlhandske	5 guardamano	5 rempujo	5 repucho
6 nål og tråd	6 ago e spago	6 aguja e hilo de velas, filástica	6 agulha e linha
7 tragt med filter	7 imbuto a filtro	7 embudo con filtro	7 funil com filtro
8 klæbestof	8 mastice, colla	8 adhesivo, pegamento	8 adesivo
9 isolerbånd	9 nastro isolante	9 cinta aislante	9 fita isoladora

ENGLISH	FRANÇAIS	DEUTSCH	NEDERLANDS
Tools	**Outils**	**Werkzeuge**	**Gereedschappen**
1 saw	1 scie	1 Säge	1 zaag
2 plane	2 rabot	2 Hobel	2 schaaf
3 chisel	3 ciseau à bois	3 Meißel	3 beitel
4 brace and bits	4 vilebrequin et mèches	4 Brustleier mit Einsätzen	4 booromslag en boren
5 vice	5 étau	5 Schraubstock	5 bankschroef
6 hammer	6 marteau	6 Hammer	6 hamer
7 screwdriver	7 tournevis	7 Schraubenzieher	7 schroevedraaier
8 hand drill and bits	8 chignolle à main avec forets	8 Drillbohrer und Bohrer	8 handboor met boren
9 hacksaw	9 scie à métaux	9 Metallsäge	9 metaalzaag
10 file	10 lime	10 Feile	10 vijl
11 wire cutters	11 pinces coupantes	11 Drahtschere	11 draadschaar
12 rule	12 règle	12 Lineal	12 lineaal
13 square	13 équerre	13 Winkel	13 tekenhaak
14 spokeshave	14 racloire, vastringue	14 Ziehklinge	14 spookschaaf
15 pliers	15 pinces	15 Drahtzange	15 buigtang, vouwtang
16 bradawl	16 poinçon	16 Nagelbohrer	16 els
17 gimlet	17 vrille	17 Frittbohrer	17 spitsboor
18 punch	18 chasse-clou	18 Dorn	18 pons
19 carborundum stone	19 pierre à aiguiser, à affûter	19 Karborund-Abziehstein	19 carborundum steen
20 grease gun	20 pompe de graissage	20 Fettspritze, Schmierpresse	20 vetspuit
21 oil can	21 burette	21 Ölkanne	21 oliekan
22 feeler gauge	22 feuilles d'épaisseur	22 Rachenlehre	22 voelermaat
23 spanner	23 clé anglaise	23 Engländer	23 sleutel
24 wrench	24 clé à écrous, tourne à gauche	24 Schraubenschlüssel	24 waterpomptang

DANSK	ITALIANO	ESPAÑOL	PORTUGUÊS
Værktøj	**Utensili**	**Herramientas**	**Ferramenta**
1 sav	1 sega	1 sierra	1 serra
2 høvl	2 pialla	2 cepillo	2 plaina
3 mejsel	3 scalpello	3 formón	3 cinzel, escôpro
4 svingbor og sneglebor	4 menaraole e punta	4 berbiquí y broca	4 arco de pua e brocas
5 skruestik	5 morsa	5 mordaza	5 tôrno, prensa
6 hammer	6 martello	6 martillo	6 martelo
7 skruetrækker	7 cacciavite	7 destornillador	7 chave de parafuso
8 håndbor og drilbor	8 trapano a mano	8 taladro y broca	8 barbequim manual e brocas
9 nedstryger	9 seghetto	9 serrucho	9 serrote para metal
10 file	10 lima	10 lima	10 lima
11 trådsaks, boltsaks	11 cesoie	11 cortafrio	11 alicate para cortar arame
12 tommestok	12 riga	12 regla	12 régua
13 vinkel	13 squadra	13 escuadra	13 esquadro
14 bugthøvl	14 piattello	14 cabilla	14 cortchet
15 tang	15 pinze	15 alicates	15 alicate
16 platbor	16 punteruolo ad estremità piatta	16 barrena	16 buril
17 vridbor	17 succhiello	17 barrenita	17 verruma
18 dorn	18 punzone	18 punzón	18 punção, furador
19 karborundumsten	19 carburo	19 carborundo	19 pedra de esmeril de carborundum
20 fedtsprøjte	20 ingrassatore	20 engrasador a presión	20 bomba de lubrificação
21 oliekande	21 recipiente dell'olio, oliatore	21 aceitera	21 almotolia
22 søger	22 spessimetro	22 calibres de huelgo	22 canivete de folgas
23 nøgle	23 chiave	23 llave	23 chave
24 rørtang	24 chiave inglese	24 llave inglesa	24 chave inglesa

ENGLISH	FRANÇAIS	DEUTSCH	NEDERLANDS
On deck	**Sur le pont**	**An Deck**	**Aan dek**
1 pulpit	1 balcon avant	1 Bugkorb	1 preekstoel
2 stern pulpit, pushpit	2 balcon arrière	2 Heckkorb	2 hekstoel
3 guardrail, lifeline	3 filière, garde-corps	3 Seereling	3 zeereling
4 stanchion	4 chandelier	4 Relingsstütze	4 steun, scepter
5 samson post, bitts	5 bitte d'amarrage	5 Beting, Poller	5 voorbolder
6 ventilator	6 dorade, manche à air	6 Lüfter	6 ventilator
7 skylight	7 claire-voie	7 Oberlicht	7 koekoek, vallicht
8 porthole	8 hublot	8 Bullauge	8 patrijspoort
9 fender	9 défense, pare-battage	9 Fender	9 stootkussen
10 bow fender, noseband	10 défense d'étrave	10 Bugfender	10 neuswaring
11 boathook	11 gaffe	11 Bootshaken	11 pikhaak
12 sounding pole	12 sondeur	12 Peilstock	12 slaggaard
13 legs	13 béquilles	13 Stützen (die verhindern, daß das ẞoot beim Trockenfallen umkippt)	13 stutten
14 davits	14 porte-manteau, bossoir	14 Davits	14 davits
15 ladder	15 échelle	15 Leiter	15 trap
16 sail cover	16 prélart, taud, bâche	16 Segelpersenning	16 zeilkleed
17 awning	17 tente	17 Sonnensegel	17 zonnetent
18 tarpaulin	18 bâche, taud, prélart	18 Persenning	18 presenning
19 bucket	19 seau	19 Pütz	19 emmer
20 mop	20 vadrouille, faubert	20 Dweil	20 stokdweil
21 scrubbing brush	21 brosse à récurer	21 Schrubber	21 schrobborstel
22 wheel	22 roue	22 Steuerrad	22 stuurrad
23 steering wires	23 drosses	23 Ruderleitung	23 stuurlijnen
24 oilskins	24 cirés	24 Ölzeug	24 oliegoed
25 sou'wester	25 suroît	25 Sudwester	25 zuidwester

DANSK	ITALIANO	ESPAÑOL	PORTUGUÊS
På dækket	**In coperta**	**En cubierta**	**No convez**
1 prædikestol	1 pulpito	1 púlpito	1 guarda proeiro
2 prædikestol agter	2 pulpito poppiero	2 púlpito de popa	2 varandim
3 rundlist	3 battagliola	3 pasamano	3 balaustrada
4 lønnings-sceptre	4 candelieri	4 candelero	4 balaústre
5 samson post	5 monachetto, bitta	5 bitón	5 abita
6 ventilator	6 manica a vento, ventilatore	6 ventilador	6 ventilador
7 skylight	7 osteriggio	7 lumbrera	7 lanternim
8 koøje	8 oblò	8 portillo	8 vigia
9 fender	9 parabordo, paglietto	9 defensa	9 defensa, molhelha
10 stævnskinne	10 guardalato	10 defensa de proa	10 barra da roda de proa
11 bådshage	11 gaffa, mezzo marinaio	11 bichero	11 croque
12 lodde-stok (stage)	12 canna per scandagliare	12 varilla de sonda	12 vara de sondagem
13 støtter	13 puntelli	13 escora	13 escoras
14 davider	14 gruette	14 pescante	14 turcos
15 leider	15 scaletta	15 escala	15 escada
16 sejl-presenning	16 cappa della vela	16 funda	16 capa da vela
17 solsejl	17 tenda	17 toldo	17 toldo
18 presenning	18 copertone incerato	18 encerado	18 capa
19 pøs	19 bugliolo	19 balde	19 balde
20 dvejl	20 redazza	20 lampazo	20 lambaz
21 skurebørste	21 frettazzo	21 escoba de fregar	21 escôva
22 rat	22 ruota del timone	22 rueda del timón	22 roda do leme
23 styre-wire	23 frenello del timone	23 guardín	23 gualdropes
24 olietøj	24 tenute incerate	24 chubasquero, ropa de agua	24 oleados
25 sydvest	25 sudovest	25 montera impermeable	25 sueste

ENGLISH	FRANÇAIS	DEUTSCH	NEDERLANDS
Winch	**Winch, treuil**	**Winde, Winsch**	**Lier**
1 barrel	1 poupée	1 Trommel	1 trommel
2 pawl	2 cliquet d'arrêt	2 Pall	2 pal
3 winch handle	3 levier	3 Kurbel	3 zwengel
Windlass, capstan	**Guindeau, cabestan**	**Ankerwinde, Ankerspill, Gangspill**	**Ankerlier, kaapstander**
4 warping drum	4 poupée	4 Spillkopf	4 verhaalkop
5 gipsy	5 barbotin	5 Barbotin-Ring	5 kettingschijf
6 crank handle	6 manivelle	6 Kurbel	6 zwengel
7 spindle	7 mèche	7 Achse, Welle	7 spil
8 brake	8 frein	8 Bremse	8 rem
9 ratchet	9 rochet	9 Pallkranz, Sperrad	9 ratelsleutel of -hefboom
Bilge pump	**Pompe de cale**	**Lenzpumpe**	**Lenspomp**
1 centrifugal pump	1 pompe centrifuge	1 Zentrifugalpumpe, Kreiselpumpe	1 centrifugaal pomp
2 diaphragm pump	2 pompe à diaphragme	2 Membranpumpe	2 membraam pomp
3 semi-rotary pump	3 pompe semi-rotative	3 Flügelpumpe	3 vleugelpomp
4 double-action pump	4 pompe à double effet	4 doppeltwirkende Pumpe	4 dubbelwerkende pomp
5 self-priming pump	5 pompe auto-amorçante	5 selbstansaugende Pumpe	5 zelfaanzuigende pomp
6 capacity	6 capacité, débit	6 Leistungsfähigkeit	6 capaciteit
7 plunger	7 piston, plongeur	7 Kolben	7 plunjer
8 valve	8 soupape	8 Ventil	8 klep, afsluiter
9 washer	9 cuir, joint	9 Dichtungsscheibe	9 leertje
10 impeller	10 rotor	10 Kreisel	10 waaier
11 suction pipe	11 tuyau d'aspiration	11 Ansaugrohr	11 zuigpijp
12 strum box	12 crépine	12 Saugkorb	12 zuigkorf

DANSK	ITALIANO	ESPAÑOL	PORTUGUÊS
Spil	**Verricello**	**Winche, chigre**	**Guincho**
1 spilkop	1 tamburo, campana	1 tambor	1 saia
2 pal	2 scontro	2 linguete, pal	2 linguete
3 spil-håndtag	3 manovella	3 palanca del winche	3 alavanca, manivela
Ankerspil, gangspil	**Argano a salpare, argano**	**Molinete, chigre, cabrestante**	**Molinete do ferro, cabrestante**
4 spilkop	4 tamburo per tonneggio	4 tambor	4 saia, tambor
5 kædehjul	5 barbotin	5 tamborete	5 gola
6 håndtag	6 aspa a manovella	6 maquinilla	6 manivela
7 aksel	7 albero, fusto	7 mecha	7 eixo, peão
8 bremse	8 freno	8 freno	8 travão
9 palring	9 castagna, dente	9 molinete	9 roquete
Lænsepumpe	**Pompa di sentina**	**Bombas de achique**	**Bomba de esgoto**
1 centrifugal pumpe	1 pompa centrifuga	1 bomba centrífuga	1 bomba centrífuga
2 membran-pumpe	2 pompa a diaframma	2 bomba de diafragma	2 bomba de diafragma
3 nikke-pumpe	3 pompa simplex, a mano	3 bomba de palanca	3 bomba de relógio
4 dobbeltvirkende pumpe	4 pompa a doppio effetto	4 bomba de doble efecto	4 bomba de efeito duplo
5 selvansugende pumpe	5 pompa autoinnescante	5 bomba de cebado automático	5 bomba de ferrar automáticamente
6 kapacitet	6 portata	6 capacidad	6 capacidade, débito
7 pumpestempel	7 pistone, stantuffo	7 émbolo	7 êmbolo
8 ventil	8 valvola	8 válvula	8 válvula
9 spændskive	9 guarnizione	9 arandela	9 anel
10 impeller, impuls, vinge	10 girante	10 impelente	10 impulsor
11 sugerør	11 tubo aspirante	11 tubo de aspiración	11 tubo de aspiração
12 sugekurv	12 succhiarola	12 alcachofa	12 caixa de lôdo

47

ENGLISH	FRANÇAIS	DEUTSCH	NEDERLANDS
Anchor	**Ancre**	**Anker**	**Anker**
1 bower anchor	1 ancre de bossoir	1 Buganker	1 boeganker
2 kedge	2 ancre à jet	2 Warpanker, Reserveanker	2 werpanker, hulpanker
3 fisherman's anchor	3 ancre à jas	3 Stockanker	3 stokanker
4 stock	4 jas	4 Stock	4 stok
5 shank	5 verge	5 Schaft	5 schacht
6 flukes	6 pattes	6 Flunken	6 vloeien
7 ring	7 organeau	7 Ring	7 roering
8 C.Q.R. or plough anchor	8 C.Q.R., ou ancre charrue	8 Pflugscharanker	8 ploegschaaranker
9 Danforth	9 ancre à bascule	9 Danforthanker	9 Danforth
10 sea anchor	10 ancre flottante	10 Seeanker, Treibanker	10 zeeanker, drijfanker
11 anchor warp	11 aussière, câblot	11 Ankertrosse	11 ankertros
12 chain, cable	12 chaîne ou câble d'ancre	12 Ankerkette	12 ankerketting
13 link	13 maille, maillon	13 Kettenglied	13 schalm
14 stud-link	14 maille à étai	14 Stegkette	14 damketting
15 navel pipe	15 écubier de pont	15 Kettenklüse	15 kettingkoker
16 anchor buoy	16 bouée de corps-mort	16 Ankerboje	16 ankerboei
17 tripping line	17 orin, lève-nez	17 Bojereep	17 neuringlijn
To anchor	**Mouiller**	**Vor Anker gehen, ankern**	**Ankeren**
1 let go the anchor	1 jeter l'ancre	1 Anker fallen lassen	1 anker laten vallen
2 run out the anchor	2 faire porter l'ancre par un canot	2 einen Anker ausfahren	2 een anker uitbrengen
3 fouled	3 surjalée, surpattée	3 unklar	3 onklaar
4 dragging anchor	4 chasser sur l'ancre	4 der Anker schleppt	4 het anker krabt
5 holding anchor	5 l'ancre croche, tient	5 der Anker hält	5 het anker houdt
6 lie to an anchor	6 être au mouillage	6 vor Anker liegen	6 voor anker liggen
7 break out an anchor	7 décrocher, déraper l'ancre	7 den Anker ausbrechen	7 anker uitbreken
8 to weigh anchor	8 appareillage	8 Ankerauf gehen, Anker hieven oder lichten	8 ankerop gaan, hieuwen opankeren, lichten
9 to slip the anchor	9 filer par le bout	9 den Anker schlippen	9 anker slippen

DANSK	ITALIANO	ESPAÑOL	PORTUGUÊS
Anker	**Ancora**	**Ancla**	**Ferro**
1 sværdanker	1 ancora di posta	1 ancla principal	1 ferro de amura, de leva
2 varpanker	2 ancorotto	2 anclote	2 ancorote
3 stokanker	3 ferro da imbarcazione	3 ancla de cepo	3 âncora com cêpo
4 ankerstok	4 ceppo	4 cepo	4 cêpo do ferro
5 ankerlæg	5 fuso	5 cana	5 haste do ferro
6 fligen	6 patte	6 uñas	6 unhas do ferro
7 ankerring	7 maniglione, cicala	7 arganeo	7 anete do ferro
8 C.Q.R., plovanker	8 C.Q.R.	8 C.Q.R./Arado	8 tipo C.Q.R., de charrua
9 Danforth	9 Danforth	9 Danforth	9 tipo Danforth
10 drivanker	10 ancora galleggiante	10 ancla flotante	10 âncora flutuante
11 ankertrosse	11 cavo da tonneggio	11 amarra del ancla	11 espia do ferro
12 ankerkæde	12 catena, cavo, gomena	12 cadena, cable del ancla	12 amarra
13 kædeled	13 maglia	13 eslabón	13 elo
14 stolpekæde	14 maglia con traversino	14 eslabón de contrete	14 elo com estai
15 kædebrønd	15 discesa del pozzo delle catene	15 escobén	15 gateira
16 ankerbøje	16 gavitello	16 boyarín del orinque	16 bóia do arinque
17 bøjereb	17 grippiale	17 orinque	17 arinque
At ankre	**Ancorarsi**	**Fondear**	**Fundear**
1 lad falde anker	1 dare fondo all'ancora	1 dar fondo	1 largar o ferro
2 føre et anker ud med jolle	2 stendere un'ancora	2 atoar el ancla	2 espiar um ferro
3 uklar	3 ancora impigliata, inceppata	3 encepada	3 ferro prêso, ensarilhado
4 i drift for ankeret	4 ancora che ara	4 ancla garreando	4 ferro a garrar
5 ankeret holder	5 ancora che agguanta	5 ancla agarrada	5 ferro unhado
6 at ligge til ankers	6 stare all'ancora	6 aguantarse con un ancla	6 fundeado
7 at brække et anker los	7 spedare l'ancora	7 desatrincar	7 arrancar o ferro
8 at lette ankeret	8 salpare l'ancora	8 levar el ancla	8 suspender a amarra
9 at stikke ankeret fra sig med bøje på	9 gettare l'ancora	9 perder el ancla	9 picar a amarra

ENGLISH	FRANÇAIS	DEUTSCH	NEDERLANDS
Below deck	**Sous le pont**	**Unter Deck**	**Onderdeks**
1 mattress	1 matelas	1 Matratze	1 matras
2 cushions	2 coussin	2 Sitzkissen, Polster	2 zitkussen
3 pillow and case	3 oreiller et taie	3 Kopfkissen und Bezug	3 kussen, kussensloop
4 sleeping bag	4 sac de couchage	4 Schlafsack	4 slaapzak
5 sheet	5 drap	5 Bettlaken	5 laken
6 blanket	6 couverture	6 Decke	6 wollen deken
7 leeboard	7 planche ou toile de roulis	7 Kojenbrett, Kojensegel	7 kooiplank
8 chart table	8 table à cartes	8 Kartentisch	8 kaartentafel
9 fiddle	9 violon, rebord	9 Schlingerleiste	9 slingerlat
10 W.C., heads,	10 W.C., toilettes,	10 Pumpklosett, Toilette	10 W.C., Closet
11 non-return valve	11 soupape de retenue	11 Rückschlagventil	11 terugslagklep
12 flap valve	12 soupape à clapet	12 Schwenkhahn	12 tuimelklep
13 discharge piping	13 tuyau de débit	13 Abflußrohr	13 uitlaatpijp
14 seacock	14 vanne	14 Seeventil	14 buitenboordskraan
15 lavatory paper	15 papier hygiénique	15 Toilettepapier	15 toilet-papier
16 wash basin	16 lavabo	16 Waschbecken	16 wasbak, waskom
17 towel	17 serviette	17 Handtuch	17 handdoek
18 soap	18 savon	18 Seife	18 zeep
19 lock and key	19 serrure et clef	19 Schloß und Schlüssel	19 slot en sleutel
20 flush handle	20 poignée noyée	20 versenkter Griff	20 verzonken handel
21 hinge	21 charnière	21 Scharnier	21 scharnier
22 ashtray	22 cendrier	22 Aschbecher	22 asbakje
23 knife and fork	23 couteau et fourchette	23 Messer und Gabel	23 mes en vork
24 spoon	24 cuiller	24 Löffel	24 lepel
25 cup and saucer	25 tasse et soucoupe	25 Tasse und Untertasse	25 kop en schotel
26 plate	26 assiette	26 Teller	26 bord
27 glass	27 verre	27 Glas	27 glas
28 mug	28 quart	28 Becher	28 kroes
29 bowl	29 bol	29 Schale	29 schaal

DANSK	ITALIANO	ESPAÑOL	PORTUGUÊS
Under dæk	**Sotto coperta**	**Bajo cubierta**	**No interior**
1 madras	1 strapuntino	1 colchón	1 colchão
2 puder	2 cuscini	2 cojínes	2 almofadas
3 hovedpude, pudevår	3 cuscino e federa	3 almohada y funda	3 almofada e fronha
4 sovepose	4 sacco a pelo	4 saco de dormir	4 saco de dormir
5 lagen	5 lenzuolo	5 sábana	5 lençol
6 tæppe	6 coperta	6 manta, frazada	6 cobertor
7 køjebrædder	7 piastra di deriva	7 gualdera	7 resguardo do beliche
8 kortbord	8 tavolo da carteggio	8 mesa de cartas	8 mesa das cartas
9 slingebrædder	9 tavola di rollio	9 balancera	9 régua de balanço
10 toilet	10 locale igienico, W.C.	10 WC, sanitario	10 W.C., retrete
11 kontraventil	11 valvola di ritegno	11 válvula de retención	11 válvula sem retôrno
12 klapventil	12 valvola a cerniera	12 válvula de charnela	12 válvula de portinhola
13 afløbsrør	13 scarichi a mare	13 tubo de descarga	13 tubo de descarga
14 stophane	14 valvola di arresto	14 llave de paso	14 torneira de segurança
15 toiletpapir	15 carta igienica	15 papel higiénico	15 papél higiénico
16 håndvask	16 lavabo, lavandino	16 lavabo	16 lavatório
17 håndklæde	17 asciugamano	17 toalla	17 toalha
18 sæbe	18 sapone	18 jabón	18 sabonete
19 lås og nøgle	19 serratura e chiave	19 cerradura y llave	19 fechadura e chave
20 indfældet dørhåndtag	20 maniglia a paro	20 asa a ras	20 pega embebida
21 hængsel	21 cerniera	21 charnela, bisagra	21 dobradiça
22 askebæger	22 portacenere	22 cenicero	22 cinzeiro
23 kniv og gaffel	23 coltello e forchetta	23 cuchilla y tenedor	23 faca e garfo
24 ske	24 cucchiaio	24 cuchara	24 colher
25 kop og underkop	25 tazza e piattino	25 taza y platillo	25 chávena e pires
26 tallerken	26 piatto	26 plato	26 prato
27 glas	27 bicchiere	27 vaso	27 copo
28 krus	28 boccale	28 pote	28 caneca
29 skål	29 scodella, ciotola	29 tazón	29 tigela

ENGLISH	FRANÇAIS	DEUTSCH	NEDERLANDS
Galley	**Cuisine**	**Kombüse**	**Kombuis**
1 pressure stove	1 réchaud à pétrole	1 Petroleumkocher	1 petroleumgas-toestel
2 pressure gauge	2 jauge de pression	2 Manometer	2 drukmeter
3 flexible metal pipe	3 tuyau souple en métal	3 biegsamer Metallschlauch	3 buigzame pijp
4 paraffin tank	4 réservoir à pétrole	4 Petroleumtank	4 petroleumtank
5 self-pricking	5 à débouchage	5 automatische Düsenreini-	5 automatische doorsteek-
		gung, selbstreinigend	inrichting
6 pricker	6 déboucheur	6 Pricker	6 staaldraadnaaldje
7 methylated spirits	7 alcool à brûler	7 Brennspiritus	7 spiritus
8 gas stove	8 réchaud à gaz	8 Propangaskocher, Gasherd	8 gastoestel
9 cylinder	9 bouteille	9 Gasflasche	9 fles
10 gimbals	10 à la Cardan	10 kardanische Aufhängung	10 cardanische ophanging
11 sink	11 évier	11 Abwaschbecken	11 gootsteen
12 plug	12 bouchon	12 Stöpsel	12 stop
13 tap	13 robinet	13 Hahn	13 kraan
14 washer	14 joint	14 Dichtungsring	14 leertje
15 washing-up liquid	15 détergent	15 Abwaschmittel	15 afwasmiddel
16 frying pan	16 poêle à frire	16 Bratpfanne	16 braadpan
17 saucepan	17 casserole, poêlon	17 Kochtopf	17 steelpan
18 pressure cooker	18 casserole à pression,	18 Schnellkochtopf	18 drukpan, snelkookpan
	cocotte-minute		
19 kettle	19 bouilloire	19 Kessel	19 ketel
20 tin	20 boîte	20 Dose	20 blik
21 tin opener	21 ouvre-boîtes	21 Dosenöffner	21 blikopener
22 bottle	22 bouteille	22 Flasche	22 fles
23 corkscrew	23 tire-bouchon	23 Korkenzieher	23 kurketrekker
24 matches	24 allumettes	24 Streichhölzer	24 lucifers
25 salt	25 sel	25 Salz	25 zout
26 pepper	26 poivre	26 Pfeffer	26 peper
27 mustard	27 moutarde	27 Senf	27 mosterd

DANSK	ITALIANO	ESPAÑOL	PORTUGUÊS
Kabys	**Cucina**	**Fogón**	**Cozinha**
1 tryk-komfur	1 fornello a pressione	1 cocina de petróleo	1 fogão de pressão
2 tryk-måler	2 manometro	2 manómetro	2 manómetro de pressão
3 bøjelig metal-slange	3 tubo metallico flessibile	3 tubo flexible de metal	3 tubo flexível metálico
4 petroleums-tank	4 latta, bidone di petrolio	4 tanque de petróleo	4 depósito de petróleo
5 selvrensende	5 spinotto autopulitore	5 auto-limpiador	5 espevitador automático
6 rensenål	6 scovolatore per fornello	6 punzón del quemador	6 agulha
7 sprit	7 alcool denaturato	7 alcohol desnaturalizado	7 alcool para queimar
8 gasovn	8 fornello a gas	8 cocina de gas	8 fogão a gás
9 cylinder	9 bombola	9 cilindro, carga de gas	9 cilindro, bidão do gás
10 kardansk ophæng	10 sospensione cardanica	10 balancera, cardan	10 suspensão cardan
11 vask	11 acquaio	11 fregadero	11 lava-loiça
12 prop	12 tappo	12 tapón	12 bujão, tampa
13 hane	13 rubinetto	13 grifo	13 torneira
14 pakning, underlags-skive	14 guarnizione a rondella	14 arandela	14 anel, válvula da torneira
15 opvaskemiddel	15 detersivo liquido per rigovernatura	15 detergente	15 detergente líquido para lavar a loiça
16 stegepande	16 padella	16 sartén	16 frigideria
17 kasserolle	17 casseruola	17 cacerola, cazo	17 panela
18 trykkoger	18 pentola a pressione	18 olla de presión	18 panela de pressão
19 kedel	19 bricco	19 caldero	19 chaleira
20 dåse	20 scatola di latta	20 lata	20 lata
21 dåseåbner	21 apriscatole	21 abrelatas	21 abre-latas
22 flaske	22 bottiglia	22 botella	22 garrafa
23 proptrækker	23 cavatappi	23 sacacorchos	23 saca-rolhas
24 tændstikker	24 fiammiferi	24 cerillas	24 fósforos
25 salt	25 sale	25 sal	25 sal
26 peber	26 pepe	26 pimienta	26 pimenta
27 sennep	27 senape	27 mostaza	27 mustarda

ENGLISH	FRANÇAIS	DEUTSCH	NEDERLANDS
Lights	**Feux**	**Lampen**	**Lichten**
1 navigation lights	1 feux de navigation, de route, de position	1 Positionslaternen, Seitenlaternen	1 navigatielicht
2 stern light	2 feu arrière ou de poupe	2 Hecklicht	2 heklicht
3 riding light	3 feu de mouillage	3 Ankerlicht	3 ankerlicht
4 masthead light	4 feu de tête de mât	4 Dampferlicht, Topplicht	4 toplicht
5 lens, plain, dioptric, prismatic	5 lentille, simple, fraisenelle, à facettes	5 Linse, gewöhnliche, dioptrische, prismatische	5 lens, enkelvoudig, dioptrisch, prismatisch
6 wick	6 mèche	6 Docht	6 kousje
7 watertight socket	7 socket étanche	7 wasserdichte Steckdose	7 waterdicht stop-contact
Interior lighting	**Éclairage**	**Innenbeleuchtung**	**Kajuitverlichting**
1 candle	1 bougie	1 Kerze	1 kaars
2 paraffin lamp	2 lampe à pétrole	2 Petroleumlampe	2 petroleumlamp
3 chimney	3 verre	3 Zylinder	3 lampeglas
4 vaporizing lamp, Tilley	4 lampe à pression	4 Petroleumdrucklampe	4 petroleumgaslamp
5 mantle	5 manchon	5 Glühstrumpf	5 kousje
6 electric torch	6 torche électrique	6 Taschenlampe, Stablampe	6 zaklantaarn
7 dry battery	7 pile sèche	7 Trockenbatterie	7 batterij
8 bulb	8 ampoule	8 Glühlampe	8 lampje
Electric lighting	**Eclairage électrique**	**Elektrische Beleuchtung**	**Elektrische verlichting**
9 switch	9 commutateur	9 Schalter	9 schakelaar
10 wiring	10 câblage électrique	10 Leitung	10 elektrische leidingen
11 junction box	11 boîte de raccordement	11 Verteilerkasten	11 verdeeldoos
12 current	12 courant	12 Strom	12 stroom
13 voltage	13 voltage, tension	13 Spannung	13 spanning
14 short circuit	14 court-circuit	14 Kurzschluß	14 kortsluiting
15 blown fuse	15 fusible fondu, plomb sauté	15 durchgebrannte Sicherung	15 doorgebrande zekering

DANSK	ITALIANO	ESPAÑOL	PORTUGUÊS
Lanterner	**Fanali, luci**	**Luces**	**Luzes**
1 lanterneføring	1 fanali di via	1 luz de navegación, luz de situación	1 faróis de navegação
2 agterlanterne	2 fanale di coronamento	2 luz de alcance, de popa	2 farol de pôpa
3 ankerlanterne	3 fanale di fonda	3 luz de fondeado	3 farol de navio fundeado
4 signallys på mastetoppen	4 fanale di via bianco	4 luz de tope	4 farol do tôpo do mastro
5 linse, glat, dioptrik, prismatik	5 lente, piana, diottrica, prismatica	5 lente, plana, dioptrica, prismatica	5 lente, simples, dióptrica, prismática
6 væge	6 stoppino	6 mecha torcida	6 torcida
7 vandtæt stikkontakt-dåse	7 presa o attacco di corrente stagna	7 enchufe estanco	7 tomada estanque
Belysning under dæk	**Illuminazione interna**	**Alumbrado interior**	**Iluminação interior**
1 et lys	1 candela	1 vela	1 vela
2 petroleumslampe	2 lampada a petrolio	2 lámpara de petróleo	2 candieiro de petróleo
3 lampeglas	3 tubo di lume	3 mambrú, tubo de chimenea	3 vidro ou chaminé
4 Optimus lampe	4 lume a vapori di petrolio	4 lámpara de vapor	4 candieiro de pressão
5 glødenæt	5 reticella Auer	5 camisa	5 camisa
6 stavlygte	6 torcia elettrica	6 linterna	6 lanterna eléctrica portátil
7 tørbatteri	7 batteria a secco	7 pila seca	7 pilha sêca
8 elektrisk pære	8 lampadina	8 bombilla	8 lâmpada
Elektrisk belysning	**Illuminazione elettrica**	**Alumbrado electrico**	**Instalação eléctrica**
9 strømafbryder	9 interruttore	9 interruptor	9 interruptor
10 elektrisk installation	10 cavi	10 instalación	10 conjunto dos circuitos eléctricos
11 fordelerkasse	11 cassetta di giunzione	11 caja de juntas	11 caixa de derivação
12 strøm	12 corrente	12 corriente	12 corrente
13 spænding	13 voltaggio	13 voltaje	13 voltagem
14 kortslutning	14 corto circuito	14 corto circuito	14 curto-circuito
15 smelte sikring	15 valvola bruciata, saltata	15 fusible fundido	15 fusível queimado

ENGLISH	FRANÇAIS	DEUTSCH	NEDERLANDS
Chandlery and ship's chandler	**Quincaillerie, accastillage et fournisseur de marine**	**Beschläge, Schiffsausrüster**	**Beslag en scheepsleverancier**
1 cleat	1 taquet	1 Klampe	1 klamp, kikker
2 jam cleat	2 taquet coinceur, coinceur d'écoute	2 Curryklemme, Schotklemme	2 schootklem
3 mooring bitts	3 bitte d'amarrage	3 Poller	3 beting
4 belaying pin	4 cabillot	4 Beleg-, Koffeynagel	4 korvijnagel
5 fairlead	5 chaumard	5 Lippe, Verholklüse	5 verhaalkam
6 roller fairlead	6 chaumard à réa	6 Rollenklampe	6 verhaalklamp met rol
7 sheet lead	7 filoire d'écoute	7 Leitöse	7 leioog
8 adjustable sheet lead	8 filoire d'écoute réglable	8 verstellbare Leitöse	8 verstelbaar schootleioog
9 swivelling sheet lead	9 filoire à émerillon	9 drehbare Leitöse	9 wartelleioog
10 eye bolt	10 piton de filière	10 Augbolzen	10 oogbout
11 block	11 poulie	11 Block	11 blok
12 sheave	12 réa	12 Scheibe	12 schijf
13 single block	13 poulie simple	13 einscheibiger Block	13 eenschijfsblok
14 double block	14 poulie double	14 zweischeibiger Block	14 tweeschijfsblok
15 with becket	15 à ringot, à œil	15 mit Hundsvott	15 met hondsvot
16 fiddle block	16 poulie violon	16 Violinblock	16 vioolblok
17 shackle and pin	17 manille et vis, manille et clavette	17 Schäkel und Bolzen	17 sluiting met bout
18 'D' shackle	18 manille droite	18 'U' Schäkel	18 rechte sluiting
19 harp shackle	19 manille violon	19 Bügelschäkel	19 harp sluiting
20 snap shackle	20 mousqueton à ressort	20 Schnapp-, Patentschäkel	20 patentsluiting
21 swivel	21 émerillon	21 Wirbel	21 wartel
22 thimble	22 cosse	22 Kausch	22 kous
23 wire rope or Bulldog grip	23 serre-câble à étrier	23 Seilklemme	23 staaldraadklem
24 hank	24 mousqueton	24 Stagreiter	24 knipleuver, musketonhaak
25 jubilee clip	25 collier de serrage	25 Schlauchklemme, Schlauchschelle	25 slangklem

DANSK	ITALIANO	ESPAÑOL	PORTUGUÊS
Skibsinventar, skibshandler	**Articoli navali, fornitore navale**	**Pertrechos y almacén de efectos navales**	**Ferragem de embarcações e fornecedor de navios**
1 klampe	1 galloccia	1 cornamusa	1 cunho
2 beknebklampe	2 strozzacavi	2 barbeta	2 mordente para escota
3 fortøjningspullert	3 bitta da ormeggio	3 bitas	3 abita
4 kofilnagle	4 caviglia	4 cabilla	4 malagueta
5 klyds	5 passacavo a bocca di rancio	5 galápago, guía	5 castanha
6 klyds med rulle	6 passacavo con rullo	6 galápago de rolete	6 tamanca
7 skødeviser	7 passascotte	7 escotera	7 guia de escota
8 indstillelig skødeviser	8 passascotte scorrevole	8 escotera regulable	8 guia de escota ajustável
9 drejelig skødeviser	9 passascotte a molinello	9 escotera giratoria	9 guia de escota de tornél
10 øjebolt	10 golfare	10 cáncamo de argolla	10 olhal de trapas
11 blok	11 bozzello	11 motón	11 moitão
12 skive	12 puleggia	12 roldana	12 roldana
13 enkel blok	13 bozzello semplice	13 motón sencillo, single	13 moitão singelo, simples
14 dobbelt blok	14 bozzello doppio	14 motón doble	14 cadernal
15 med hundsvot	15 con anello o stroppo	15 con manzanillo	15 moitão alçeado
16 violinblok	16 a violino	16 motón de briol	16 polé
17 sjækkel og bolt	17 maniglione e perno	17 grillete y pasador o perno	17 manilha e cavirão
18 'D' sjækkel	18 maniglione o grillo	18 grillete en D	18 manilha direita
19 'H' eller harpesjækkel	19 maniglione o grillo	19 grillete de mucho ojo	19 manilha de ferradura, de borracha
20 tryksjækkel	20 maniglione o grillo	20 grillete de enganche	20 manilha de mola
21 hvirvel	21 molinello	21 giratorio	21 tornél
22 kovs	22 redancia	22 guardacabo	22 sapatilho
23 wirelås	23 morsetto metallico	23 trinca de cable	23 grampas
24 fokkehage, karabinhage	24 moschettone, garroccio	24 garrucho, mosquetón	24 garruncho
25 slangebinder	25 fascetta a vite	25 abrazadera	25 abraçadeira ajustável

ENGLISH	FRANÇAIS	DEUTSCH	NEDERLANDS
Shipyard, maintenance	**Chantier naval, entretien**	**Yachtwerft, Instandhaltung**	**Scheepswerf, onderhoud**
1 scrub the bottom	1 nettoyer la carène à la brosse	1 das Unterwasserschiff reinigen	1 onderwater schoonmaken
2 draw the keel bolts	2 enlever ou sortir les boulons de quille	2 die Kielbolzen herausschlagen	2 kielbouten trekken
3 caulk the seams	3 calfater les coutures	3 die Nähte kalfatern	3 de naden breeuwen
4 overhaul	4 revision	4 überholen	4 reviseren
5 strengthen	5 renforcer	5 verstärken	5 versterken
6 replace	6 remplacer	6 erneuern	6 vervangen
7 make watertight	7 étancher, rendre étanche	7 wasserdicht machen	7 waterdicht maken
8 stop a leak	8 aveugler une voie d'eau	8 Leck abdichten	8 een lek dichten
9 check	9 contrôler	9 kontrollieren, nachsehen	9 kontroleren
Laying up	**Désarmement**	**Auflegen**	**Aftuigen**
1 haul out	1 tirer à terre, au sec	1 an Land holen	1 op de wal halen
2 winter storage	2 hivernage	2 Winterlager	2 winterberging, winterstalling
3 under cover	3 sous abri	3 abgedeckt, in einer Halle	3 in loods
4 mud berth	4 en vasière	4 im Schlick liegen	4 ligplaats op modderbank
5 unstep the mast	5 démâter	5 den Mast herausnehmen	5 de mast uitnemen
6 cradle	6 ber, berceau	6 Slippwagen, Verladebock	6 wieg
7 to fit out	7 armer	7 ausrüsten, instandsetzen	7 uitrusten, optuigen
8 step the mast	8 mâter	8 den Mast einsetzen	8 mast inzetten
9 to launch	9 mettre à l'eau	9 zu Wasser lassen	9 te water laten

DANSK	ITALIANO	ESPAÑOL	PORTUGUÊS
Skibsbyggeri, vedligeholdelse	**Cantiere navale, manutenzione**	**Astillero, mantenimiento**	**Estaleiro, manutenção**
1 at skrubbe bunden	1 fare carenaggio	1 limpiar fondos	1 escovar, limpar o fundo
2 at slå kølbolte ud	2 estrarre i bulloni della chiglia	2 sacar los pernos de la quilla	2 retirar cavilhas do patilhão
3 at kalfatre nåderne	3 calafatare	3 calafatear las costuras	3 calafetar as bainhas
4 at efterse	4 fare lavori di manutenzione	4 recorrer, revisar	4 fazer revisão, rever
5 at forstærke	5 rinforzare	5 reforzar	5 reforçar
6 at forny	6 rimpiazzare	6 reemplazar	6 substituir, repôr
7 at gøre vandtæt	7 assicurare la tenuta d'acqua	7 hacer estanco	7 tornar estanque
8 at stoppe en lækage	8 turare le vie d'acqua	8 taponar	8 tapar uma entrada de água
9 kontrollere	9 verificare	9 comprobar	9 verificar
Lægge op	**Mettere in disarmo**	**Desarmar**	**Encalhar, pôr em sêco**
1 hale på land	1 alare in secco	1 varar	1 alar, encalhar
2 lægge op	2 rimessa per l'inverno	2 invernada	2 encalhar para o inverno
3 i hus	3 al coperto	3 sombrajo	3 pôr em barracão
4 vinterplads i mudder	4 ormeggio in secco	4 cama de fango	4 encalhar no lôdo
5 tage mast ud	5 disalberare	5 abatir el palo	5 desmontar o mastro
6 afstivning, vugge	6 culla, invasatura	6 cuna, calzo	6 berço
7 udruste, klargøring	7 armare	7 alistar	7 armar
8 rejse masten	8 alberare	8 arbolar el palo	8 montar, armar o mastro
9 søsætte	9 mettere a mare, varare	9 botar, lanzar al agua	9 desencalhar, pôr na água

ENGLISH	FRANÇAIS	DEUTSCH	NEDERLANDS
Painting	**Peinture**	**Anstrich**	**Schilderen**
1 burn off	1 brûler	1 abbrennen	1 afbranden
2 rub down	2 poncer	2 schleifen	2 schuren
3 stop	3 enduire	3 spachteln	3 plamuren
4 primer	4 couche d'impression	4 Grundanstrich	4 grondverf, primer
5 undercoat	5 sous-couche	5 Vorstreichfarbe	5 grondlaag
6 enamel paint	6 émail	6 Glanzanstrich	6 glansverf
7 varnish	7 vernis	7 Lack	7 lak
8 anti-fouling paint	8 peinture antisalissante ou antifouling	8 anwuchsverhütende Farbe	8 aangroeiwerendeverf
9 boot-topping	9 bande de flottaison	9 Wasserpaß-Farbe	9 waterlijnverf
10 non-slip deck paint	10 peinture anti-dérapante	10 rutsch-und trittfester Decksanstrich	10 antislipverf
11 stripper, paint remover	11 décapant	11 Abbeizer	11 afbijtmiddel
12 blow lamp	12 lampe à souder	12 Lötlampe	12 benzinelamp
13 paint brush	13 pinceau	13 Pinsel	13 kwast
14 scraper	14 grattoir	14 Schraper	14 schraper
15 sandpaper	15 papier de verre	15 Sandpapier	15 schuurpapier
Dinghy, tender	**Annexe, youyou**	**Beiboot**	**Bijboot, volgboot**
1 oar, scull, sweep	1 aviron, rame, godille	1 Riemen	1 riemen
2 rowlock	2 dame de nage	2 Dolle, Zepter, Rundsel	2 dol
3 painter	3 bosse	3 Fangleine	3 vanglijn
4 fender	4 bourrelet, boudin	4 Wieling	4 kabelaring, fender
5 bow or nose fender	5 défense d'étrave	5 Maus, Bugfender	5 leguaan, stevenkap
6 bottom boards	6 plancher	6 Bodenbretter	6 buikdenning
7 gunwale	7 plat-bord	7 Dollbord	7 dolboord
8 thwart	8 banc	8 Ducht	8 doft
9 to scull	9 godiller	9 wriggen	9 wrikken
10 to tow	10 remorquer	10 schleppen	10 slepen
11 to row	11 nager, ramer	11 pullen, rudern	11 roeien

DANSK	ITALIANO	ESPAÑOL	PORTUGUÊS
Male	**Pitturare**	**Pintado**	**Pintura**
1 brænde af	1 bruciare via la pittura	1 quemar con soplete	1 queimar
2 slibe i bund	2 raschiare	2 lijar	2 passar à lixa
3 spartle	3 stuccare	3 boza, estopor	3 encher
4 grundfarve	4 prima mano	4 imprimación	4 primário
5 understryge	5 mano di fondo	5 primera mano de pintura	5 aparelho
6 emaille farve	6 pittura a smalto	6 pintura de esmalte	6 tinta de esmalte
7 fernis	7 vernice	7 barniz	7 verniz
8 patentfarve	8 pittura sottomarina	8 pintura de patente,	8 tinta anti-vegetativa
	antincrostazione	anti-incrustante	
9 vandlinie maling	9 pittura protettiva	9 pintura de la flotación	9 boot-topping, tinta para
			faixa da linha de água
10 skridsikker dæksmaling	10 pittura da ponti anti-	10 pintura antideslizante	10 tinta anti escorregante
	sdrucciolevole		para convez
11 afstryger	11 sverniciatore	11 decapan	11 decapante
12 blæselampe	12 lampada a benzina	12 soplete	12 maçarico
13 malerpensel	13 pennello, pennellesse	13 brocha	13 pincel, brocha
14 skraber	14 raschietta	14 rasqueta	14 raspa
15 sandpapir	15 cartavetro	15 papel de lija	15 lixa
Jolle	**Dinghy, battellino**	**Chinchorro, bote**	**Bote, escaler, embarcação**
1 årer, vrikke-åre, styreåre	1 remo, battana, remo sensile	1 remo, remo de singar,	1 remo
		espadilla	
2 åregaffel	2 scalmo	2 tolete, horquilla	2 forqueta
3 fangeline	3 barbetta	3 boza	3 boça
4 fender	4 parabordo, guardalato	4 defensa	4 defensa, molhelha
5 stævnfender	5 parabordo di prora	5 defensa de proa	5 molhelha da prôa
6 bundtøj	6 paglioli	6 cuartel, enjaretado	6 paneiros
7 iærlng, lønning	7 capo di banda, frisata	7 borda, regala	7 alcatrate, borda
8 tofte	8 banco	8 bancada	8 banco, bancada
9 at vrikke	9 vogare di poppa	9 singar	9 remar à gingar
10 at slæbe	10 rimorchiare	10 remolcar	10 rebocar
11 at ro	11 remare, vogare	11 bogar, remar	11 remar

ENGLISH	FRANÇAIS	DEUTSCH	NEDERLANDS
Racing dinghy	**Dériveur léger**	**Rennjolle**	**Wedstrijdjol**
1 measurement certificate	1 certificat de jauge	1 Meßbrief	1 meetbrief
2 buoyancy bag	2 volume gonflable	2 Auftriebskörper	2 luchtzaak
3 buoyancy compartment	3 caisson étanche	3 Lufttank	3 luchtkast
4 centreboard	4 dérive	4 Mittelschwert	4 midzwaard
5 centreboard case	5 puits de dérive	5 Schwertkasten	5 zwaardkast
6 dagger plate	6 sabre	6 Steckschwert	6 steekzwaard
7 mast groove	7 gorge, rainure	7 Keep des Mastes	7 mastsleuf
8 drop rudder	8 safran relevable, mobile	8 Senkruder	8 klaproer
9 pintle	9 aiguillot	9 Ruderzapfen	9 roerpen
10 gudgeon	10 fémelot	10 Fingerling	10 vingerling
11 tiller extension	11 allonge de barre	11 Pinnenverlängerung	11 helmstok uithouder
12 whisker pole	12 tangon	12 Fockausbaumer	12 fokkeloet
13 paddle	13 pagaie	13 Paddel	13 peddel
14 toe straps	14 sangles	14 Hängegurte	14 hangbanden
15 sitting out	15 en rappel, en-dehors	15 hinauslehnen, ausreiten	15 hangen
16 sliding seat	16 planche escamotable	16 Gleitsitz	16 uitschuifzit
17 trapeze	17 trapèze	17 Trapez	17 trapeze
18 plane	18 planer	18 gleiten	18 planeren
19 capsize	19 chavirer	19 kentern	19 omslaan
20 to right	20 redresser	20 aufrichten	20 oprichten
21 bailer	21 écope	21 Ösfaß	21 hoosvat
22 self-bailer	22 auto-videur	22 Selbstlenzer	22 zelflozer
23 bung hole	23 trou de nable	23 Spundloch, Lenzloch	23 loosgat
24 canvas boat cover	24 taud	24 Bootspersenning	24 dektent
25 trolley	25 chariot	25 Trailer	25 boattrailer

DANSK
Kapsejlads-jolle
1 målebrev
2 flydepose
3 vandtætte rum, flydetank

4 sænkekøl, sværd
5 sværdkiste
6 stiksværd
7 hulkel i mast

8 rorpladen kan sænkes og hæves
9 rortap
10 rorløkke
11 rorpind-forlænger

12 spilerstage til joller
13 pagaj
14 hængestropper
15 hænge ud
16 glidesæde
17 trapez
18 at plane
19 at kæntre, vælte
20 rejse jollen
21 øsekar
22 selvlænser
23 spuns-hul
24 presenning
25 ophalervogn

ITALIANO
Dinghy da regata
1 certificato di stazza
2 cassa d'aria
3 compartimento stagno

4 lama di deriva
5 cassa di deriva
6 deriva a coltello
7 canaletto dell'albero

8 timone a lama mobile

9 agugliotto
10 femminella
11 prolunga della barra del timone

12 asta del fiocco, tangone
13 pagaia
14 pedagne
15 sedersi sull'orlo
16 seggiolino scorrevole
17 trapezio
18 planare
19 capovolgersi, scuffiare
20 disincagliare, raddrizzare
21 sassola, gottazza
22 ombrinale (autovuotante)
23 allievo
24 cappa da imbarcazione
25 carrello

ESPAÑOL
Barco de regatas
1 Certificado de Arqueo
2 flotador
3 compartimiento estanco, caja de aire
4 orza
5 cajera de la orza
6 orza de sable
7 palo acanalado, o con esnón
8 timón regulable

9 macho del timón
10 hembra del timón
11 alargadera de la caña

12 tangoncillo
13 canalete, pala de remo
14 sujeta pies
15 hacer banda
16 asiento de corredera
17 trapecio
18 planear
19 zozobrar
20 adrizar
21 achicador
22 auto achicador
23 espiche
24 funda de bote de lona
25 carrito de varar

PORTUGUÊS
Dinghy de regatas
1 certificado de medição
2 saco de flutuação
3 caixa de ar, caixa de flutuação
4 patilhão
5 caixa do patilhão
6 patilhão de guilhotina
7 calha do mastro

8 leme móvel

9 macho
10 fêmea
11 extensão da cana

12 pau de spinnaker
13 pagaia
14 cintas para os pés
15 sentado na borda
16 banco móvel
17 trapézio
18 planar
19 virar, voltar
20 endireitar
21 bartedouro
22 esgoto automático
23 boeira
24 capa de lona
25 carro

ENGLISH	FRANÇAIS	DEUTSCH	NEDERLANDS
Safety at sea	**La sécurité**	**Sicherheit auf See**	**Veiligheid op zee**
1 fire extinguisher	1 extincteur d'incendie	1 Feuerlöscher	1 brandblusser
2 foghorn	2 corne de brume	2 Nebelhorn	2 misthoorn
3 bell	3 cloche	3 Glocke	3 scheepsbel
4 radar reflector	4 réflecteur radar	4 Radarreflektor	4 radar reflector
5 distress flares	5 feux de détresse, fusées	5 Notsignalfeuer	5 noodseinen
6 inflatable life raft	6 canot pneumatique	6 aufblasbare Rettungsinsel	6 opblaasbaar reddingsvlot
7 safety harness	7 harnais, ou ceinture de de sécurité	7 Sicherheitsgurt	7 veiligheidsriem
8 life belt	8 brassière	8 Rettungsring	8 reddingboei
9 life jacket	9 gilet de sauvetage	9 Schwimmweste	9 zwemvest
10 horseshoe lifebuoy and automatic light	10 bouée en fer à cheval avec feu	10 Rettungsweste U-förmig mit Licht	10 reddingboei in hoefijzervorm met bus
Flags	**Pavillons**	**Flaggen**	**Vlaggen**
1 ensign	1 pavillon	1 Nationalflagge	1 natie vlag, nationale vlag
2 burgee	2 guidon	2 Clubstander	2 clubstandaard
3 pennant	3 flamme	3 Wimpel	3 wimpel
4 racing flag	4 pavillon de course	4 Rennflagge	4 wedstrijd vlag
5 courtesy ensign	5 pavillon de courtoisie, pavillon du pays visité	5 Gastflagge	5 vreemde natievlag
6 flagstaff	6 mât de pavillon	6 Flaggenstock	6 vlaggestok
7 burgee stick	7 digon, hampe de fanion	7 Standerstock	7 trommelstok
8 to dress ship overall	8 envoyer le grand pavois	8 Flaggengala, über die Toppen flaggen	8 pavoiseren
9 dip the ensign	9 saluer	9 dippen	9 salueren
10 half mast	10 en berne	10 halbstock	10 half stok

DANSK

Sikkerhed på søen

1 ildslukker
2 tågehorn
3 klokke
4 radar-reflektor
5 nødlys
6 oppustelig redningsflåde
7 sikkerheds-sele
8 redningsbælte
9 redningsvest
10 hesteskoformet rednings-krans og automatisk lys

Flag

1 nationalflag
2 stander
3 vimpel
4 kapsejladsflag
5 høflighedsflag
6 flagspil
7 standerspil
8 flage over top
9 kippe med flaget
10 på halv stang

ITALIANO

Sicurezza in mare

1 estintore
2 corno da nebbia
3 campana
4 riflettore radar
5 fuochi per segnalazioni pericoli
6 zattera di salvataggio gonfiabile
7 cintura di sicurezza
8 salvagente
9 salvagente a giachetta
10 salvagente a ferro di cavallo auto luminoso

Bandiere

1 bandiera nazionale
2 guidone, bandiera sociale
3 fiamma, pennello
4 bandiera da regata
5 bandiera della nazione ospitante
6 asta della bandiera
7 asta del guidone
8 pavesare la nave, la barca
9 ammainare la bandiera nazionale
10 a mezz'asta

ESPAÑOL

Seguridad en la mar

1 extintor
2 bocina de niebla
3 campana
4 reflector de radar
5 bengala
6 balsa neumática
7 cinturón de seguridad
8 salvavidas
9 chaleco salvavidas
10 salvavidas abierto (de herradura) y luz automática

Banderas

1 pabellón, bandera nacional
2 grímpola
3 gallardete
4 grimpolón
5 bandera de cortesía, pabellón extranjero
6 asta de bandera
7 asta de grímpola
8 engalanar el buque
9 guindamaina, saludar con la bandera
10 a media asta

PORTUGUÊS

Segurança no mar

1 extintor
2 sereia de nevoeiro
3 sino
4 reflector de radar
5 fachos luminosos de socorro
6 jangada pneumática de salvação
7 cinto de segurança
8 bóia de salvação
9 cinto, colete de salvação
10 bóia de ferradura com luz automática

Bandeiras

1 bandeira nacional
2 galhardete
3 flâmula
4 galhardete de regata
5 bandeira de cortesia
6 pau de bandeira
7 pau do galhardete
8 embandeira em arco
9 arriar a bandeira nacional para cumprimentar
10 meia-haste, meia adriça

ENGLISH	FRANÇAIS	DEUTSCH	NEDERLANDS
Auxiliary	**Auxiliaire**	**Hilfsmotor**	**Hulpmotor**
1 two-stroke	1 à deux temps	1 Zweitakt	1 tweetakt
2 four-stroke	2 à quatre temps	2 Viertakt	2 viertakt
3 petrol engine	3 moteur à essence	3 Benzinmotor	3 benzinemotor
4 diesel engine	4 moteur diesel	4 Dieselmotor	4 dieselmotor
5 petrol/paraffin engine	5 moteur multicarburant	5 Vielstoffmotor	5 benzinepetroleummotor
6 serial number	6 numéro de série	6 Seriennummer	6 serienummer
7 engine number	7 numéro de moteur	7 Motornummer	7 motornummer
8 number of cylinders	8 nombre de cylindres	8 Zylinderzahl	8 aantal cilinders
9 cubic capacity	9 cylindrée	9 Zylinderinhalt	9 cilinderinhoud
10 compression ratio	10 taux de compression	10 Kompressionsverhältnis	10 compressieverhouding
11 weight	11 poids	11 Gewicht	11 gewicht
12 bore	12 alésage	12 Bohrung	12 boring
13 stroke	13 course	13 Hub	13 slag
14 revolutions per minute r.p.m.	14 tours à la minute, tr/min	14 Umdrehungen in der Minute, U/min, Drehzahl	14 omwentelingen per minuut, O.P.M.
Instruments	**Instruments**	**Instrumente**	**Instrumenten**
1 temperature gauge	1 thermomètre	1 Thermometer	1 temperatuurmeter
2 oil-pressure gauge	2 manomètre d'huile	2 Öldruckmesser	2 oliedrukmeter
3 ammeter	3 ampèremètre	3 Amperemeter	3 ampèremeter
4 fuel gauge	4 jauge de combustible	4 Tankanzeige	4 brandstofmeter
5 choke	5 starter (Fr.) choke (Belg.)	5 Choke	5 choke
6 throttle	6 accélérateur, commande des gaz	6 Drosselventil	6 manette, gashandel
7 clutch	7 embrayage	7 Kupplung	7 koppeling
8 revolution indicator	8 compte-tours	8 Drehzahlmesser	8 toerenaanwijzer
9 ignition switch	9 commutateur d'allumage	9 Zündschalter	9 ontstekingsschakelaar
10 starter button	10 bouton de démarrage	10 Anlasserknopf	10 startknop
11 gear lever	11 levier de vitesses	11 Schalthebel	11 versnellingshandel

DANSK	ITALIANO	ESPAÑOL	PORTUGUÊS
Hjælpmotor	**Motore ausiliario**	**Auxiliar**	**Motor auxiliar**
1 totakt	1 a due tempi	1 dos tiempos	1 da dois tempos
2 firetakt	2 a quattro tempi	2 cuatro tiempos	2 da quatro tempos
3 benzinmotor	3 motore a benzina	3 motor de gasolina	3 motor a gasolina
4 dieselmotor	4 motore diesel	4 motor diesel	4 motor diesel
5 benzin/petroleums motor	5 motore a benzina/kerosene	5 motor de gasolina/de petróleo	5 motor a gasolina/petróleo
6 serienummer	6 numero di serie	6 número de serie	6 número de série
7 maskin-nummer	7 numero del motore	7 número del motor	7 número do motor
8 cylinderantal	8 numero dei cilindri	8 número de cilindros	8 número de cilindros
9 slagvolumen	9 cilindrata	9 cilindrada	9 cilindrada
10 kompressionsforhold	10 rapporto di compressione	10 coeficiente de compresión	10 índice de compressão
11 vægt	11 peso	11 peso	11 pêso
12 boring	12 alesaggio	12 diámetro, calibre	12 diâmetro
13 slaglængde	13 corsa	13 carrera	13 curso
14 omdrejning pr. minut O/Min	14 numero di giri al minuto giri/min	14 número de revoluciones por minuto (r.p.m.)	14 número de rotações por minuto, r.p.m.
Instrumenter	**Strumenti**	**Instrumentos**	**Instrumentos**
1 kølevandstermometer	1 termometro	1 termómetro	1 termómetro
2 olietrykmåler	2 indicatore pressione olio	2 manómetro de aceite	2 manómetro de óleo
3 amperemeter	3 amperometro	3 amperímetro	3 amperímetro
4 brændstofmåler	4 indicatore livello carburante	4 manómetro de combustible	4 indícador de combustivel
5 choker	5 controllo dell'aria	5 estrangulador, obturador	5 arranque a frio
6 gas-spjæld	6 valvola a farfalla	6 acelerador	6 acelerador
7 kobling	7 frizione	7 embrague	7 embraiagem
8 omdrejningstæller	8 conta-giri	8 contador de revoluciones	8 conta-rotações
9 tændingskontakt	9 interruttore dell'accensione	9 llave de encendido	9 interruptor de ignição
10 start knap	10 bottone di avviamento	10 botón de arranque	10 botão de arranque
11 gearstang	11 leva cambio	11 palanca de cambio de velocidades	11 alavanca de mudanças

ENGLISH

Installation

1 engine bed, seating
2 mounting
3 shims
4 propeller, screw
5 stern tube
6 stern gland
7 plummer block
8 stuffing box
9 propeller shaft
10 flexible coupling
11 driven shaft
12 gearbox
13 clutch
14 cylinder head
15 cylinder block
16 crankcase
17 sump
18 dipstick
19 oil-filler cap
20 seacock
21 water pump
22 water jacket
23 exhaust
24 silencer
25 starter motor
26 generator
27 gasket

FRANÇAIS

Installation

1 chaise, base du moteur
2 console de suspension
3 épaisseurs
4 hélice
5 tube d'étambot
6 presse-étoupe de tube d'étambot
7 palier
8 presse-étoupe
9 arbre d'hélice
10 accouplement élastique
11 arbre éntraîne
12 boîte de vitesses
13 embrayage
14 culasse
15 bloc-cylindres
16 carter
17 carter à huile
18 jauge d'huile
19 bouchon
20 vanne
21 pompe à eau
22 chemise d'eau
23 tuyau d'échappement
24 silencieux
25 démarreur
26 dynamo, génératrice
27 joint

DEUTSCH

Einbau

1 Motorfundament
2 Aufhängungskonsole
3 Unterlegscheibe
4 Schraube
5 Stevenrohr
6 Stevenrohr-Stopfbuchse
7 Tunnelwellenlager
8 Stopfbuchse
9 Schraubenwelle
10 elastische Kupplung
11 Antriebswelle
12 Getriebekasten
13 Kupplung
14 Zylinderkopf
15 Zylinderblock
16 Kurbelgehäuse
17 Ölwanne
18 Ölmeßstab
19 Oleinfüllverschluß
20 Seeventil
21 Wasserpumpe
22 Wassermantel
23 Auspuffrohr
24 Schalldämpfer
25 Anlasser
26 Lichtmaschine
27 Dichtung

NEDERLANDS	DANSK	ITALIANO	ESPAÑOL	PORTUGUÊS
Installatie	**Maskininstallation**	**Installazione del motore**	**Instalación**	**Instalação do motor**
1 fundatie	1 maskinfundament	1 basamento	1 bancada, polín	1 fixe do motor
2 motorsteun	2 beslag	2 supporti	2 soporte	2 suporte dos mancais
3 vulring	3 mellemslæg	3 zeppa, spessori	3 suplemento	3 calços
4 schroef	4 propeller, skrue	4 elica	4 hélice	4 hélice
5 schroefaskoker	5 stævnrør	5 astuccio dell'asse dell'elica	5 bocina	5 manga
6 pakkinggland	6 stopbøsning	6 premistoppe	6 prensa-estopa de la bocina	6 bucim
7 asblok	7 pandeleje	7 cuscinetto	7 chumacera	7 chumaceira
8 pakkingbus	8 pakdåse	8 pressatreccia	8 prensa-estopa	8 caixa do bucim, empanque
9 schroefas	9 skrue-aksel	9 albero dell'elica	9 árbol de la hélice	9 veio do hélice
10 flexibele koppeling	10 fleksibel kobling	10 accoppiamento flessibile	10 conexión flexible	10 engrenagem flexível
11 drijfas	11 drivaksel	11 albero secondario	11 eje guiado	11 veio motor
12 versnellingsbak	12 gearkasse	12 cambio	12 caja de cambio	12 caixa de velocidades
13 koppeling	13 kobling	13 frizione	13 embrague	13 embraiagem
14 cilinderkop	14 topstykke	14 testata (dei cilindri)	14 culata	14 cabeça do motor
15 cilinderblok	15 cylinderblok	15 blocco cilindri	15 bloque de cilindros	15 bloco do motor
16 carter	16 krumtap-hus	16 carter	16 cárter	16 carter
17 oliecarter	17 bundkar	17 coppa dell'olio	17 cárter de aceite	17 carter do óleo
18 oliepeilstok	18 målepind-olie	18 asta di livello dell'olio	18 varilla de sondar	18 vareta
19 olievuldop	19 hætte til oliepåfyldning	19 tappo del bocchetone dell'olio	19 tapa de tanque de aceite	19 tampa de entrada de óleo
20 buitenboordskraan	20 søhane	20 valvola di presa dell'acqua di mare	20 grifo de fondo	20 válvula de fundo
21 waterpomp	21 vandpumpe	21 pompa dell'acqua	21 bomba de agua	21 bomba de água
22 koelmantel	22 kølekappe	22 camicia d'acqua	22 camisa	22 camisa de água
23 uitlaatpijp	23 udblæsningsrør	23 tubo di scappamento	23 tubo de escape	23 tubo de escape
24 knalpot, geluidsdemper	24 lydpotte	24 silenziatore	24 silencioso	24 silencioso
25 startmotor	25 startmotør	25 motorino d'avviamento	25 motor de arranque	25 motor de arranque
26 dynamo	26 generator	26 generatore	26 dinamo	26 gerador, dínamo
27 pakking	27 pakning	27 guarnizione	27 empaquetadura junta	27 junta

ENGLISH

1 cylinder
2 liner
3 piston
4 compression ring
5 oil or scraper ring
6 gudgeon pin
7 connecting rod
8 big-end bearing
9 crankshaft
10 main bearing
11 flywheel
12 timing chain
13 tappet
14 camshaft
15 pushrod
16 rocker arm
17 inlet valve
18 exhaust valve
19 valve spring
20 valve seat
21 valve guide
22 oil pump
23 oil-pressure relief valve
24 port
25 transfer port
26 starting handle

FRANÇAIS

1 cylindre
2 chemise
3 piston
4 segment de compression
5 racleur d'huile
6 axe de piston
7 bielle
8 palier de grosse tête de bielle
9 vilebrequin
10 palier
11 volant
12 chaîne de distribution
13 poussoir, taquet
14 arbre à came
15 tige du culbuteur
16 culbuteur
17 soupape d'admission
18 soupape d'echappement
19 ressort de soupape
20 siège de soupape
21 guide de soupape
22 pompe à huile
23 clapet de décharge
24 lumière, orifice
25 orifice de transfert
26 manivelle

DEUTSCH

1 Zylinder
2 Buchse
3 Kolben
4 Kompressionsring
5 Abstreifring
6 Kolbenbolzen
7 Pleuelstange
8 Pleuelstangenlager
9 Kurbelwelle
10 Kurbelwellenlager
11 Schwungrad
12 Steuerkette
13 Stößel
14 Nockenwelle
15 Stoßstange
16 Kipphebel
13 Einlaßventil
18 Auslaßventil
19 Ventilfeder
20 Ventilsitz
21 Ventilführung
22 Ölpumpe
23 Ölüberdruckventil
24 Öffnung
25 Überstromkanal
26 Anlaßkurbel

NEDERLANDS	DANSK	ITALIANO	ESPAÑOL	PORTUGUÊS
1 cilinder	1 cylinder	1 cilindro	1 cilindro	1 cilindro
2 voering	2 foringer	2 camicia	2 camisa	2 camisa
3 zuiger	3 stempel	3 pistone	3 émbolo	3 pistéo, êmbolo
4 compressieveer	4 kompressionsring	4 fascia elastica	4 aro de compresion	4 segmento de compressão
5 olieschraapveer	5 oliering	5 raschiaolio	5 rascador	5 segmento de óleo
6 zuigerpen	6 stempelpind	6 perno, spinotto	6 pasador, perno	6 cavilhão
7 zuigerstang, drijfstang	7 plejlstang	7 biella	7 biela	7 biela
8 bigend lager	8 plejlstanglejer	8 cuscinetto di biella	8 cojinete de cabeza de biela	8 bronze da biela
9 krukas	9 krummtapaksel	9 albero a gomiti	9 cigüeñal	9 cambota
10 krukaslager	10 hovedlejer	10 cuscinetto di banco	10 cojinete principal	10 bronze da cambota
11 vliegwiel	11 svinghjul	11 volano	11 volante	11 volante
12 distributieketting	12 knastakselkæde	12 catena della distribuzione	12 cadena de distribución	12 corrente de distribuição
13 klepstoter	13 medbringer-knast	13 punteria	13 taqué	13 touche
14 nokkenas	14 knastaksel	14 albero a camme	14 árbol de levas	14 árvore de cames
15 klepstoterstang	15 ventilløfter	15 asta di comando del bilanciere	15 varilla de distribución	15 haste de comando do balancim
16 tuimelaar	16 vippearm	16 bilanciere	16 balancin	16 balancim
17 inlaat klep	17 indsugningsventil	17 valvola di aspirazione	17 válvula de admisión	17 válvula de admissão
18 uitlaat klep	18 udblæsningsventil	18 valvola di scarico	18 válvula de escape	18 válvula de escape
19 klepveer	19 ventilfjeder	19 molla della valvola	19 muelle de válvula	19 mola de válvula
20 klepzitting	20 ventilsæde	20 sede, seggio	20 asiento	20 sede de válvula
21 klepgeleider	21 ventilstyr	21 guida valvola	21 guia	21 guia de válvula
22 oliepomp	22 oliepumpe	22 pompa dell'olio	22 bomba de aceite	22 bomba de óleo
23 oliedrukafblaasventiel	23 sikkerhedsventil olietryk	23 valvola regolatrice della pressione dell'olio	23 válvula de seguridad	23 válvula de segurança para pressão de óleo
24 poort	24 åbning	24 luce	24 lumbrera	24 janela
25 overstroompoort	25 oliekanal	25 luce di travaso	25 lumbrera de paso	25 janelas do ar de lavagem
26 aanzetslinger	26 starthåndtag	26 manovella per l'avviamento	26 manivela de arranque	26 manivela de arranque

ENGLISH

Petrol engine

1 fuel tank
2 fuel lines
3 fuel pump
4 air filter
5 **carburettor**
6 float chamber
7 needle valve
8 main jet
9 slow-running jet

10 air-correction jet
11 compensating jet
12 throttle, butterfly
13 strangler
14 choke tube
15 throttle lever
16 accelerator pump
17 mixture, rich/weak
18 to adjust

Diesel engine

19 injection pump
20 injector
21 nozzle
22 pressure pipe
23 leak-off
24 overflow valve
25 governor
26 fuel filter
27 control sleeve

FRANÇAIS

Moteur à essence

1 réservoir de combustible
2 conduites de combustible
3 pompe à combustible
4 filtre à air
5 **carburateur**
6 cuve du flotteur
7 pointeau
8 gicleur principal
9 gicleur de ralenti
10 gicleur d'automaticité
11 gicleur d'équilibre
12 papillon des gaz
13 volet de départ
14 buse ou tuyau d'air
15 levier de papillon
16 pompe de reprise
17 mélange, riche/pauvre
18 régler

DEUTSCH

Benzinmotor

1 Kraftstofftank
2 Kraftstoffleitungen
3 Kraftstoffpumpe
4 Luftfilter
5 **Vergaser**
6 Schwimmerkammer
7 Nadelventil
8 Hauptdüse
9 Leerlaufdüse
10 Luftkorrekturdüse
11 Ausgleichsdüse
12 Drosselklappe
13 Luftklappe
14 Luftrichter
15 Drosselhebel
16 Beschleunigungspumpe
17 Gemisch, reich/mager
18 einstellen

Moteur diesel

19 pompe d'injection
20 injecteur
21 gicleur
22 tuyau d'injection
23 conduite de retour d'huile
24 clapet de trop-plein
25 régulateur
26 filtre à combustible
27 douille de réglage

Dieselmotor

19 Einspritzpumpe
20 Einspritzdüse
21 Düse
22 Druckleitung
23 Überströmleitung
24 Überströmventil
25 Regler
26 Ölfilter, Kraftstofffilter
27 Regelhülse

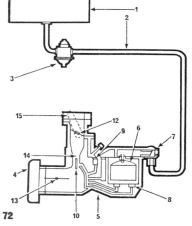

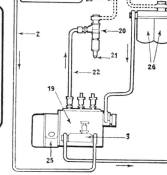

NEDERLANDS	DANSK	ITALIANO	ESPAÑOL	PORTUGUÊS
Benzinemotor	**Benzinmotor**	**Motore a benzina**	**Motor de gasolina**	**Motor a gasolina**
1 brandstoftank	1 brændstoftank	1 serbatoio del combustibile	1 tanque de combustible	1 depósito de combustível
2 brandstofleidingen	2 brændstof-ledninger	2 tubazione del combustibile	2 tuberia de alimentación	2 tubagem de combustível
3 brandstofpomp	3 brændstofpumpe	3 pompa d'alimentazione	3 bomba de alimentación	3 bomba de combustível
4 luchtfilter	4 luftfilter	4 filtro dell'aria	4 filtro de aire	4 filtro de ar
5 **carburateur**	5 **carburator**	5 **carburatore**	5 **carburador**	5 **carburador**
6 vlotterkamer	6 svømmehus	6 vaschetta	6 cámara del flotador	6 câmara do flutudor
7 vlotternaald	7 nåleventil	7 valvola a spillo	7 válvula de aguja	7 válvula de nível
8 hoofdsproeier	8 hovedstrålespids	8 getto principale	8 surtidor principal	8 gicleur do máximo
9 stationaire sproeier	9 tomgangsdyse	9 getto del minimo	9 surtidor de ralenti	9 gicleur do relantie
10 remluchtsproeier	10 luftdyse	10 calibratore dell'aria	10 boquilla automática	10 gicleur de correcção do ar
11 compensatiesproeier	11 kompensations-strålespids	11 getto del compensatore	11 surtidor compensador	11 gicleur do compensação
12 smoorklep	12 gasspjæld	12 farfalla	12 mariposa	12 borboleta
13 luchtklep, chokeklep	13 startspjæld	13 valvola di chiusura dell'aria	13 estrangulador	13 estrangulador
14 luchttrechter	14 luftblandingskontrolrør	14 diffusore dell'aria	14 difusor de aire	14 tubo do ar, cone do ar
15 smoorklephefboompje	15 spjældarm på gas	15 leva, comando del gas	15 palanca de mando de gases	15 alavanca do acelerador
16 acceleratiepomp	16 accelerationspumpe	16 pompa di accelerazione	16 bomba de aceleración	16 bomba de aceleração
17 mengsel, rijk/arm	17 blanding, fed/mager	17 miscela, ricca/povera	17 mezcla, rica/pobre	17 mistura, rica/pobre
18 afstellen	18 justere, indstille	18 messa a punto, regolare	18 ajustar, reglar	18 para ajustar
Dieselmotor	**Dieselmotor**	**Motore diesel**	**Motor diesel**	**Motor diesel**
19 brandstofinspuitpomp	19 indsprøjtningspumpe	19 pompa d'iniezione	19 bomba de inyección	19 bomba de injecção
20 inspuiter	20 injektor	20 iniettore	20 inyector	20 injector
21 verstuiver	21 strålerør	21 polverizzatore	21 pulverizador	21 vaporizador
22 drukpijp	22 tryk-ledning	22 tubo di pressione	22 tubo de presión	22 tubo de pressão
23 overstroomaansluiting	23 overflods-rør	23 valvola di spurgo	23 tubo de retorno	23 tubo de retôrno
24 overstroomventiel	24 overløbs-ventil	24 valvola di troppo pieno	24 válvula del sobrante	24 válvula de descarga
25 regulateur	25 regulator	25 regolatore	25 regulador	25 regulador
26 brandstoffilter	26 brændstof-filter	26 filtro del combustibile	26 filtro de combustible	26 filtro de combustível
27 regelhuls	27 kontrol-føring	27 zoccolo di comando	27 manguito de mando	27 válvula de camisa para contrôle

ENGLISH

Electrical system

1 battery
2 positive terminal
3 negative terminal
4 earth
5 dynamo
6 commutator
7 armature
8 fuse box

Ignition

9 sparking plug
10 electrodes
11 distributor
12 contacts
13 contact breaker
14 rotor arm
15 carbon brush
16 condenser
17 cable, lead
18 coil
19 core
20 winding
21 gap
22 spark
23 timing
24 advance
25 retard
26 firing order
27 high/low tension

FRANÇAIS

Système électrique

1 batterie
2 borne positive
3 borne négative
4 masse, terre
5 dynamo
6 commutateur
7 induit
8 boîtier à fusibles

Allumage

9 bougie
10 electrodes
11 distributeur
12 contacts
13 interrupteur, rupteur
14 doigt de distributeur
15 balai
16 condensateur
17 câble
18 bobine
19 noyau
20 bobinage
21 écartement
22 étincelle
23 réglage d'allumage
24 avancer
25 retarder
26 ordre d'allumage
27 haute/basse tension

DEUTSCH

Elektrische Anlage

1 Batterie
2 Pluspole
3 Minuspole
4 Erdung
5 Lichtmaschine
6 Kollektor
7 Anker
8 Sicherungskasten

Zündung

9 Zündkerze
10 Elektroden
11 Zündverteiler
12 Kontakte
13 Unterbrecherkontakt
14 Verteilerfinger
15 Kohlebürste
16 Kondensator
17 Kabel
18 Zündspule
19 Kern
20 Wicklung
21 Abstand
22 Funke
23 Zündeinstellung
24 früh
25 spät
26 Zündzeitfolge
27 Hoch-
   Schwachstromspannung

NEDERLANDS	DANSK	ITALIANO	ESPAÑOL	PORTUGUÊS
Elektrische installatie	**Elektrisk anlæg**	**Impianto elettrico**	**Instalación electrica**	**Circuito eléctrico**
1 accu	1 batteri	1 batteria	1 bateria	1 batería
2 positieve pool	2 positiv pol	2 morsetto positivo	2 borna positiva	2 terminal positivo
3 negatieve pool	3 negativ pol	3 morsetto negativo	3 borna negativa	3 terminal negativo
4 aarding	4 stel, jord	4 massa, terra	4 masa	4 terra
5 dynamo	5 dynamo	5 dinamo	5 dinamo	5 dínamo
6 commutator	6 kommutator	6 collettore	6 conmutador	6 comutador
7 anker	7 armatur	7 indotto	7 inducido	7 armadura, induzido
8 zekeringskast	8 sikringsdåse	8 scatola dei fusibili	8 caja de fusibles	8 caixa de fusiveis

NEDERLANDS	DANSK	ITALIANO	ESPAÑOL	PORTUGUÊS
Ontsteking	**Tænding**	**Accensione**	**Encendido**	**Ignição**
9 bougie	9 tændrør	9 candela	9 bujia	9 vela
10 electroden	10 elektrode	10 elettrodi	10 electrodos	10 polo
11 verdeler	11 strømfordeler	11 spinterogeno	11 distribuidor	11 distribuidor
12 contacten	12 kontakter	12 puntine, contatti	12 contactos	12 platinados
13 contactonderbreker	13 afbryder	13 ruttore	13 ruptor	13 interruptor
14 rotor	14 rotor arm	14 spazzola rotante	14 rotor, brazo del ruptor	14 rotor
15 koolborstel	15 kulbørste	15 spazzola	15 escobilla de carbón	15 escôva
16 condensator	16 kondensator	16 condensatore	16 condensador	16 condensador
17 kabel	17 elektrisk ledning	17 cavo	17 cable	17 cabo
18 spoel	18 spole	18 bobina	18 bobina	18 bobina
19 kern	19 kærne	19 nucleo	19 núcleo	19 núcleo
20 wikkeling	20 vikling	20 avvolgimento	20 arroyamiento	20 bobinagem
21 afstand	21 gnistafstand	21 intraferro	21 juego	21 folga
22 vonk	22 gnisten	22 scintilla	22 chispa	22 faísca
23 het regelen van de ontsteking	23 indstilling	23 messa in fase	23 regulación	23 regulação
24 vervroegen	24 fortænding	24 anticipo	24 avance	24 avanço
25 vertragen	25 eftertænding	25 ritardo	25 retardo	25 retardar
26 ontstekingsvolgorde	26 tændfølge	26 ordine di accensione	26 orden del encendido	26 ordem de ignição
27 hoog/laagspanning	27 høj/lav spænding	27 alta/bassa tensione	27 alta/baja tensióne	27 alta/baixa tensão

ENGLISH	FRANÇAIS	DEUTSCH	NEDERLANDS
Propeller	**Hélice**	**Schraube**	**Schroef**
1 blade	1 pale, aile	1 Flügel	1 blad
2 pitch	2 pas	2 Steigung	2 spoed
3 feathering propeller	3 mise en drapeau	3 verstellbare Schraube	3 schroef met vaanstand
4 variable-pitch propeller	4 pas variable	4 Umstellschraube	4 omkeerbare schroef
5 right-handed	5 pas à droite	5 rechtsdrehende Schraube	5 rechtsdraaiend
6 left-handed	6 pas à gauche	6 linksdrehende Schraube	6 linksdraaiend
Gearbox	**Boîte de vitesses**	**Getriebekasten**	**Versnellingsbak**
1 reverse and reduction	1 renversement et réduction de marche	1 Wende- und Untersetzungsgetriebe	1 reductie-keerkoppeling
2 ahead	2 marche avant	2 vorwärts	2 voorwaarts
3 astern	3 marche arrière	3 rückwärts	3 achteruit
4 neutral	4 point mort	4 Leerlauf	4 vrijloop
Clutch	**Embrayage**	**Kupplung**	**Koppeling**
1 lining	1 garniture	1 Belag	1 voering
2 disc clutch	2 embrayage à disque	2 Scheibenkupplung	2 platenkoppeling
3 dog clutch	3 embrayage à clabots	3 Klauenkupplung	3 klauwkoppeling
4 centrifugal clutch	4 embrayage centrifuge	4 Fliehkraftkupplung	4 centrifugaalkoppeling
Outboard engine	**Moteur hors-bord**	**Außenbordmotor**	**Buitenboordmotor**
1 pull rope	1 cordelette de démarrage	1 Anreißleine	1 aanslagkabel
2 twist-grip throttle	2 commande des gaz par poignée	2 Handgas	2 handgas
Turbo-jet	**Turbine**	**Turbo-Düse**	**Turbine straalmotor**
1 impellers	1 pales de turbine	1 Antriebsschaufeln	1 voortstuwers
2 nozzle	2 gicleur	2 Düse, Leitschaufel	2 straalpijp
3 stators	3 stators	3 Statoren	3 statoren

DANSK

Skruen
1 skrueblade
2 stigning
3 selvindstillelige
4 stilbar skrue
5 højregående
6 venstregående

Gearkasse
1 bak- og reduktionsgear

2 frem
3 bak
4 neutral, frigear

Kobling
1 belægning
2 pladekobling
3 klokobling
4 centrifugal-kobling

Påhængsmotor
1 startsnor
2 gas-regulering i styrehåndtag

Turbo-jet
1 vinge (pumpe)
2 dysse
3 stator

ITALIANO

Elica
1 pala
2 passo
3 elica a pale articolate
4 elica a passo variabile
5 elica destrorsa
6 elica sinistrorsa

Cambio di velocità
1 invertitore e riduttore ad ingranaggi
2 marcia avanti
3 marcia indietro
4 posizione di folle

Frizione
1 ferodo
2 frizione a disco
3 innesto a denti
4 frizione centrifuga

Motore fuoribordo
1 cavetto per l'avviamento
2 comando manopola del gas

Motore a turbogetto
1 girante della turbina
2 ugello
3 statori

ESPAÑOL

Hélice
1 pala
2 paso de la hélice
3 hélice en bandera
4 paso variable
5 paso a la derecha
6 paso a la izquierda

Caja de cambio
1 inversor-reductor

2 marcha avante
3 atrás
4 punto muerto

Embrague
1 revestimiento
2 embrague de disco
3 embrague dentado
4 embrague centrífugo

Motor fuera de borda
1 cabo de arranque
2 acelerador de puño

Turbina
1 rotor de turbina
2 boquilla
3 estatores

PORTUGUÊS

Hélice
1 pá
2 passo
3 hélice de pás reguláveis
4 hélice de passo variável
5 hélice de passo direito
6 hélice de passo esquerdo

Caixa de velocidades
1 caixa inversora-redutora

2 marcha a vante
3 marcha a ré
4 neutro, ponto morto

Embraiagem
1 ferodo, calços
2 embraiagem de disco
3 união de dentes
4 embraiagem centrífuga

Motor de fora de borda
1 cabo de arranque
2 acelerador manual

Turbo jacto
1 impulsionadores
2 ejector
3 estatores

ENGLISH	FRANÇAIS	DEUTSCH	NEDERLANDS
Components, etc.	**Pièces détachées, etc.**	**Bestandteile, u.s.w.**	**Bestanddelen**
1 screw	1 vis	1 Schraube	1 schroef
2 bolt	2 boulon	2 Bolzen	2 bout
3 nut	3 écrou	3 Mutter	3 moer
4 locknut	4 contre-écrou	4 Gegen-, Sicherungsmutter	4 borgmoer
5 wing nut	5 vis papillon	5 Flügelmutter	5 vleugelmoer
6 washer	6 rondelle	6 Unterlegsscheibe	6 ring
7 spring washer	7 rondelle élastique	7 Federring	7 veerring
8 spindle	8 broche	8 Spindel, Achse	8 spil
9 shaft	9 arbre	9 Welle	9 as
10 spring	10 ressort	10 Feder	10 veer
11 lever	11 levier	11 Hebel	11 hefboom
12 bush	12 bague, buselure	12 Buchse	12 bus
13 bearing	13 palier	13 Lager	13 lager
14 ball bearing	14 roulement à billes	14 Kugellager	14 kogellager
15 split pin	15 goupille fendue	15 Splint	15 splitpen
16 gasket	16 garniture, joint	16 Dichtung	16 pakking
17 spacer	17 anneau d'écartement	17 Abstandsring	17 afstandsring
18 gear wheel	18 pignon, roue d'engrenage	18 Zahnrad	18 tandwiel
19 belt	19 courroie	19 Riemen	19 riem
20 pulley	20 poulie	20 Riemenscheibe	20 riemschijf
21 drain tap	21 robinet de vidange	21 Ablaßhahn	21 aftapkraan
22 grease cup	22 pot de graissage	22 Schmierkopf	22 vetpot
23 torque	23 couple	23 Drehmoment	23 koppel
24 friction	24 friction	24 Reibung	24 wrijving
25 suction	25 aspiration, succion	25 Ansaugung	25 zuiging
26 pressure	26 pression	26 Druck	26 druk
27 combustion	27 combustion	27 Verbrennung	27 verbranding
28 compression	28 compression	28 Kompression	28 compressie

DANSK	ITALIANO	ESPAÑOL	PORTUGUÊS
Tilbehør	**Parti componenti etc.**	**Componentes etcétera**	**Peças**
1 skrue	1 vite	1 tornillo	1 parafuso
2 bolt	2 bullone	2 perno	2 parafuso de porca
3 møtrik	3 dado	3 tuerca	3 porca
4 kontramøtrik	4 contradado	4 contratuerca	4 contraporca
5 fløjmøtrik	5 galletto	5 tuerca de orejas	5 porca de orelhas
6 spændeskive	6 rondella	6 arandela	6 anilha
7 fjederskive	7 rondella elastica	7 arandela de muelle	7 anilha de mola
8 spindel	8 fuso, alberino	8 eje	8 fuso
9 aksel	9 asse	9 eje, árbol	9 veio
10 fjeder	10 molla	10 resorte, muelle	10 mola
11 vægtstang	11 leva	11 palanca	11 alavanca
12 bøsning	12 boccola	12 buje, casquillo	12 casquilho
13 leje	13 cuscinetto	13 cojinete	13 chumaceira
14 kugleleje	14 cuscinetto a sfere	14 cojinete de bolas	14 rolamento de esferas
15 split	15 coppiglia	15 pasador abierto, chaveta	15 troço
16 pakning	16 guarnizione	16 empaquetadura junta	16 junta
17 afstandsstykke	17 distanziatore	17 anillo de distancia	17 espaçador
18 gear	18 ingranaggio	18 piñón, rueda dentada	18 engrenagem
19 drivrem	19 cinghia	19 correa	19 correia
20 remskive	20 puleggia	20 polea	20 roldana
21 aftapningshane	21 tappo di scarico	21 válvula de drenage	21 torneira de drenagem
22 fedtkop	22 ingrassatore	22 engrasador	22 copo de lubrificação
23 drejningsmoment	23 momento, coppia torcente	23 par	23 binário
24 friktion	24 frizione	24 fricción	24 fricção, atrito
25 sugning	25 aspirazione	25 aspiración	25 aspiração, sucção
26 tryk	26 pressione	26 presión	26 pressão
27 forbrænding	27 combustione	27 combustión	27 combustão
28 kompression	28 compressione	28 compresión	

ENGLISH	FRANÇAIS	DEUTSCH	NEDERLANDS
Faults and repairs	**Défauts et réparations**	**Defekte und Reparaturen**	**Gebreken en reparaties**

ENGLISH	FRANÇAIS	DEUTSCH	NEDERLANDS
1 broken	1 cassé	1 gebrochen	1 gebroken
2 damaged	2 endommagé	2 beschädigt	2 beschadigd
3 worn	3 usé	3 abgenutzt	3 versleten
4 pitted	4 piqué	4 angefressen	4 ingevreten
5 blocked	5 bouché, bloqué	5 verstopft	5 geblokkeerd
6 loose	6 desserré	6 lose	6 los
7 stall	7 caler	7 abwürgen	7 vastlopen
8 vibrate	8 vibrer	8 vibrieren	8 trillen, vibreren
9 knock	9 cogner	9 klopfen	9 kloppen
10 leak	10 fuir, s'échapper	10 lecken	10 lekken
11 overheat	11 surchauffer	11 überhitzen	11 oververhitten, warmlopen
12 misfire	12 raté d'allumage	12 fehlzünden	12 overslaan
13 to oil	13 huiler, lubrifier	13 ölen	13 olien
14 to grease	14 graisser	14 schmieren	14 invetten
15 to change the oil	15 faire la vidange d'huile	15 das Öl wechseln	15 de olie verversen
16 to charge the battery	16 charger la batterie	16 Batterie aufladen	16 de accu laden
17 to top up the battery	17 remplir la batterie	17 Batterie auffüllen	17 de accu bijvullen
18 to overhaul	18 revision, remettre à neuf	18 überholen	18 reviseren
19 to test	19 vérifier	19 prüfen	19 beproeven, testen
20 to adjust	20 régler	20 einstellen	20 afstellen
21 to clean	21 nettoyer	21 reinigen	21 schoonmaken
22 to tighten	22 serrer, bloquer	22 anziehen	22 aandraaien
23 to loosen	23 desserrer, libérer	23 nachlassen, lockern	23 losmaken, losdraaien
24 to decarbonize	24 décalaminer	24 entkohlen	24 ontkolen
25 to grind in valves	25 roder ou rectifier les soupapes	25 Ventile einschleifen	25 klep inslijpen
26 to bleed	26 purger d'air	26 entlüften	26 ontluchten
27 to reline	27 regarnir	27 wieder ausfüllen	27 van nieuwe voering voorzien

DANSK	ITALIANO	ESPAÑOL	PORTUGUÊS
Fejl og reparationer	**Avarie e riparazioni**	**Averías y reparaciones**	**Defeitos e reparações**
1 knækket	1 rotto	1 roto	1 partido
2 beskadiget	2 danneggiato	2 averiado	2 danificado
3 slidt	3 usurato, consumato	3 gastado	3 gasto
4 tilsodet	4 vaiolato, cariato	4 picado	4 picado
5 blokeret	5 bloccato, chiuso	5 obstruido	5 obstruído
6 løs	6 lasco, lento	6 flojo	6 solto
7 at gå i stå	7 fermarsi	7 detenerse	7 afogar, parar
8 at vibrere	8 vibrare	8 vibrar	8 vibrar
9 at banke	9 battere	9 golpear	9 bater
10 at lække	10 avere una perdita	10 gotear	10 perder líquido, verter
11 at løbe varm	11 surriscaldare	11 recalentar	11 sobreaquecer
12 at tænde forkert	12 dare accensioni irregolari	12 encendido defectuoso	12 falhar, ratés
13 at smøre	13 lubrificare	13 lubricar	13 meter óleo
14 at smøre med fedt	14 ingrassare	14 engrasar	14 lubrificar
15 at skifte olie	15 cambiare l'olio	15 cambiar el aceite	15 mudar o óleo
16 oplade batteri	16 caricare la batteria	16 cargar la batería	16 carregar bateria
17 fylde batteriet op	17 riempire la batteria	17 rellenar la batería	17 atestar bateria
18 at efterse	18 revisionare	18 revisión	18 fazer revisão
19 at prøve	19 controllare	19 probar	19 ensaiar
20 indstille	20 regolare	20 ajustar, regular	20 regular
21 at rense	21 pulire	21 limpiar	21 limpar
22 at spænde	22 stringere	22 apretar	22 apertar
23 at opgå	23 allascare, allentare	23 aflojar	23 desapertar
24 afkoksning	24 disincrostare	24 descarbonizar	24 descarbonisar
25 at slibe ventiler	25 smerigliare le valvole	25 esmerilar las válvulas	25 rodar ou rectificar válvulas
26 at lufte ud	26 spurgare	26 purgar	26 sangrar
27 ny foring	27 sostituire i ferodi	27 renovar los forros	27 calçar de novo

ENGLISH	FRANÇAIS	DEUTSCH	NEDERLANDS
Fuel, etc.	**Combustible, etc.**	**Kraftstoff u.a.**	**Brandstof**
1 fuel consumption	1 consommation	1 Kraftstoffverbrauch	1 brandstofverbruik
2 petrol	2 essence	2 Benzin	2 benzine
3 paraffin	3 pétrole	3 Petroleum	3 petroleum
4 diesel oil	4 gas-oil, mazout	4 Dieselöl	4 dieselolie
5 engine oil	5 huile	5 Schmieröl	5 olie
6 grease	6 graisse	6 Fett	6 vet
7 distilled water	7 eau distillée	7 destilliertes Wasser	7 gedistilleerd water
8 hydraulic fluid	8 liquide hydraulique	8 Hydrauliköl	8 hydraulische olie
9 antifreeze	9 anti-gel	9 Frostschutzmittel	9 antivries

Trailer **Motor car**	**Remorque** **Voiture**	**Pkw-Anhänger** **Auto**	**Boottrailer** **Auto**
1 serial number	1 numéro de série	1 Fabriknummer	1 serienummer
2 chassis number	2 numéro de châssis	2 Fahrgestellnummer	2 chassisnummer
3 overall length	3 longueur hors-tout	3 Gesamtlänge	3 grootste lengte
4 overall width	4 largeur totale	4 Breite	4 grootste breedte
5 height	5 hauteur	5 Höhe	5 hoogte
6 wheelbase	6 empattement	6 Achsstand	6 wielbasis
7 weight	7 poids	7 Gewicht	7 gewicht
8 registration	8 numéro d'immatriculation	8 Zulassungsnummer	8 kenteken

Garage	**Garage**	**Tankstelle**	**Garage**
1 repair a puncture	1 réparer une crevaison	1 einen Reifen flicken	1 een band plakken
2 change a wheel	2 remplacer une roue	2 ein Rad wechseln	2 een wiel verwisselen
3 fill up with petrol	3 faire le plein	3 volltanken	3 met benzine vullen
4 tyre pressure	4 pression des pneus	4 Reifendruck	4 bandenspanning
5 put on chains	5 mettre les chaînes	5 Schneeketten anlegen	5 sneeuwkettingen aanbrengen

DANSK	ITALIANO	ESPAÑOL	PORTUGUÊS
Brændstof	**Combustibile**	**Combustible**	**Combustível**
1 brændstof-forbrug	1 consumo di combustibile	1 consumo de combustible	1 consumo de combustível
2 benzin	2 benzina	2 gasolina	2 gasolina
3 petroleum	3 petrolio	3 petróleo	3 petróleo
4 dieselolie	4 motorina, combustibile per diesel, gasolio	4 gasoil	4 gasóleo
5 maskinolie	5 olio lubrificante	5 aceite de motor	5 óleo de motor
6 fedt	6 grasso	6 grasa	6 massa
7 destilleret vand	7 acqua distillata	7 agua destilada	7 água destilada
8 hydraulisk vædske	8 liquido idraulico	8 aceite hidráulico	8 óleo para sistema hidráulico
9 frysevædske	9 anticongelante	9 anticongelante	9 anti-congelante
Trailer	**Carrello, rimorchio**	**Remolque**	**Carro, para reboque**
Bil	**Automobile**	**Automóvil**	**Automóvel**
1 serienummer	1 numero di serie	1 número de serie	1 número de série
2 chassis number	2 numero di chassis	2 número del chassis	2 número de chassis
3 størstelængde	3 lunghezza totale	3 longitud total	3 comprimento máximo
4 største bredde	4 larghezza totale	4 anchura total	4 largura máxima
5 højde	5 altezza	5 altura	5 altura
6 akselafstand	6 passo	6 batallo, anchura entre ruedas	6 distância entre eixos
7 vægt	7 peso	7 peso	7 pêso
8 indregistrerings-nummer	8 numero di identificazione	8 número de registro	8 número de matrícula de registo
Garage	**Rimessa, garage**	**Garage**	**Garagem**
1 reparation af punktering	1 riparare una bucatura	1 reparar un pinchazo	1 consertar o furo
2 udskifte et hjul	2 cambiare una ruota	2 cambiar una rueda	2 mudar a roda
3 påfylde benzin	3 fare il pieno	3 llenar con gasolina	3 encher com gasolina
4 trykket i bil-dækkene	4 pressione dei pneumatici	4 presión de neumático	4 pressão dos pneus
5 sætte snekæder på	5 mettere le catene per la neve	5 poner cadenas (nieve)	5 montar correntes para neve

ENGLISH	FRANÇAIS	DEUTSCH	NEDERLANDS
Motor car	**Voiture**	**Auto**	**Auto**
1 steering wheel	1 volant	1 Lenkrad	1 stuurwiel
2 accelerator	2 accélérateur	2 Gaspedal	2 gaspedaal
3 foot brake	3 frein à pied	3 Fußbremse	3 rempedaal
4 hand brake	4 frein à main	4 Handbremse	4 handrem
5 clutch pedal	5 pédale d'embrayage	5 Kupplungspedal	5 koppelingspedaal
6 windscreen	6 pare-brise	6 Windschutzscheibe	6 voorruit
7 windscreen wiper	7 essuie-glace	7 Scheibenwischer	7 ruitenwisser
8 windscreen washer	8 lave-glace	8 Scheibenwaschanlage	8 ruitensproeier
9 direction indicators	9 indicateurs de direction	9 Winker	9 richtingaanwijzer
10 brake lights	10 feux de freins	10 Bremslichter	10 stoplichten
11 side lights	11 feux de position	11 Parklichter	11 stadslichten
12 rear lights	12 feux arrière	12 Rücklichter	12 achterlichten
13 headlights	13 phares	13 Scheinwerfer	13 grootlichten, koplampen
14 horn	14 klaxon, avertisseur	14 Hupe	14 claxon
15 number plate	15 plaque minéralogique	15 Nummernschild	15 nummerplaat
16 bonnet	16 capot	16 Motorhaube	16 motorkap
17 door	17 porte	17 Tür	17 portier
18 lock	18 serrure	18 Schloß	18 slot
19 boot	19 coffre	19 Kofferraum	19 kofferruimte
20 bumper	20 pare-choc	20 Stoßstange	20 bumper
21 brake drum	21 tambour de frein	21 Bremstrommel	21 trommel
22 lining	22 garniture	22 Bremsbelag	22 remvoering
23 axle	23 essieu	23 Achse	23 as
24 shock absorber	24 amortisseur	24 Stoßdämpfer	24 schokbreker
25 spring	25 ressort	25 Feder	25 veer
26 steering	26 direction	26 Lenkung	26 stuurinrichting
27 radiator	27 radiateur	27 Kühler	27 radiateur
28 tyre	28 pneu	28 Reifen	28 band
29 tubeless tyre	29 tubeless (pneu sans chambre à air)	29 schlauchloser Reifen	29 tubeless band

DANSK	ITALIANO	ESPAÑOL	PORTUGUÊS
Bil	**Auto**	**Automóvil**	**Automóvel**
1 rat	1 volante	1 volante	1 volante
2 speeder	2 acceleratore	2 acelerador	2 acelerador
3 fodbremse	3 freno pedale	3 freno de pedal	3 travão de pé
4 håndbremse	4 freno a mano	4 freno de mano	4 travão de mão
5 koblingspedal	5 pedale della frizione	5 pedal de embrague	5 pedal de embraiagem
6 vindspejl	6 parabrezza	6 parabrisas	6 parabrisas
7 vindspejlvisker	7 tergicristallo	7 limpia parabrisas	7 limpa parabrisas
8 vindspejl-vasker	8 spruzzavetro	8 lava parabrisas	8 lavador do parabrisas
9 afviser	9 lampeggiatori, indicatori di direzione	9 intermitentes	9 indicadores de direcção
10 stoplygte	10 fanali dello stop	10 luz de pare	10 luzes de travão
11 parkeringslygte	11 fanali di posizione	11 luz posición	11 farolins
12 baglygte	12 fanali posteriori	12 luz trasera	12 farolins trazeiros
13 forlygte	13 fari	13 faros	13 faróis
14 horn	14 clacson, tromba	14 bocina	14 bozina, claxon
15 nummerplade	15 targa	15 matrícula	15 chapa de matrícula
16 motorhjelm	16 cofano	16 capot	16 capot
17 dør	17 porta	17 puerta	17 porta
18 lås	18 serratura	18 cerradura	18 fechadura
19 bagage-rum	19 portabagagli	19 maleta	19 mala
20 kofanger	20 paraurti	20 parachoques	20 pára-choques
21 bremsetromle	21 tamburo per il freno	21 tambor de freno	21 tambor de travão
22 belægning	22 ferodo, spessore	22 forro	22 calços de travão
23 aksel	23 asse	23 eje	23 eixo
24 støddæmper	24 ammortizzatore	24 amortiguador	24 amortecedor
25 fjeder	25 molla	25 ballestas	25 mola
26 styretøj	26 guida, sterzo	26 dirección	26 direcção
27 køleren	27 radiatore	27 radiador	27 radiador
28 dæk	28 pneumatico	28 neumático	28 pneumático, pneu
29 dæk uden slange	29 pneumatico senza camera d'aria	29 neumático sin cámara	29 pneu sem câmara de ar

ENGLISH	FRANÇAIS	DEUTSCH	NEDERLANDS
Points of sailing	**Les allures**	**Die Kurse zum Wind**	**Koersen**
1 **Head wind**	1 **Vent debout**	1 **Gegenwind**	1 **wind tegen**
2 head to wind	2 nez dans le vent	2 in den Wind	2 stik-in-de-wind, recht in de wind
3 the tack	3 bordée, bord	3 Schlag, Überstaggehen	3 slag
4 port tack	4 bâbord amures	4 Steuerbordbug	4 stuurboordsboeg, over stuurboord
5 starboard tack	5 tribord amures	5 Backbordbug	5 bakboordsboeg, over bakboord
6 to beat	6 tirer des bords, louvoyer	6 kreuzen	6 laveren, kruisen
7 to go about	7 virer au vent	7 über Stag gehen, wenden	7 overstag gaan, wenden, door de wind gaan
8 'Ready about'	8 'Paré à virer'	8 'Klar zum Wenden'	8 'Klaar om te wenden'
9 'Lee-o'	9 'Envoyez'	9 'Ree'	9 'Ree'
10 close hauled	10 au plus près	10 hoch am Wind	10 bij-de-wind
11 on the wind	11 au près	11 am Wind, beim Wind	11 aan-de-wind
12 full and by	12 au près bon plein	12 voll und bei	12 vol-en-bij
13 **wind abeam**	13 **vent de travers, de côté**	13 **halber Wind**	13 **wind dwars, halve wind**
14 reaching	14 largue	14 raumschots	14 ruimschoots zeilen
15 **wind free**	15 **vent arrière ou portant**	15 **raumer Wind**	15 **ruime wind**
16 wind on the quarter	16 vent de la hanche, largue	16 Backstagsbrise	16 bakstagwind
17 running	17 vent arrière	17 vor dem Wind	17 voor de wind zeilen
18 dead before the wind	18 plein vent arrière	18 platt vor dem Wind	18 vlak of pal voor de wind
19 run by the lee	19 sous le vent, sur la panne	19 vor dem Wind nach Lee segeln	19 binnen de wind zeilen
20 to gybe	20 empanner, gambeyer	20 halsen	20 gijpen
21 accidental gybe	21 empannage involontaire, gambeyage accidentel	21 unfreiwilliges Halsen, giepen	21 onvrijwillige gijp
22 heading wind	22 le vent refuse	22 schralender Wind	22 schralende wind
23 freeing wind	23 le vent adonne	23 raumender Wind	23 ruimende wind
24 windward/leeward	24 au vent/sous le vent	24 luvwärts/leewärts	24 loefwaarts/lijwaarts boven/beneden

DANSK	ITALIANO	ESPAÑOL	PORTUGUÊS
Sejlads	**Andature**	**Mareaje**	**Mareações**
1 **modvind**	1 **vento di prora**	1 **viento de proa**	1 **vento de prôa**
2 vindret	2 prua al vento	2 proa al viento	2 aproado ao vento
3 vending	3 il bordo	3 bordada	3 o bordo
4 på bagbords halse	4 con mure a sinistra	4 amurado a babor	4 amuras a bombordo
5 på styrbords halse	5 con mure a dritta	5 amurado a estribor	5 amuras a estibordo
6 at krydse	6 bolinare, andare di bolina	6 barloventear, ceñir	6 bolinar
7 at vende	7 virare di bordo	7 virar	7 virar por de vante
8 'Klar til at vende'	8 'pronto a virare'	8 'listo para virar'	8 'claro a virar'
9 'Vende'	9 'vira'	9 '¡vira!'	9 'vira'
10 kloshalet	10 di bolina	10 ciñendo	10 bolina cerrada
11 bidevind	11 al vento	11 de bolina	11 bolinando
12 bidevind og godt fuldt	12 di bolina stretta	12 en viento	12 de bolina
13 **vinden tværs**	13 **vento a mezza nave o al traverso**	13 **viento de través**	13 **vento pelo través**
14 slør, rumskøds	14 lasco	14 a un largo	14 a um largo
15 **fri vind**	15 **a vento largo**	15 **viento libre**	15 **vento aberto, largo**
16 vind agten for tværs	16 al giardinetto	16 viento de aleta	16 vento pela alhêta
17 lænse	17 in poppa, in fil di ruota	17 en popa	17 navegar com vento à pôpa
18 med vinden ret agterind	18 vento esattamente in poppa	18 en pura empopada	18 à pôpa razada
19 lige før man bommer	19 scarrocciare sottovento	19 tomar por la lua	19 correr à pôpa com vento já por sotavento
20 at bomme	20 strambare, abbattere	20 trasluchar	20 cambar
21 bomme ved et uheld	21 strambata involontaria abbatuta involontaria	21 trasluchada involuntaria	21 cambar involuntáriamente
22 vinden spidser	22 vento che rifiuta	22 escasear el viento	22 vento que casseia
23 vinden rummer	23 vento che ridonda	23 alargarse el viento	23 vento que alarga
24 luv/læ	24 sopravento, sottovento	24 barlovento/sotavento	24 barlavento/sotavento

ENGLISH	FRANÇAIS	DEUTSCH	NEDERLANDS
Setting sails	**Etablir les voiles**	**Segel setzen**	**Het zetten van de zeilen**
1 bend on the sails	1 enverguer les voiles	1 die Segel anschlagen	1 de zeilen aanslaan
2 hank on the jib	2 endrailler le foc	2 die Stagreiter einpicken	2 de fok inpikken
3 put in the battens	3 enfiler les lattes	3 Segellatten einsetzen	3 zeillatten inbrengen
4 pull out the foot	4 étarquer le point d'écoute	4 das Unterliek ausholen	4 voetlijk strekken
5 reeve the sheets	5 passer les écoutes dans les margouillets	5 die Schoten einscheren	5 de schoten inscheren
6 tighten the topping lift	6 peser sur la balancine	6 andirken	6 kraanlijn doorzetten
7 hoist the sail	7 hisser, établir la voile	7 Segel vorheißen	7 zeil hijsen
8 sweat up the halyard	8 étarquer la drisse	8 das Fall steif durchsetzen	8 de vallen doorzetten
9 change a sail	9 changer une voile	9 ein Segel auswechseln	9 een zeil verwisselen
10 to shackle on	10 emmailler, maniller	10 einschäkeln	10 met sluiting vastzetten
11 lower, hand a sail	11 amener, baisser ou rentrer une voile	11 ein Segel bergen	11 een zeil strijken, innemen
12 to furl	12 serrer, ferler	12 auftuchen, bändseln	12 opdoeken
13 in stops	13 à envergures-cassantes ou bosses-cassantes	13 aufgetucht	13 opgestopt
Sail trimming	**Régler, tendre les voiles**	**Segel trimmen**	**Trimmen, bedienen**
14 to sheet a sail	14 border les voiles	14 ein Segel schoten	14 schoot van een zeil vastzetten
15 to make fast, belay	15 amarrer; tourner ou frapper une amarre	15 festmachen, belegen	15 vastmaken, beleggen
16 to ease out, pay out	16 choquer, filer, mollir	16 fieren, schricken, auffieren	16 vieren, uitvieren
17 to coil a rope	17 lover	17 ein Tau aufschießen	17 opschieten
18 to take a turn	18 frapper un tour, donner un tour	18 einen Rundtörn machen	18 een torn nemen
19 to haul in, harden	19 embraquer, haler; peser sur, souquer, border	19 dichtholen	19 schoot doorzetten
20 cast off	20 larguer, démarrer	20 losschmeissen, loswerfen	20 loswerpen, losgooien

DANSK	ITALIANO	ESPAÑOL	PORTUGUÊS
Sætte sejl	**Messa in vela, vele alzate**	**Dar la vela**	**Içar os panos**
1 at slå sejl under	1 inferire le vele	1 envergar las velas	1 envergar os panos
2 at slå fokken under	2 inferire il fiocco	2 envergar el foque	2 envergar o estai
3 at sætte sejlpindene i	3 mettere le stecche	3 colocar los sables	3 meter as réguas
4 at strække underliget	4 alare la linea di scotta	4 tesar el pujamen	4 esticar o punho da escota
5 at skære skøderne i	5 spassare le scotte	5 guarnir las escotas	5 gornir o cabo da escota
6 at sætte bomdirken	6 tesare a ferro l'amantiglio	6 tesar el amantillo	6 esticar o amantilho
7 at hejse sejlet	7 alzare la vela	7 izar la vela	7 içar a vela
8 at strække faldet	8 metter in forza la drizza	8 tesar bien la driza	8 entesar a adriça
9 at skifte sejl	9 cambiare una vela	9 cambiar una vela	9 mudar uma vela
10 at sjækle på	10 ammanigliare	10 engrilletar	10 emanilhar
11 at bjærge et sejl	11 ammainare una vela	11 arriar una vela	11 arriar a vela
12 at rulle sammern	12 serrare	12 aferrar	12 ferrar
13 i knækgarn	13 vele serrate con i matafioni	13 enjuncar, enchorizar	13 rafiar
Trimning af sejl	**Orientamento delle vele**	**Marear las velas**	**Mareação dos panos**
14 at skøde et sejl	14 fissare le scotte di una vela	14 cazar una vela	14 caçar a vela
15 at gøre fast	15 dare volta ad un cavo	15 amarrar	15 amarrar, passar volta a um cunho
16 at slække på skøderne	16 filare	16 amollar, filar	16 folgar a vela
17 at skyde en ende op	17 raccogliere un cavo	17 adujar un cabo	17 colher um cabo
18 at tage en tørn på en klampe	18 prendere una volta	18 tomar una vuelta	18 passar uma volta
19 at hale hjem på skødet	19 cazzare, tesare a ferro	19 cazar	19 caçar
20 at smide los	20 mollare	20 largar	20 largar

ENGLISH	FRANÇAIS	DEUTSCH	NEDERLANDS
Under sail	**Sous voiles**	**Unter segel**	**Onder zeil**
1 full, drawing	1 pleine, portante	1 vollstehend, ziehend	1 vol
2 lifting	2 faseyer	2 killen	2 killen
3 aback	3 à contre	3 backstehen	3 bak
4 slatting	4 battante, fouettante	4 schlagen	4 klapperen
5 to let fly	5 larguer	5 fliegen lassen	5 laten vieren
6 to back the jib	6 contrebrasser, porter le foc au vent	6 Fock backhalten	6 fok bakhouden
7 boom out or wing out	7 voile en ciseau	7 ausbaumen	7 te loevert zetten
Characteristics	**Caractéristiques**	**Eigenschaften**	**Zeileigenschappen**
1 seaworthy	1 marin, qui tient bien la mer	1 seetüchtig	1 zeewaardig
2 stability	2 stabilité	2 Stabilität	2 stabiliteit
3 to heel	3 gîter	3 krängen, überliegen	3 hellen, overhellen
4 stiff	4 raide à la toile	4 steif	4 stijf
5 tender	5 gîtard	5 rank	5 slap
6 to point well	6 tenir bon cap	6 hoch am Wind segeln	6 hoog aan-de-wind zeilen
7 weather helm	7 être ardent	7 luvgierig	7 loefgierig
8 lee helm	8 être mou	8 leegierig	8 lijgierig
9 to pitch	9 tanguer	9 einsetzen, stampfen	9 stampen
10 to roll	10 rouler	10 rollen	10 rollen
11 to yaw	11 faire des embardées	11 gieren	11 gieren
To run aground	**Échouer**	**Auf Grund laufen**	**Vastlopen**
1 aground	1 échoué	1 auf Grund sitzen	1 aan de grond
2 high and dry	2 au sec	2 hoch und trocken	2 droogvallen
3 to heel the boat	3 faire gîter le bateau	3 das Boot krängen	3 de boot krengen
4 to refloat	4 dégager, deséchouer	4 wieder flottmachen	4 van de grond brengen

DANSK	ITALIANO	ESPAÑOL	PORTUGUÊS
Under sejl	**In vela**	**A la vela**	**Navegar à vela**
1 sejlet står fuldt og trækker	1 piene, che portano	1 llena, portando	1 cheia, cheio, a puxar
2 sejlet lever	2 che si alza	2 tocando	2 encher por sotavento
3 sejlet bakker	3 a collo	3 en facha	3 aquartelado
4 blafre	4 che sbattono, che sfileggiano	4 flamear	4 bater pano
5 at lade gå	5 mollare e lasciar sbattere	5 arriar en banda	5 largar o pano
6 at bakke fokken	6 mettere il fiocco a collo	6 acuartelar el foque	6 aquartelar o estai
7 at spile forsejlene	7 con il fiocco a farfalla	7 a orejas de mulo	7 armar em borboleta
Egenskaber	**Caratteristiche**	**Caracteristicas**	**Qualidades**
1 sødygtig	1 qualità marine	1 navegabilidad	1 qualidades de mar
2 stabilitet	2 stabilità	2 estabilidad	2 estabilidade
3 at krænge	3 ingavonarsi, sbandarsi	3 escorar	3 inclinar
4 stiv	4 dura	4 duro	4 com muita estabilidade
5 kilden	5 cedevole	5 blando	5 com pouca estabilidade
6 at holde højt	6 stringere molto il vento	6 bolinero	6 bolinar bem
7 luvgerrig	7 orziera	7 ardiente	7 leme com tendência para orçar
8 lægerrig	8 puggiera	8 propenso a la arribada	8 leme com tendência para arribar
9 at stampe	9 beccheggiare	9 cabecear, arfar	9 balanço longitudinal
10 at slingre	10 rollare	10 balancear	10 balanço transversal
11 at gire	11 straorzare	11 guiñar	11 guinar
Gå på grund	**Andare in secca**	**Varar, encallar**	**Encalhar**
1 på grund	1 arenato, incagliato	1 varado, encallado	1 encalhado
2 højt og tørt	2 completamente in secco	2 estar en seco	2 ficar em sêco
3 at krænge båden over	3 ingavonare, sbandare	3 tumbar, dar la banda	3 inclinar o barco
4 at få båden let	4 rimettere a galla, rigalleggiare	4 poner a flote	4 pôr a flutuar

ENGLISH	FRANÇAIS	DEUTSCH	NEDERLANDS
To steer	**Gouverner**	**Steuern**	**Sturen**
1 helm	1 barre, gouvernail	1 Ruder	1 roer
2 put up the helm	2 mettre la barre dessus	2 Ruder nach Luv	2 afhouden
3 bear away	3 abattre, laisser arriver	3 abfallen	3 afhouden, afvallen
4 sail fuller	4 abattre, venir sous le vent	4 voller segeln	4 voller zeilen, lager sturen
5 put down the helm	5 mettre la barre dessous	5 Ruder nach Lee	5 oploeven
6 luff up	6 lofer	6 anluven	6 oploeven, opsturen
7 to point higher	7 venir au vent, remonter	7 höher anliegen	7 hoger sturen
8 pinching	8 fìnasser, faire trop bon cap	8 kneifen	8 knijpen
9 to meet her	9 rencontrer	9 aufkommen	9 opvangen
10 on course	10 maintenir le cap,	10 auf Kurs	10 op koers
11 off course	11 ne pas suivre la route	11 vom Kurs abgewichen	11 van koers
12 alter course	12 changer de cap	12 Kurs ändern	12 koers veranderen
13 to answer the helm	13 obéir à la barre	13 dem Ruder gehorchen	13 naar het roer luisteren
Under way	**En route**	**In Fahrt**	**Vaart houden**
1 to have way	1 avoir de l'erre, lancée	1 Fahrt voraus machen	1 gang houden
2 to make headway	2 avancer, fìler	2 Fahrt über Grund machen	2 vooruit lopen
3 to stem the tide	3 remonter la marée	3 den Strom aussegeln	3 het tij doodzeilen
4 becalmed	4 encalminé	4 bekalmt	4 in katzwijm
5 to drift	5 dériver	5 treiben, abtreiben	5 afdrijven
6 sternway	6 culer	6 Achterausfahrt	6 deinzen
7 bow wave	7 moustaches	7 Bugwelle	7 boeggolf
8 stern wave, wake, wash	8 lame de sillage, sillage	8 Heckwelle, Kielwasser	8 hekgolf, kielzog
9 way enough	9 erre suffìsante	9 genug Fahrt	9 genoeg vaart
10 full ahead	10 en avant toute	10 volle Fahrt voraus	10 volle kracht vooruit
11 slow astern	11 arrière lentement	11 langsame Fahrt zurück	11 langzaam achteruit
12 lose way	12 perdre de l'erre, casser son erre	12 Fahrt verlieren	12 vaart verliezen

DANSK	ITALIANO	ESPAÑOL	PORTUGUÊS
At styre	**Governare**	**Gobernar**	**Governar, fazer leme**
1 roret	1 il timone	1 caña	1 o leme
2 at lægge roret op	2 mettere il timone alla puggia	2 levantar la caña	2 leme de encontro
3 at holde af	3 puggiare	3 arribar	3 arribar
4 at sejle mere fuldt	4 puggiare un tantino	4 marear la vela	4 navegar mais arribado
5 at lægge roret ned	5 metter il timone all'orza	5 meter la caña	5 leme de ló
6 at luffe	6 orzare	6 orzar	6 orçar
7 at holde højere	7 stringere di più	7 ceñir más	7 orçar mais
8 at holde for højt hele tiden	8 governare quasi a sfileggiare	8 orzar a fil de roda	8 à trinca
9 at støtte båden	9 scontrare il timone	9 gobernar al encuentro	9 levar ao encontro
10 på kursen	10 in rotta	10 a rumbo	10 estar no rumo
11 ude af kurs	11 fuori rotta	11 fuera de rumbo	11 estar fora do rumo
12 at ændre kurs	12 cambiare rotta, accostare	12 cambiar el rumbo	12 alterar o rumo
13 at lystre roret	13 ubbidire al timone	13 responder bien al timón	13 obedecer ao leme
Båden er let	**In navigazione**	**Navegando**	**Em andamento**
1 at have styrefart	1 guadagnare cammino	1 llevar camino, ir avante	1 ter andamento
2 at skyde over stævn	2 avere abbrivio in avanti	2 hacer camino	2 ganhar andamento
3 at bove strømmen	3 risalire la corrente	3 vencer la marea	3 vencer a corrente
4 ligger i vindstille	4 abbonacciato	4 encalmado	4 encalmado
5 at drive med strømmen	5 derivare	5 derivar	5 andar à deriva
6 sakke	6 abbrivio indietro	6 navegar hacia atrás, ciar	6 andamento a ré
7 bovbølge	7 onda di prora	7 bigote	7 onda da proa
8 hækbølge, kølvand	8 onda di poppa, scia	8 bigote de aleta	8 onda da pôpa, esteira
9 fart nok	9 abbrivio sufficiente	9 salida	9 andamento suficiente
10 fuld kraft frem	10 avanti tutta	10 avante toda	10 tôdo avante
11 langsomt bak	11 indietro adagio	11 atrás despacio	11 a ré devagar
12 tabe fart	12 perdere cammino	12 perder marcha	12 perder andamento

ENGLISH	FRANÇAIS	DEUTSCH	NEDERLANDS
Mooring	**Corps-mort, s'amarrer**	**Vermuren, Festmachen**	**Meren**
1 pick up a mooring	1 prendre, s'amarrer sur une bouée de corps-mort	1 eine Ankerboje aufnehmen	1 op een boei meren
2 slip the mooring	2 larguer un corps-mort	2 die Ankerboje loswerfen	2 meerboei slippen
3 wind rode	3 éviter au vent	3 im Wind liegen, schwojen	3 op de wind liggend
4 tide rode	4 éviter au courant	4 im Strom liegen, schwojen	4 voor tij liggend
5 lie alongside	5 accoster, s'amarrer le long de . . .	5 längsseits liegen	5 langszij liggen
6 put out fenders	6 munir de défenses	6 Fender ausbringen	6 stootkussens of willen uithangen
7 make fast	7 amarrer, capeler, frapper	7 festmachen	7 vastmaken, vastzetten
8 cast off	8 dégager, larguer	8 loswerfen, ablegen, los-schmeißen	8 losgooien
9 fend off	9 écarter	9 absetzen, abstoßen	9 afduwen
10 piles	10 poteaux	10 Festmachepfahl	10 palen, remmingwerk
11 jetty	11 jetée	11 Anlegestelle, kleine Pier	11 pier
12 Yacht Club	12 Yacht Club, Club Nautique	12 Yachtclub	12 Jacht Club, Zeilvereniging
13 Harbour Master	13 Chef ou Capitaine de port	13 Hafenkapitän	13 havenmeester
14 harbour dues	14 droits de port	14 Hafengebühr	14 havengelden
15 speed limit	15 vitesse maximum autorisée	15 Geschwindigkeitsbegren-zung	15 snelheidsbeperking
16 depth alongside pier	16 profondeur le long de la jetée	16 Wassertiefe längsseits der Pier	16 diepte naast de pier
17 traffic signals	17 signaux de mouvements de navires	17 Verkehrssignale (in Tidenhäfen)	17 verkeersseinen
18 Is there enough water?	18 Y a-t-il du fond?	18 Ist dort Wasser genug?	18 Is er genoeg water?
19 Where can I moor?	19 Où puis-je accoster?	19 Wo kann ich festmachen?	19 Waar kan ik vastmaken?

ENGLISH	FRANÇAIS	DEUTSCH	NEDERLANDS
Spring a leak	**Voie d'eau**	**Leck schlagen**	**Lek springen**
1 to make water	1 faire de l'eau	1 Wasser machen	1 water maken
2 to ship water	2 embarquer de l'eau	2 vollschlagen	2 water overnemen
3 pump the bilges	3 pomper, vider, assécher	3 Bilge lenzen	3 lenzen, lens pompen
4 bail out	4 écoper	4 ausösen	4 uithozen

(handwritten at top) to anchore — fondear, anclar
anchor (N) — ancla

DANSK	ITALIANO	ESPAÑOL	PORTUGUÊS
Fortøjning	**Ormeggio**	**Amarraje**	**Amarração**
1 at tage en fortøjning	1 prendere un ormeggio, ormeggiarse	1 tomar la amarra de un muerto	1 apanhar a amarração
2 at lade fortøjningen gå	2 lasciare l'ormeggio	2 largar, lascar la amarra	2 largar a amarração
3 vindret	3 orientato con la prora al vento (all'ancora)	3 caer por el viento	3 aproado ao vento
4 strømret	4 orientato con la prora alla corrente (all'ancora)	4 caer por la marea	4 aproado à maré, à corrente
5 side om side, langs med	5 affiancato	5 atracar de costado	5 atracado
6 at hænge fendere ud	6 mettere fuori i parabordi	6 poner las defensas	6 pôr as defensas
7 at gøre fast	7 ormeggiarsi	7 amarrar firme	7 amarrar
8 at smide los	8 mollare	8 largar amarras	8 largar
9 at fendre af	9 scostarsi	9 abrir	9 defender
10 fortøjningspæle	10 piloni	10 estaca	10 estacas, duques de alba
11 mole	11 molo	11 muelle	11 molhe
12 Yacht Klub	12 Yacht Club, Circolo Velico, Circolo Nautico	12 Club Náutico, Club Marítimo	12 Clube Náutico
13 Havnefoged	13 Comandante del Porto	13 Capitán de Puerto, Comandante de Marina	13 Capitão do Pôrto
14 havneafgift	14 tassa d'ormeggio	14 derechos de puerto	14 taxa de estadia no pôrto
15 fart-begrænsning	15 limite di velocità	15 velocidad máxima	15 limite de velocidade
16 dybde langs pieren	16 fondale lungo il molo	16 calado del muelle	16 altura de água junto ao cais
17 trafiksignaler	17 segnali di traffico	17 señales de tráfico	17 sinais de trânsito
18 Er der vand nok?	18 C'e sufficiente acqua?	18 ¿Hay bastante calado?	18 Há altura de água suficiente?
19 Hvor skal jeg fortøje?	19 Dove posso ormeggiarmi?	19 ¿Dónde puedo amarrar?	19 Aonde posso amarrar?
At få en læk	**Via d'acqua**	**Descubrir un agua**	**Verter**
1 at trække vand	1 fare acqua	1 hacer agua	1 fazer água
2 at tage vand ind	2 imbarcare acqua	2 embarcar agua	2 meter água
3 at pumps læns	3 pompare le sentine	3 achicar la sentina	3 esgotar com bomba
4 at øse læns	4 sgottare	4 achicar	4 esgotar com bartedouro

95

ENGLISH	FRANÇAIS	DEUTSCH	NEDERLANDS
Act of God, etc.	**Fortune de mer, etc.**	**Höhere Gewalt u.s.w.**	**Force majeure**
1 collision	1 abordage	1 Kollision	1 aanvaring
2 shipwreck	2 naufrage	2 Schiffbruch	2 schipbreuk
3 man overboard	3 homme à la mer	3 Mann über Bord	3 man overboord
4 capsize	4 chavirer	4 kentern	4 omslaan, kapseizen
5 stove in	5 défoncé	5 eingeschlagen	5 ingeslagen
6 dismasted	6 démâté	6 entmastet	6 mast overboord
7 abandon ship	7 quitter, abandonner	7 Schiff aufgeben	7 schip verlaten

Heavy weather	**Gros temps**	**Schweres Wetter**	**Zwaar weer**
1 tie down a reef	1 prendre un ris, ariser une voile	1 ein Reff einbinden	1 een rif steken, reven
2 roll down a sail	2 prendre des tours de rouleau	2 das Segel einrollen	2 het zeil oprollen
3 shorten sail	3 réduire la voile	3 Segel verkleinern	3 zeil minderen
4 close reefed	4 au bas ris	4 dicht gerefft	4 dicht gereefd
5 shake out a reef	5 larguer un ris	5 ausreffen, Reffs ausschütten	5 uitreven, een rif uitnemen
6 under bare poles	6 à sec de toile	6 vor Topp und Takel	6 voor top en takel
7 stream a sea anchor	7 mouiller sur une ancre flottante	7 einen Treibanker ausbringen	7 zeeanker uitbrengen
8 stream a warp	8 filer une aussière en remorque	8 eine Trosse nach-schleppen	8 tros achteruitbrengen en slepen
9 strike the topmast	9 saluer un grain, rentrer le flèche	9 die Toppstenge streichen	9 de topmast strijken
10 heave to	10 capeyer, mettre à la cape, prendre la cape	10 beiliegen, beidrehen	10 bijleggen
11 ride out a storm	11 étaler une tempête	11 Sturm abreiten	11 een storm afrijden
12 blow out a sail	12 déchirer, perdre une voile	12 ein Segel fliegt aus den Lieken	12 een zeil uit de lijken waaien
13 ship a green sea	13 embarquer un paquet de mer	13 grünes Wasser übernehmen	13 een zee overnemen
14 weather bound	14 bloqué par le temps	14 eingeweht	14 door het weer opgehouden

DANSK	ITALIANO	ESPAÑOL	PORTUGUÊS
Force majeure	**Incidente**	**Accidentes**	**Casos imprevistos**
1 kollision	1 collissione	1 colisión, abordaje	1 colisão, abalroamento
2 skibbrud	2 relitto	2 naufragio	2 naufrágio
3 mand over bord	3 uomo a mare	3 hombre al agua	3 homem ao mar
4 at kæntre	4 capovolgersi	4 zozobrado	4 virar-se
5 havareret	5 falla o bugna	5 pasado por ojo	5 ter um rombo
6 riggen over bord	6 disalberato	6 desarbolado	6 partir o mastro
7 at forlade skibet	7 abbandonare la nave	7 abandonar el buque	7 abandonar o navio
Hårdt vejr	**Cattivo tempo**	**Mal tiempo**	**Mau tempo**
1 at stikke et reb i	1 prendere una mano di terzaruolo	1 tomar un rizo	1 rizar
2 at rulle på	2 diminuire la superfice velica	2 arrizar	2 enrolar a vela
3 at mindske sejl	3 ridurre la velatura	3 reducir paño	3 reduzir o pano
4 klosrebet	4 terzaruolato al massimo	4 llevar todos los rizos	4 muito rizado
5 at stikke et reb ud	5 mollare un terzaruolo	5 largar los rizos	5 desrizar
6 for den bare rig	6 rimanere senza vele	6 a palo seco	6 em árvore sêca
7 at sætte et drivanker	7 filare una ancora galeggiante	7 largar un ancla flotante	7 deitar a âncora flutuante
8 at stikke et varp ud	8 filare un cavo di tonneggio	8 largar una estacha por popa	8 deitar ao mar um cabo a servir de âncora flutuante
9 at stryge topmasten	9 sghindare l'alberetto	9 calar el mastelero	9 arriar o mastaréu
10 at dreje under	10 mettersi alla cappa, stare alla cappa	10 fachear, capear	10 meter de capa
11 at ride en storm af	11 sostenere bene una burrasca	11 aguantar un mal tiempo	11 aguentar um temporal
12 at få et sejl blæst ud af ligene	12 strappare una vela	12 rifar una vela	12 desfazer uma vela
13 at tage en grøn sø over	13 prendere una incappellata	13 embarcar un golpe de mar	13 embarcar grande massa de água
14 indeblæst	14 trattenuto in porto dal maltempo	14 detenido por mal tiempo	14 abrigado, aguardando melhoria de tempo

ENGLISH	FRANÇAIS	DEUTSCH	NEDERLANDS
Ship's company	**L'équipage**	**Schiffsbesatzung**	**Scheepsbemanning**
1 skipper	1 chef de bord, skipper	1 Kapitän, Schiffsführer	1 schipper
2 navigator	2 navigateur	2 Navigator	2 navigator
3 mate	3 second, chef de quart	3 Bestmann, Steuermann	3 stuurman
4 bo'sun, boatswain	4 quartier-maître, bosco	4 Bootsmann	4 bootsman
5 cook	5 cuisinier	5 Koch	5 kok
6 helmsman	6 barreur, timonier	6 Rudergänger	6 roerganger
7 crew	7 équipage	7 Mannschaft	7 bemanning
8 foredeck hand	8 focquier	8 Vorschotmann	8 dekhulp
9 port watch	9 quart de bâbord, les bâbordais	9 Backbordwache	9 bakboordswacht
10 starboard watch	10 quart de tribord, les tribordais	10 Steuerbordwache	10 stuurboordswacht
11 landlubber	11 éléphant, terrien	11 Landratte	11 landrob
Ship's papers, etc	**Papiers de bord, etc.**	**Schiffspapiere**	**Scheepsdocumenten**
1 Certificate of Registry	1 Certificat de Francisation, Lettre de mer	1 Registrierungs-Zertifikat	1 Zeebrief
2 Ship's Articles	2 Rôle d'équipage	2 Musterrolle	2 Monsterrol
3 Ship's Log	3 Livre de bord	3 Schiffstagebuch, Logbuch	3 Journaal
4 Bill of Health	4 Patente de santé	4 Gesundheitspaß	4 gezondheidsbewijs
5 pratique	5 libre-pratique	5 freie Verkehrserlaubnis	5 pratique
6 insurance certificate	6 certificat d'assurance	6 Versicherungspolice	6 verzekeringsbewijs
7 charter party	7 charte-partie	7 Chartervertrag	7 charterparty
8 customs clearance	8 libre-sortie, congé de douane	8 Zollabfertigung	8 bewijs van klaring door douane
9 bonded stores	9 provisions entreposées, en franchise, sous douane	9 unter Zollverschluß	9 belastingvrije goederen
10 passport	10 passeport	10 Reisepaß	10 paspoort
11 rating certificate	11 certificat de jauge	11 Meßbrief	11 meetbrief

DANSK	ITALIANO	ESPAÑOL	PORTUGUÊS
Fartøjets besætning	**Equipaggio**	**Compania naviera**	**Tripulaçao**
1 skipper	1 padrone	1 patrón, capitán	1 patrão
2 navigator	2 ufficiale di rotta	2 navegante	2 navegador
3 styrmand	3 secondo, prodiere	3 segundo, piloto	3 imediato
4 bådsmand	4 nostromo	4 contramaestre	4 mestre
5 kokken	5 cuoco	5 cocinero	5 cozinheiro
6 rorsmand	6 timoniere	6 timonel	6 homem do leme, timoneiro
7 mandskab	7 equipaggio	7 tripulación	7 tripulaçao
8 forgast	8 mozzo, marinaio	8 tripulante de cubierta de proa	8 prôa, tripulante que faz a manobra à prôa
9 bagbords vagt	9 vedetta di sinistra	9 guardia de babor	9 componentes do 1° quarto
10 styrbords vagt	10 vedetta di dritta	10 guardia de estribor	10 componentes do 2° quarto
11 landkrabbe	11 marinaio d'acqua dolce	11 zapatero	11 homem que não esta habituado ao mar

DANSK	ITALIANO	ESPAÑOL	PORTUGUÊS
Skibspapirer, etc.	**Pratiche di bordo, etc.**	**Documentación**	**Documentação do Barco, etc**
1 Indregistrerings-certifikat	1 Certificato del Registro Navale	1 Patente de Navegación	1 Certificado de Registo
2 Mønstringsliste	2 Ruolo dell'equipaggio	2 Rol	2 Rol da Equipagem
3 Logbog	3 Giornale di Chiesuola	3 Cuaderno de bitácora	3 Diário de Bordo
4 Sundhedspas	4 Patente Sanitaria	4 Patente de Sanidad	4 Certificado de Saúde
5 praktika, tilladelse til at sejle	5 libera pratica	5 plática	5 livre prática
6 assurance police	6 certificato, polizza d'assicurazione	6 póliza de seguro	6 certificado de seguro
7 certeparti	7 contratto di noleggio	7 contrato de flete	7 fretador
8 toldklarering	8 pratica di sdoganamento	8 despacho de aduana	8 despacho
9 varer fra frilager	9 magazzini doganali	9 víveres precintados	9 mantimentos desalfandegados
10 pas	10 passaporto	10 pasaporte	10 passaporte
11 målebrev	11 certificato di stazza	11 certificado de 'Rating' (ventaja)	11 certificado de abôno

99

ENGLISH	FRANÇAIS	DEUTSCH	NEDERLANDS
Navigational equipment	**Instruments de navigation**	**Navigationsausrüstung**	**Navigatie instrumenten**
1 Pilot	1 Instructions Nautiques	1 Seehandbuch	1 Zeemansgids
2 Nautical Almanac	2 Almanach Nautique	2 Nautischer Almanach	2 Almanak
3 Tide Tables	3 Annuaire des Marées	3 Gezeitentafeln	3 Getijtafel
4 Tidal Stream Atlas	4 Atlas des Marées	4 Stromatlas	4 Stroomatlas
5 List of Lights	5 Livre des Phares	5 Leuchtfeuerverzeichnis	5 Lichtlijst, Lichtenlijst
6 Notices to Mariners	6 Avis aux Navigateurs	6 Nachrichten für Seefahrer	6 Berichten aan Zeevarenden
7 deviation table	7 courbe des déviations	7 Deviationstabelle	7 stuurtafel
8 parallel ruler	8 règles parallèles	8 Parallellineal	8 parallellineaal
9 protractor	9 rapporteur	9 Winkelmesser	9 gradenboog
10 triangular protractor	10 rapporteur triangulaire	10 Kursdreieck	10 driehoek
11 pencil	11 crayon	11 Bleistift	11 potlood
12 rubber	12 gomme	12 Radiergummi	12 vlakgom
13 dividers	13 pointes sèches	13 Kartenzirkel	13 verdeelpasser
14 binoculars	14 jumelles	14 Fernglas, Doppelglas	14 kijker
Sextant	**Sextant**	**Sextant**	**Sextant**
1 horizon, index glass	1 petit, grand miroir	1 Horizont-, Indexspiegel	1 kimspiegel, grote spiegel
2 index error	2 erreur de l'alidade	2 Indexfehler	2 indexfout
3 shades	3 filtres	3 Schattengläser	3 gekleurde glazen
4 micrometer drum	4 tambour micrométrique	4 Trommel	4 micrometer trommel
5 arc	5 limbe	5 Gradbogen	5 cirkelboog
Patent log	**Loch enregistreur, sillomètre**	**Patentlog**	**Patent log**
1 rotator	1 hélice	1 Propeller	1 drijver, vin
2 log line	2 ligne du loch	2 Logleine	2 loglijn
3 register	3 enregistreur, compteur	3 Meßuhr	3 klokje, telwerk
4 record on the log	4 enregistrer	4 loggen	4 logaanwijzing
5 stream the log	5 mouiller le loch	5 das Log ausbringen	5 de log uitzetten
6 speed-variation indicator	6 speedomètre	6 Speedometer, Geschwindigkeitsmesser	6 snelheidsmeter

DANSK	ITALIANO	ESPAÑOL	PORTUGUÊS
Navigations udstyr	**Apparecchiature per la Condotta delle navigazione**	**Instrumentos de navegación**	**Equipamento de navegação**
1 Den Danske Lods	1 Portolano	1 Derrotero	1 Pilôto, Roteiro da costa
2 Nautisk Almanak	2 Effemeridi Nautiche	2 Almanaque Náutico	2 Almanaque Náutico
3 Tidevands-tabeller	3 Tavole di Marea	3 Tabla de Mareas	3 Tabela de Marés
4 Tidevandskort	4 Atlanti delle correnti	4 Atlas de Mareas	4 Atlas das Marés
5 Fyrliste	5 Elenco Fari	5 Cuaderno de Faros	5 Lista de Faróis
6 Efterretninger for søfarende	6 Avvisi ai Naviganti	6 Aviso a los Navegantes	6 Avisos aos Navegantes
7 Deviationstabel	7 Tabella della Deviazioni	7 Table de desviós	7 Tábua de desvios
8 parallellinial	8 parallela a snodo	8 paralelas	8 régua de paralelas
9 transportør	9 goniometro	9 transportador	9 transferidor
10 trekantet transportør	10 squadretta nautica	10 transportador triangular	10 transferidor triangul
11 blyant	11 matita	11 lapiz	11 lápis
12 viskelæder	12 gomma	12 goma	12 borracha
13 passer	13 compassi	13 compás de puntas	13 compasso de bicos
14 kikkert	14 binocoli	14 gemelos, prismáticos	14 binóculos
Sekstant	**Sestante**	**Sextante**	**Sextante**
1 horisont, alide spejl	1 specchietto, specchio grande	1 espejo pequeño, espejo grande	1 espelho pequeno, espelho grande
2 index fejl	2 errore d'indice	2 error de índice	2 êrro de índice
3 blændglasset	3 vetrini colorati	3 vidrios de color	3 vidros corados
4 mikrometer-skrue	4 tamburo micrometrico	4 tornillo micrométrico	4 micrómetro
5 buen	5 lembo	5 arco, limbo	5 limbo
Patent log	**Solcometro ad elica**	**Corredera de Patente**	**Odómetro**
1 rotator, rotoren	1 pesce	1 hélice	1 hélice
2 logline	2 sagola del solcometro	2 cordel de la corredera	2 linha do odómetro
3 log-ur	3 contatore	3 registrador	3 contador
4 loggens registrering	4 solcometro registratore	4 registrar las millas	4 registar no odómetro
5 at sætte loggen	5 filare il solcometro	5 largar la corredera	5 lançar o odómetro
6 fart-indikator	6 tachimetro	6 indicador de velocidad	6 indicador de velocidade

ENGLISH	FRANÇAIS	DEUTSCH	NEDERLANDS
Compass	**Compas**	**Kompaß**	**Kompas**
1 bowl	1 boîtier	1 Kessel	1 ketel
2 glass	2 verre	2 Glas	2 glas
3 card, rose	3 rose des vents	3 Rose	3 kompasroos
4 lubber line	4 ligne de foi	4 Steuerstrich	4 zeilstreep
5 binnacle	5 habitacle	5 Kompaßhaus	5 nachthuis
6 grid steering compass	6 compas à grille	6 Gridkompaß Gitterkompaß	6 stuurkompas met instelbare koersring
7 ring sight	7 alidade	7 Peildiopter	7 peiltoestel
8 pelorus	8 taximètre	8 Peilscheibe	8 pelorus
9 hand bearing compass	9 compas de relèvement	9 Handpeilkompaß	9 handpeilkompas
10 swing a compass	10 établir la courbe de déviation	10 Deviationsbestimmung	10 kompas zwaaien
11 adjust a compass	11 compenser un compas	11 kompensieren	11 een kompas bijstellen
12 heeling error	12 déviation à la gîte	12 Krängungsfehler	12 hellingsfout
13 North (N); South (S)	13 Nord (N); Sud (S)	13 Nord (N); Süd (S)	13 Noord (N); Zuid (Z)
14 East (E); West (W)	14 Est (E); Ouest (O)	14 Ost (E); West (W)	14 Oost (O); West (W)
15 North-East (NE)	15 Nordé (NE)	15 Nordost (NE)	15 Noord-oost (NO)
16 North-North-East (NNE)	16 Nord-nordé (NNE)	16 Nordnordost (NNE)	16 Noord-noord-oost (NNO)
17 North by East	17 Nord quart Nordé N4NE	17 Nord zu Ost (NzE)	17 Noord ten oosten (N-t-O)
18 point	18 quart	18 Strich	18 streek
19 degree	19 degré	19 Grad	19 graad
To sound	**Sonder**	**Loten**	**Loden**
1 lead	1 plomb de sonde	1 Lot	1 lood
2 sounding pole	2 barre de sonde	2 Peilstock	2 slaggaard
3 echo sounder	3 échosondeur	3 Echolot	3 echolood

DANSK
Kompas
1 kompaskop
2 glas
3 rose
4 styrestreg
5 kompashus
6 parallel-styring
7 pejlediopter
8 pejleskive
9 håndpejle-kompas
10 rette kompas
11 rette, regulere
12 krængnings-fejl
13 Nord (N); Syd (S)
14 Øst (Ø); Vest (V)
15 Nordøst (NØ)
16 Nord-nordøst (NNØ)
17 Nord til øst (N t Ø)
18 streg
19 grad

At lodde
1 lod
2 målestang
3 ekkolod

ITALIANO
Bussola
1 mortaio
2 vetro
3 rosa graduata
4 linea di fede
5 chiesuola
6 bussola con indica-
   tore di rotta
7 cerchio azimutale
8 peloro, grafometro
9 bussoletta portatile
   per rilevamenti
10 fare i giri di bussola
11 ritoccare la
   compensazione
12 deviazone di
   sbandamento
13 Nord (N); Sud (S)
14 Est (E); Ovest (O)
15 Nord-est (NE)
16 Nord-nord-est (NNE)
17 Nord una quarta a
   est (N q E)
18 quarta
19 grado

Scandagliare
1 scandaglio
2 canna per scandagliare
3 scandaglio ultra-
   sonoro

ESPAÑOL
Compas, aguja
náutica
1 mortero
2 vidrio
3 rosa
4 línea de fé
5 bitácora
6 ——
7 circulo de marcar
8 taxímetro
9 aguja de marcar
10 hallar los desvios de
   la aguja
11 ajustar, compensar
   el compás
12 error de escora
13 Norte (N); Sur (S)
14 Este, Leste (E);
   Oeste (W)
15 Nordeste (NE)
16 Nornordeste (NNE)
17 Norte cuarta al
   Este (N $\frac{1}{4}$ NE)
18 cuarta
19 grado

Sondar
1 escandallo, plomo
2 sonda de varilla
3 sonda acústica

PORTUGUÊS
Bússola, agulha
1 morteiro
2 tampa de vidro
3 rosa dos ventos
4 linha de fé
5 bitácula
6 agulha com indicador
   de rumo
7 quadrante graduado
   com aparelho de marcar
8 pelorus
9 agulha de marcar
   portátil
10 regular a agulha
11 regular, ajustar
12 desvio devido à
   inclinação
13 Norte (N); Sul (S)
14 Este (E);
   Oeste (O ou W)
15 Nordeste (NE)
16 Nor-nordeste (NNE)
17 Norte quarta leste
   (N4NE)
18 quarta
19 grau

Sondar
1 sonda, prumo de mão
2 vara para sondagem
3 sondador acústica

ENGLISH	FRANÇAIS	DEUTSCH	NEDERLANDS
Radio receiver	**Poste récepteur**	**Empfangsgerät**	**Radio-ontvangtoestel**
1 radio broadcasting station	1 station d'émission	1 Rundfunksender	1 radio omroep station
2 radio telegraph station	2 station radio-télégraphique	2 FT-Station	2 radiotelegraafstation
3 radio mast	3 pylône de T.S.F.	3 Funkmast	3 radiomast
4 radio beacon	4 radiophare	4 Funkfeuer	4 radiobaken
5 radar station	5 station radar	5 Radarstation	5 radarstation
6 radar reflector	6 réflecteur radar	6 Radarreflektor	6 radar reflector
7 receive	7 recevoir	7 empfangen	7 ontvangen
8 transmit	8 émettre	8 senden	8 zenden
9 frequency	9 fréquence	9 Frequenz	9 frequentie
10 wavelangth	10 longueur d'ondes	10 Wellenlänge	10 golflengte
11 long wave	11 longues ondes	11 Langwelle	11 lange golf
12 short wave	12 ondes courtes	12 Kurzwelle	12 korte golf
13 radio telephone	13 radio-téléphone	13 Sprechfunkgerät	13 radio telefoon
14 D.F. wireless	14 récepteur gonio-métrique	14 Funkpeiler	14 radio peil-toestel
15 aerial	15 antenne	15 Antenne	15 antenne
16 ferrite rod	16 barreau de ferrite	16 Ferritstab	16 ferrite staaf
17 loop	17 anneau	17 Peilrahmen	17 peilraam
18 headphones	18 écouteur	18 Kopfhörer	18 koptelefoon
19 loudspeaker	19 haut-parleur	19 Lautsprecher	19 luidspreker
20 call sign	20 indicatif	20 Rufzeichen	20 roepsein
21 operating time	21 heure d'émission	21 Sendezeit	21 seintijd
22 range	22 portée	22 Bereich, Reichweite	22 bereik, reikwijdte
23 period	23 fréquence, période	23 Wiederkehr	23 periode
24 tune	24 syntoniser	24 einstellen	24 afstemmen
25 null	25 secteur d'extinction	25 Minimum, Null	25 nul
26 time signal	26 signal horaire, top horaire	26 Zeitzeichen	26 tijdsein

DANSK
Radiomodtager
1 radiofonistation
2 radiotelegrafstation
3 radiomast
4 radiopejlstation
5 radarstation
6 redarreflektor
7 modtage
8 afsende
9 hyppighed
10 bølgelængde
11 lange bølger
12 korte bølger
13 radiotelefon
14 radio pejler
15 antenne
16 ferrit pejlestav
17 pejleantenne
18 hovedtelefon
19 højtaler
20 kalde-signaler
21 sendetid
22 rækkevidde
23 periode
24 at indstille
25 nul
26 tidssignal

ITALIANO
Radioricevitore
1 stazione radio-trasmittente
2 stazione radio-telegrafica
3 antenna radio
4 radiofaro
5 stazione radar
6 riflettore radar
7 ricevere
8 trasmettere
9 frequenza
10 lunghezza d'onda
11 onda lunga
12 onda corta
13 radiotelefono
14 radiogoniometro
15 aereo, antenna
16 barretta di ferrite
17 antenna a quadro
18 cuffia
19 altoparlante
20 nominativo di chiamata
21 orario di lavoro
22 portata
23 periodo
24 sintonizzare
25 zona di silenzio
26 segnale orario, stop orario

ESPAÑOL
Receptor de radio
1 estación de radio-difusión
2 estación radio-telegráfica
3 antenas T.S.H.
4 radiofaro
5 estación de radar
6 reflector radar
7 recibir
8 transmitir
9 frecuencia
10 longitud de onda
11 onda larga
12 onda corta
13 radio teléfono
14 radio goniometro
15 antena
16 varilla de ferrite
17 espira
18 auricular
19 altavoz
20 señal de llamada
21 hora de servicio
22 alcance
23 periodo
24 sintonizar
25 anulado, nulo
26 señal horaria

PORTUGUÊS
Receptor T.S.F.
1 estação radiodifusora
2 estação radio-telegráfica
3 antenas de TSF
4 radiofarol
5 estação de radar
6 reflector de radar
7 receber
8 transmitir
9 frequência
10 comprimento de onda
11 onda longa
12 onda curta
13 radio telefone
14 radio goniómetro
15 antena
16 antena de ferrite
17 quadro
18 oscultador de cabeça
19 alti-falante
20 sinal de chamada
21 hora de funcionamento
22 alcance
23 período
24 sintonisar
25 ponto de intensidade mínima
26 sinal horário

ENGLISH	FRANÇAIS	DEUTSCH	NEDERLANDS
Charts	**Cartes marines**	**Seekarten**	**Zeekaarten**
1 title	1 titre	1 Titel	1 titel
2 scale	2 échelle	2 Maßstab	2 schaal
3 latitude/longitude	3 latitude/longitude	3 Breite/Länge	3 breedte/lengte
4 meridian	4 méridien	4 Meridian	4 meridiaan
5 minute	5 minute	5 Minute, Bogenminute	5 minuut
6 nautical mile	6 mille marin	6 Seemeile	6 zeemijl
7 correction	7 correction	7 Berichtigung	7 correctie
Dangers	**Dangers**	**Gefahren**	**Gevaren**
1 rock awash at the level of chart datum	1 roche à fleur d'eau au niveau de zéro des cartes	1 Fels in Höhe des Kartennulls	1 rots, ligt op reductievlak
2 rock which covers and uncovers, height above chart datum	2 roche, hauteur au-dessus du niveau de zéro des cartes	2 Fels trockenfallend, Höhe über KN	2 rots, hoogte boven reductievlak
3 sunken rock	3 roche submergée	3 Unterwasserklippe (Klp.)	3 blinde klip
4 wreck	4 épave	4 Wrack (WK)	4 wrak (Wk.)
5 bank (B^k·)	5 banc (B^c·)	5 Bank	5 bank (Bk.)
6 shoal	6 haut fond (H^t· F^d·)	6 Untiefe (Untf.)	6 droogte, ondiepte (Dr^e·)
7 reef (R^f·)	7 récif (R^f·)	7 Riff (R.)	7 rif
8 obstruction (Obs^n·)	8 obstruction (Obs.)	8 Schiffahrtshindernis(se) (Sch-H.)	8 belemmering van de vaart, hindernis (Obstr.)
9 overfalls, tide-rips	9 remous et clapotis	9 Stromkabbelung	9 stroomrafeling
10 eddies	10 tourbillons	10 Stromwirbel	10 draaikolken
11 breakers	11 brisants (Br.)	11 Brandung (Brdg.)	11 branding, brekers
12 sea-weed, kelp	12 algues, herbes marines	12 Seetang, Seegras	12 zeewier
13 dries (Dr.)	13 assèche	13 trockenfallend (trfall.)	13 droogvallend
14 covers (Cov.)	14 couvre	14 bedeckt	14 ondervloeiend
15 uncovers (Uncov.)	15 découvre	15 unbedeckt	15 droogvallend
16 limiting danger line	16 limite des dangers	16 Gefahrengrenze	16 gevaarlijn
17 isolated danger	17 danger isolé	17 einzeln liegende Gafahr	17 losliggend gevaar

DANSK	ITALIANO	ESPAÑOL	PORTUGUÊS
Søkort	**Carte**	**Cartas náuticas**	**Cartas Hidrográficas**
1 titel	1 titolo	1 título	1 título
2 skala	2 scala	2 escala	2 escala
3 bredde/længde	3 latitudine/longitudine	3 latitud/longitud	3 latitude/longitude
4 meridian	4 meridiano	4 meridiano	4 meridiano
5 minut	5 primo	5 minuto	5 minuto
6 sømil	6 miglio nautico	6 milla marítima	6 milha marítima
7 rettelse	7 correzione	7 corrección	7 correcção
Fare	**Pericoli**	**Peligros**	**Perigos**
1 skær, tørt ved daglig vande	1 scoglio, a fior d'acqua rispetto al datum	1 piedra a flor de agua en marea escorada	1 rocha que aflora na baixa-mar
2 skær, højde over daglig vande	2 scoglio, alto sopra il datum	2 piedra, altura sobre la bajamar escorada	2 rocha, altura acima de baixa-mar
3 undervandsskær	3 scoglio sommerso	3 roca siempre cubierta	3 rocha submersa
4 vrag	4 relitto, scafo	4 naufragio (Nauf.)	4 navio naufragado
5 banke	5 banco (B^{co}·)	5 banco (B^{co}·)	5 banco
6 grund (GR.)	6 basso fondale, secca	6 bajo (B^{o}·)	6 baixo
7 rev	7 scogliera (Sc^{ra}·)	7 arrecife (Arr^{e}·)	7 recife
8 hindring	8 ostruzione, ostacolo (Ost.)	8 obstrucción (Obst$^{on}_{.}$)	8 obstrução
9 strømsø	9 frangenti di marea	9 escarceos, hileros	9 bailadeiras
10 strømhvirler	10 vortici	10 remolinos	10 redemoínhos
11 brænding	11 frangenti	11 rompientes	11 rebentação
12 tang, søgræs	12 alga natante	12 algas, hierbas marinas	12 algas, sargaços
13 tørt	13 affiorante (Aff.)	13 que vela en bajamar	13 fica em sêco
14 overskylles	14 coperto (Cop.)	14 cubre	14 cobre
15 bliver synligt	15 emerso (Em.)	15 descubre	15 descobre
16 ydergrænse farelinie	16 limite di pericoli	16 límite de peligro	16 limite de perigo
17 isoleret hindring	17 pericolo isolato	17 peligro aislado	17 perigo isolado

ENGLISH	FRANÇAIS	DEUTSCH	NEDERLANDS
Buoys and beacons	**Bouées et balises**	**Tonnen und Baken**	**Tonnen en Bakens**
1 cardinal system	1 système cardinal	1 Kardinalsystem	1 cardinaal stelsel
2 lateral system	2 système latéral	2 Lateralsystem	2 lateraal stelsel
3 light buoy	3 bouée lumineuse	3 Leuchttonne	3 lichtboei
4 whistle buoy	4 bouée sonore à sifflet	4 Heultonne (Hl-Tn)	4 brulboei (Brul)
5 bell buoy	5 bouée sonore à cloche	5 Glockentonne (Gl-Tn)	5 belboei (Bel)
			6 stompe ton
6 can buoy	6 bouée plate, cylindrique; cylindre	6 Stumpftonne	7 spitse ton
			8 bolton
7 conical buoy	7 bouée conique, cône	7 Spitztonne	9 sparboei
8 spherical buoy	8 bouée sphérique, disque	8 Kugeltonne	10 torenboei
			11 drum, ton
9 spar buoy	9 bouée à espar	9 Spierentonne	12 topteken
10 pillar buoy	10 bouée à fuseau	10 Bakentonne	13 meerboei
11 barrel buoy	11 bouée tonne, tonne	11 Faßtonne	
12 topmark	12 voyant	12 Toppzeichen	14 kopbaken
13 mooring buoy	13 coffre d'amarrage, corps-mort	13 Festmachetonne	15 drijfbaken
			16 steekbakens
14 fixed beacon	14 balise fixe	14 Bake	17 geblokt (Gb)
15 floating beacon	15 balise flottante	15 Bakentonne	18 horizontaal gestreept (HS)
16 perches	16 perches, pieux	16 Pricken	19 verticaal gestreept
17 chequered (Cheq.)	17 à damiers (dam.)	17 gewürfelt	
18 horizontal stripes (H.S.)	18 à bandes horizontales	18 waagerecht gestreift	
19 vertical stripes (V.S.)	19 à bandes verticales	19 senkrecht gestreift	

DANSK

Sømærker

1 hovedaf mærkning
2 sideafmærkning
3 lystønde (LT.)
4 fløjtetønde (Fl.T.)
5 klokke-tønde (Kl.T.)
6 stumptønde
7 spidstønde
8 kugletønde
9 spirtønde
10 tønde med stage
11 fadtønde
12 topbetegnelse
13 fortøjningstønde

14 båke
15 flydende sømærke
16 pind-stage
17 tærnet
18 vandret stribet

19 lodret stribet

ITALIANO

Boe e mede

1 sistema cardinale
2 sistema laterale
3 boa luminosa
4 boa a fischio
5 boa a campana
6 boa cilindrica
7 boa conica
8 boa sferica
9 boa ad asta
10 boa a fuso
11 boa a barile
12 miraglio
13 boa da ormeggio

14 meda fissa
15 meda galleggiante
16 palo
17 boa a scacchi
18 boa a strisce
    orizzontali
19 boa a strisce verticali

ESPAÑOL

Boyas y balizas

1 sistema cardinal
2 sistema lateral
3 boya luminosa
4 boya de silbato
5 boya de campana
6 boya cilíndrica
7 boya cónica
8 boya esférica
9 boya de espeque
10 boya de huso
11 barril
12 marca de tope
13 boya de amarre,
    muerto
14 baliza fija
15 baliza flotante
16 marca
17 damero, a cuadros
18 franjas horizontales

19 franjas verticales

PORTUGUÊS

Bóias e balizas

1 sistema cardeal
2 sistema lateral
3 bóia luminosa
4 bóia de apito
5 bóia de sino
6 bóia cilíndrica
7 bóia cónica
8 bóia esférica
9 bóia de mastro
10 bóia de pilar
11 bóia de barril
12 alvo
13 bóia de amarração

14 baliza fixa
15 baliza flutuante
16 estaca
17 aos quadrados (x.)
18 faixas horizontais (F.H.)

19 faixas verticais (F.V.)

ENGLISH	FRANÇAIS	DEUTSCH	NEDERLANDS
Lights	**Feux**	**Leuchtfeuer**	**Lichten**
1 lighthouse (Lt Ho)	1 phare	1 Leuchtturm (Lcht-Tm.)	1 licht-, vuurtoren (Lt.)
2 lightship, light vessel (Lt v)	2 bateau-phare	2 Feuerschiff (F-Sch.)	2 lichtschip
3 fixed light (F)	3 feu fixe (F.f.)	3 Festfeuer (F.)	3 vast licht (V.)
4 flashing light (Fl)	4 feu à éclats (F.é.)	4 Blinkfeuer (Blk.)	4 schitterlicht (S.)
5 quick flashing light (Q)	5 feu scintillant (F.sc.)	5 Funkelfeuer (Fkl.)	5 flikkerlicht (Fl.)
6 occulting light (Oc)	6 à occultations (F.o.)	6 unterbrochenes Feuer (Ubr.)	6 onderbroken licht (O.)
7 group occulting light (Oc)	7 à occultations groupées (F.2.o.)	7 unterbrochenes Gruppenfeuer (Ubr. [2])	7 groeponderbroken licht (G.o.)
8 alternating light (Al.)	8 à changement de coloration (F.alt.)	8 Wechselfeuer (Wchs.)	8 alternerend kleurwisselend (Alt.)
9 intermittent	9 feu intermittent	9 periodisches Feuer	9 intermitterend (Int.)
10 interrupted quick flashing (I Q)	10 feu interrompu	10 unterbrochenes Funkelfeuer (Fkl. unt.)	10 onderbroken flikkerlicht (Int. Fl.)
11 fixed and flashing (F Fl)	11 fixe blanc varié par un éclat (F.b.é.)	11 Mischfeuer: Festfeuer und Blinke (Mi.)	11 vast en schitter licht (V. & S.)
12 period	12 période	12 Wiederkehr	12 periode
13 leading light	13 feu d'alignement	13 Richtfeuer (Rcht-F.)	13 geleidelicht
14 upper light	14 supérieur (S.)	14 Oberfeuer (O-F.)	14 boven-, hogelicht
15 lower light	15 inférieur (I.)	15 Unterfeuer (U-F.)	15 beneden-, lagelicht
16 sector	16 secteur (Sect./S.)	16 Sektor	16 sector
17 obscured	17 masqué	17 verdunkelt (vdklt.)	17 duister
18 visible, range	18 portée (vis.)	18 Sichtweite, Tragweite	18 reikwijdte
Coastline	**Contour de la côte**	**Küstenlinien**	**De Kustlijn**
1 steep coast	1 côte escarpée	1 Steilküste	1 steile kust
2 cliffy coastline	2 côte à falaises	2 Kliffküste	2 klipkust
3 stony or shingly	3 cailloux ou galets	3 Stein-oder Kiesküste	3 grind of kiezelstrand
4 sand hills, dunes	4 dunes	4 Sandhügel, Dünen	4 duinen
5 foreshore	5 côte découvrant à marée basse	5 Küstenvorland	5 droogvallend strand

DANSK	ITALIANO	ESPAÑOL	PORTUGUÊS
Fyr	**Segnalmento luminoso**	**Luces**	**Farolagem**
1 fyrtårn	1 faro	1 faro	1 farol
2 fyrskib	2 battello fanale	2 buque faro	2 barco-farol
3 fast fyr (Fst.)	3 luce fissa (F., F.f)	3 luz fija (f.)	3 luz fixa (F.)
4 blink (Blk.)	4 luce a lampi (Lam.)	4 luz de destellos (dest.)	4 relâmpagos (Rl.)
5 hurtig blink (Q. Blk.)	5 luce scintillante (Sc.)	5 luz centelleante	5 relâmpagos rápidos
6 formørkelser (Fmk.)	6 intermittente (Int.)	6 luz de ocultaciones (oc.)	6 ocultações (Oc.)
7 gruppe-formørkelser (Gp. Fmk.)	7 intermittente a gruppi di ecclissi (Int.)	7 luz de grupos de ocultaciones (grp. oc.)	7 grupo n. ocultações (Gp. n. Oc.)
8 vekslende (Vksl.)	8 luce alternata (Alt.)	8 luz alternativa (Alt.va)	8 alternada (Alt.)
9 periodisk	9 intermittente (Int.)	9 luz intermitente (Intr.te)	9 intermitente
10 hurtigblink med afbrydelser (Q. Blk. Int.)	10 luce scintillante intermittente (Sc. Int.)	10 luz de grupos de centelleos	10 interompida
11 fast med blink (Fst. Blk.)	11 luce fissa e a lampi (F.lam.)	11 luz fija y destellos (f.dest.)	11 fixa e com relâmpagos (F.Rl.)
12 periode	12 periodo	12 periódo	12 período
13 ledefyr	13 allineamente luminoso	13 luz de enfilación	13 farol ou farolim de enfiamento
14 øverste fyr	14 posteriore (Post.)	14 posterior	14 superior (Sup.)
15 nederste fyr	15 anteriore (Ant.)	15 anterior	15 inferior (Inf.)
16 vinkel	16 settore (set.)	16 sector (Sect.)	16 sector
17 formørket	17 oscuratori (Osc.)	17 oculto	17 obscurecido
18 synsvidde, sigtbart	18 portata, visibilità	18 alcance	18 visível
Kystinie	**Linea di costa**	**La costa**	**Linha da costa**
1 stejl kyst	1 costa scoscesa	1 costa escarpada, brava	1 costa alta
2 klippekyst	2 costa a picco	2 acantilado	2 costa escarpada
3 stenet strand	3 costa pietrosa	3 guijarro o grava	3 pedras ou seixos
4 sandhøje, klitter	4 colline sabbiose, dune	4 dunas	4 dunas de areia
5 forstrand	5 bagnasciuga	5 fondos que descubren en bajamar	5 zona entre as linhas da bm. e pm.

IALA CARDINAL

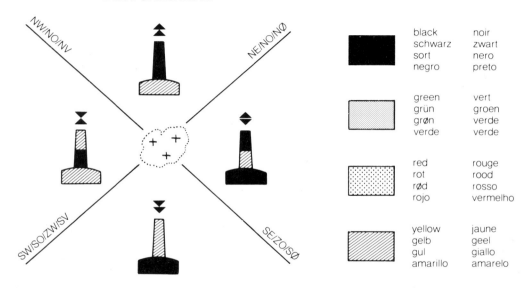

■	black schwarz sort negro	noir zwart nero preto
▢	green grün grøn verde	vert groen verde verde
▦	red rot rød rojo	rouge rood rosso vermelho
▨	yellow gelb gul amarillo	jaune geel giallo amarelo

NW/NO/NV

NE/NO/NØ

SW/SO/ZW/SV

SE/ZO/SØ

IALA LATERAL

port
bâbord
backbord
bakboord
bagbord
sinistra
babor
bombordo

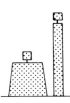

starboard
tribord
steuerbord
stuurboord
styrbord
dritta
estribor
estibordo

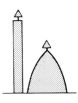

Landfall
Ansteuerung
Anduvning
Señales de recalada

Atterrisage
Verkenningstonnen
Atterragio
Aterragem

Isolated danger
Danger isolé
Einzelliegende Gefahr
Losliggend gevaar
Isoleret hindring
Pericolo isolato
Peligro aislado
Perigo isolado

Special marks
Marques spéciales
Sonder-Zeichen
Bijzondere-betonning
Special afmaerkning
Marcas especiales
Marcas especiáes
Segnali speciali

ENGLISH
Quality of the bottom
1 sand (S)
2 mud (M)
3 clay (Cy)
4 gravel (G)
5 shingle (Sn)
6 pebbles (P)
7 stones (St)
8 rock, rocky (R, r)
9 fine/coarse (f/c)
10 soft/hard (so/h)
11 small (sm)
12 large (l)
13 light/dark (lt/d)

FRANÇAIS
Nature des fonds
1 sable (S.)
2 vase (V.)
3 argile (Arg.)
4 gravier (Gr.)
5 galets (Gal.)
6 cailloux (Caill.)
7 pierres (Pi.)
8 roches (R.)
9 fin/gros (f/g)
10 mou/dur (m/d)
11 petit ($p^{it.}$)
12 grand ($g^{d.}$)
13 clair/foncé

DEUTSCH
Grundbezeichnungen
1 Sand (Sd.)
2 Schlick (Sk.)
3 Ton (T.)
4 Kies (K.)
5 grober Kies (gb.K.)
6 kleine Steine (kl.St.)
7 Steine (St.)
8 Felsen. felsig (Fls., fls.)
9 fein/grob (f./gb.)
10 weich/hart (wch./ht.)
11 klein (kl.)
12 groß (gß.)
13 hell/dunkel (h./dkl.)

NEDERLANDS
Grondsoorten
1 zand (Z.)
2 modder (M.)
3 klei (K.)
4 grind, gruis
5 grind, keisteen
6 kiezel (Kl.)
7 stenen (St.)
8 rotsgrond (R.)
9 fijn/grof (f./gr.)
10 zacht/hard (zt./h.)
11 klein
12 groot
13 licht/donker

DANSK
Bundarter
1 sand (Sd.)
2 mudder (M.)
3 ler (L.)
4 grus (G.)
5 rullesten
6 småsten
7 sten (St.)
8 klippe (K.)
9 fin/grov (f./gv.)
10 blød/hård (b.Bd./h.Bd.)
11 lille
12 stor (st.)
13 lys/mørk (l./m.)

ITALIANO
Qualità del fondo
1 sabbia (s)
2 fango (f)
3 argilla
4 ghiaia
5 ciotoli
6 sassi
7 pietre (p)
8 roccia (r)
9 fine/grosso
10 molle/duro
11 piccolo
12 grande
13 chiaro/scuro

ESPAÑOL
Naturaleza del fondo
1 arena (A)
2 fango (F)
3 arcilla (Arc.)
4 cascajo ($C^{o.}$)
5 conchuela ($C^{a.}$)
6 guijarro ($G^{o.}$)
7 piedras (P)
8 roca, rocoso (R. $R.^{so}$)
9 fino/grueso (f/g)
10 blando/duro ($b^{do.}$/d)
11 pequeño
12 grande
13 claro/oscuro (cl./o)

PORTUGUÊS
Qualidade de fundo
1 areia (A.)
2 lodo (L.)
3 argila (Ar.)
4 burgau (B.)
5 calhau (C.)
6 seixos (S.)
7 pedras (P.)
8 rocha (R.)
9 fina/grossa (f./g.)
10 mole/duro (ml./d.)
11 miuda
12 grande
13 claro/escuro (cl./e.)

ENGLISH

Fog signals
1 nautophone (Nauto)
2 diaphone (Dia)
3 gun (Gun)
4 explosive (Explos)
5 whistle (Whis)
6 bell (Bell)
7 gong (Gong)
8 siren (Siren)
9 reed (Reed)
10 submarine oscillator (SO)

11 submarine bell (Sub Bell)

FRANÇAIS

Signaux de brume
1 nautophone
2 diaphone
3 canon (Can.)
4 par explosions
5 sifflet (Sif.)
6 cloche (Cl.)
7 gong (G^g·)
8 sirène (Sir.)
9 anche
10 oscillateur sous-marin

11 cloche sous-
marine (Cl. s. m.)

DEUTSCH

Nebelsignale
1 Membransender (N-S)
2 Kolbensirene (N-S)
3 Kanone (N-S)
4 Knall (N-S)
5 Heuler (N-S)
6 Glocke (N-S)
7 Gong (N-S)
8 Sirene (N-S)
9 Zungenhorn (N-S)
10 Unterwasser-
Membransender
11 Unterwasser-
Glocke (U-Wss-Gl)

NEDERLANDS

Mistseinen
1 nautofoon
2 diafoon
3 mistkanon
4 knalmistsein
5 mistfluit
6 mistbel, mistklok
7 mistgong
8 mistsirene
9 mistfluit
10 onderwateroscillator

11 onderwaterklok

DANSK

Tågesignaler
1 nautofon (S.)
2 diafon (S.)
3 kanon
4 skud
5 fløjte (Fl.)
6 klokke (Kl.)
7 gong-gong
8 sirene (S.)
9 membran horn (H.)
10 undervandsmembran
11 undervandsklokke (TU.)

ITALIANO

Segnali da nebbia
1 nautofono (Nauto)
2 diafono
3 cannone (Cann. Neb.)
4 esplosivo
5 fischio (Fi. Neb.)
6 campana (Cam. Neb.)
7 gong
8 sirena (Sir. Neb.)
9 corno
10 oscillatore subacqueo
11 campana sottomarina
(Cam. Stm.)

ESPAÑOL

Señales de niebla
1 nautófono (N.)
2 diáfono (D.)
3 cañon
4 explosiva (E.)
5 pito
6 campana (C.)
7 gong
8 sirena (Sir.)
9 bocina (B.)
10 oscilador submarino (O.)
11 campana submarina

PORTUGUÊS

Sinais de nevoeiro
1 nautofone (Nauto.)
2 diafone (Dia.)
3 canhão
4 explosivo
5 apito (Apt.)
6 sino (Sino)
7 badalo
8 sereia (Ser.)
9 limbos
10 oscilador submarino
11 sino submarino

ENGLISH	FRANÇAIS	DEUTSCH	NEDERLANDS
Buildings, etc.	**Edifices etc.**	**Bauten aller Art u.a.**	**Gebouwen**
1 town	1 ville	1 Stadt	1 stad
2 village (Vil)	2 village (V$^{ge.}$)	2 Dorf	2 dorp
3 castle (Cas)	3 château (Ch$^{au.}$)	3 Schloß (Schl.)	3 kasteel, slot
4 church (Ch)	4 église (Egl.)	4 Kirche (Kr.)	4 kerk
cathedral (Cath)	cathédrale (Cath.)	Kathedrale	kathedraal
5 fort (F$^{t.}$)	5 fort (F$^{t.}$)	5 Fort (Ft.)	5 fort (Ft.)
6 barracks	6 caserne	6 Kaserne (Kas.)	6 kazerne
7 airport	7 aéroport (Aé.)	7 Flughafen	7 luchthaven
8 street	8 rue	8 Straße (Str.)	8 straat
9 monument (Mon$^{t.}$)	9 monument (Mon$^{t.}$)	9 Denkmal (Dkm.)	9 monument
10 tower (T$^{r.}$)	10 tour, tourelle (T$^{r.}$)	10 Turm (Tm.)	10 toren (Tr.)
11 windmill	11 moulin à vent (M$^{in.}$)	11 Windmühle (M.)	11 windmolen
12 chimney (Ch$^{y.}$)	12 cheminée (Ch$^{ee.}$)	12 Schornstein (Schst.)	12 schoorsteen (Sch$^{n.}$)
13 water tower	13 château d'eau (Ch$^{au.}$)	13 Wasserturm (Wss-Tm.)	13 watertoren (W.Tr.)
14 gasometer	14 gazomètre	14 Gasometer (Gas-T.)	14 gashouder
15 oil tank	15 réservoir à pétrole	15 Öltank (Öl-T.)	15 olietank
16 factory	16 fabrique	16 Fabrik (Fbr.)	
17 quarry	17 carrière (Carre)	17 Steinbruch	16 fabriek
18 railway (R$^{y.}$)	18 chemin de fer (Ch. de F.)	18 Eisenbahn	17 steengroeve
			18 spoorweg
19 flagstaff (F.S.)	19 mât	19 Flaggenmast (Flgmst.)	19 vlaggestok (Vs.)
		Flaggenstock (Flgst.)	
20 measured mile	20 base de vitesse	20 abgesteckte Meile	20 gemeten mijl
21 conspicuous (conspic)	21 visible, en évidence (vis.)	21 auffällig (auff.)	
			21 kenbaar
22 destroyed (dest)	22 détruit (détr.)	22 zerstört (zrst.)	22 vernield
23 prominent	23 remarquable (rem.)	23 hervorragend	23 uitstekend
24 approximate (approx)	24 approximatif (appr.)	24 ungefähr (ungf.)	24 ongeveer
25 distant (dist)	25 éloigné (él.)	25 entfernt	25 verwijderd

DANSK	ITALIANO	ESPAÑOL	PORTUGUÊS
Bygninger	**Fabricati, costruzioni**	**Edificios**	**Edificaçoes**
1 by	1 città	1 ciudad	1 cidade
2 landsby	2 villaggio (Vil⁰·)	2 pueblo, aldea	2 vila, povoação
3 slot	3 castello (Cast.)	3 castillo (Cᴵˡᵒ·)	3 castelo (Cast.)
4 kirke (K.)	4 chiesa (Ch.)	4 iglesia (Iglᵃ·)	4 igreja
domkirke	cattedrale (Catt.)	catedral (Cat.)	catedral
5 fort	5 forte	5 fuerte (Fᵗᵉ·)	5 forte
6 kaserne	6 caserna	6 cuartel	6 quartel
7 lufthavn	7 aeroporto	7 aeropuerto	7 aeroporto
8 gade	8 strada, via (V.)	8 calle	8 estrada
9 monument	9 monumento (Monᵗᵒ·)	9 monumento (Mᵗᵒ·)	9 monumento (Mon.)
10 tårn (Tn.)	10 torre (Tʳᵉ·)	10 torre (Tᵉ·)	10 moínho de vento
11 vindmølle (Ml.)	11 mulino a vento	11 molino de viento	11 tôrre
12 skorsten (Skst.)	12 fumaiolo (Fˡᵒ·)	12 chimenea (Chᵃ·)	12 chaminé (Ch.)
13 vandtårn (Vandtn.)	13 serbatoio d'acqua	13 depósito de agua	13 depósito de água (D.A.)
14 gasbeholder	14 gasometro	14 gasómetro	14 gasómetro
15 olie tank	15 serbatoio di combustibili	15 tanque de petróleo	15 depósito de combustível (D.C.)
16 fabrik (Fabr.)	16 fabbrica (Fᶜᵃ·)	16 fábrica (Fᶜᵃ·)	16 fábrica
17 stenbrud	17 cava di pietre	17 cantera	17 pedreira
18 jernbane	18 ferrovia	18 ferrocaril	18 via férrea
19 flagstang (Flagst.)	19 asta di bandiera	19 asta de bandera	19 mastro para bandeira
20 målt sømil	20 base misurata	20 milla medida	20 a milha para experiência de velocidade
21 kendelig	21 cospicuo	21 notorio, conspicuo	21 conspícuo (consp.)
22 ødelagt	22 distrutto	22 destruido (dest.)	22 destrúido (dest.)
23 fremspringende	23 prominente	23 prominente (prom.)	23 proeminente (proem.)
24 omtrentlig	24 approssimato	24 aproximado (aprox.)	24 aproximado
25 fjern	25 distante	25 distante	25 distante (dist.)

ENGLISH	FRANÇAIS	DEUTSCH	NEDERLANDS
Features	**Physionomie de la côte**	**Küstengebilde**	**Kust kenmerken**
1 bay (B)	1 baie (B$^{e.}$)	1 Bucht (B.)	1 baai (B$^{i.}$)
2 fjord (F$^{d.}$)	2 fjord (Fj$^{d.}$)	2 Fjord, Förde (Fj. Fd.)	2 fjord
3 glacier	3 glaciers	3 Gletscher (Glet.)	3 gletcher
4 lake, loch (L)	4 bras de mer (L.)	4 See, Binnensee	4 loch, meer
5 entrance	5 entrée (Ent$^{ée.}$)	5 Einfahrt (Einf.)	5 ingang, zeegat
6 passage (Pass)	6 passage, passe (Pas.)	6 Durchfahrt (Drchf.)	6 pas, doorvaart
7 estuary	7 estuaire	7 Flußmündung	7 mond
8 mouth	8 embouchure (Emb$^{re.}$)	8 Mündung (Mdg.)	8 monding
9 channel (Chan)	9 canal, chenal (C$^{al.}$)	9 Fahrwasser (Fhrwss.)	9 vaarwater
10 anchorage (Anch$^{e.}$)	10 mouillage (M$^{age.}$)	10 Ankerplatz (Ankpl.)	10 ankerplaats
11 island, -s (I, Is)	11 île, îles (I. Is.)	11 Insel(n) (I.)	11 eiland, -en (E. Eil.)
12 cape (C)	12 cap (C.)	12 Kap (K.)	12 kaap, hoek (K$^{p.}$ H$^{k.}$)
13 mountain (M$^{t.}$)	13 mont (M$^{t.}$)	13 Berg (Bg.)	13 berg
14 point (P$^{t.}$)	14 pointe (p$^{te.}$)	14 Huk (Hk.)	14 punt (p$^{t.}$)
15 hill	15 colline (Col.)	15 Hügel (Hg.)	15 heuvel
16 rocks (R$^{ks.}$)	16 rochers (R$^{ers.}$)	16 Klippe(n) (Klp.)	16 rots
Colours	**Couleurs**	**Farben**	**Kleuren**
1 black (B. blk.)	1 noir (n)	1 schwarz (s.)	1 zwart (Z.)
2 red (R.)	2 rouge (r)	2 rot (r.)	2 rood (R.)
3 green (G.)	3 vert (v)	3 grün (gn.)	3 groen (G$^{n.}$)
4 yellow (Y.)	4 jaune (j)	4 gelb (g.)	4 geel (G$^{l.}$)
5 white (W.)	5 blanc (b)	5 weiß (w.)	5 wit (W.)
6 orange (Or.)	6 orange (org)	6 orange (or.)	6 oranje (G$^{l.}$)
7 violet (Vi.)	7 violet (vio)	7 violett (viol.)	7 violet (Vi.)
8 brown	8 brun	8 braun (br.)	8 bruin
9 blue (Bl.)	9 bleu (bl)	9 blau (bl.)	9 blauw (B.)
10 grey	10 gris (gr)	10 grau (gr.)	10 grijs

DANSK
Kystkarakter
1 bugt (B.)
2 fjord (Fj.)
3 gletcher, bræ

4 indsø-fjor
5 indløb
6 rende
7 flodmunding
8 munding

9 kanal (Kan.)
10 ankerplads
11 ø, øer
12 forbjerg
13 bjerg (Bg.)
14 pynt (Pt.)
15 høj, bakke
16 klippe, skær
Farver
1 sort (s.)
2 rød (r.)
3 grøn (gr.)
4 gul (gl.)
5 hvid (hv.)
6 orange (or.)
7 violet
8 brun (br.)
9 blå (bl.)
10 grå (g.)

ITALIANO
Fisionomia della costa
1 baia (Ba.)
2 fjordo (Fdo.)
3 ghiacciaio

4 lago
5 entrata (Eta.)
6 passaggio (Pas.)
7 estuario (Eso.)
8 bocca, foce (Boc.)

9 canale (Can.)
10 ancoraggio (Anco.)
11 isola, isole (I.)
12 capo (Co.)
13 montagna (M.)
14 punta (Pta.)
15 collina (Cina.)
16 scogli (Sc.)
Colori
1 nero (n.)
2 rosso (r.)
3 verde (v.)
4 giallo (g.)
5 bianco (b.)
6 arancione (ar.)
7 violetto (vi.)
8 marrone (mar.)
9 blù, azzurro (azz.)
10 grigio (gr.)

ESPAÑOL
Acidentes de la costa
1 bahia (Ba)
2 fiord (Fd.)
3 glaciares

4 lago, laguna
5 entrada (Ent.)
6 paso (Ps.)
7 estuario, ría (Est.)
8 desembocadura
   (Desemba.)
9 canal (Can.)
10 fondeadero (Fondn.)
11 isla, islas (I, Is.)
12 cabo (C.)
13 monte (Mte.)
14 punta (Pta.)
15 colina (Col.)
16 rocas (Rs.)
Colores
1 negro (n.)
2 rojo (r.)
3 verde (v.)
4 amarillo (am.)
5 blanco (b.)
6 naranja
7 violeta
8 pardo (p.), marrón
9 azul (az.)
10 gris

PORTUGUÊS
Fisionomia da costa
1 baía (B.)
2 fiorde
3 campo do gêlo em
   movimento
4 lago, lagôa (L.)
5 entrada
6 passagem
7 estuário (Est.)
8 foz

9 canal (Can.)
10 fundeadouro
11 ilha, ilhéu (I., Il.)
12 cabo (C.)
13 monte (Mt.)
14 ponta (Pta.)
15 colina (Col.)
16 rochas (R.)
Côres
1 preto (pr.)
2 vermelho (vm.)
3 verde (vd.)
4 amarelo (am.)
5 branco (br.)
6 côr de laranja
7 violeta, lilás
8 castanho
9 azul
10 cinzento

ENGLISH	FRANÇAIS	DEUTSCH	NEDERLANDS
Ports and harbours	**Ports**	**Häfen**	**Havens**
1 yacht harbour	1 bassin pour yachts	1 Yachthafen	1 jachthaven
2 Harbour Master's Office	2 bureau du Capitaine de Port (B$^{eau.}$)	2 Hafenamt (Hfn-A)	2 havenkantoor
3 Custom house, Customs office	3 bureau de douane (D$^{ne.}$)	3 Zollamt (Zoll-A)	3 douanekantoor
4 prohibited area (Prohib$^{d.}$)	4 zone interdite	4 verbotenes Gebiet (Verb. Gbt.)	4 verboden gebied
5 dolphin (D$^{n.}$)	5 duc d'Albe	5 Dalben (Dlb.)	5 dukdalf, meerpaal
6 mooring ring	6 organeau d'amarrage	6 Festmacherring	6 meerring
7 landing steps	7 escalier de débarquement	7 Landungstreppe	7 ontschepingstrap
8 dock	8 bassin, dock	8 Hafenbecken, Dock	8 bassin, dok
9 careening grid	9 gril de carénage	9 Kielbank	9 kielplaats, bankstelling
10 slip, slipway	10 cale de halage	10 Slipp, Helling	10 sleephelling
11 breakwater	11 brise-lames	11 Wellenbrecher	11 golfbreker
12 mole	12 môle	12 Mole	12 havendam
13 Anchorage	**13 Mouillage**	**13 Ankerplatz**	**13 Ankerplaats**
14 anchorage prohibited	14 défense de mouiller	14 verbotener Ankerplatz	14 verboden ankerplaats
15 anchorage limit	15 limite de mouillage	15 Reedegrenze	15 grens ankerplaats
16 spoil ground	16 zone de déblai	16 Baggerschüttstelle	16 bagger-, stortplaats
17 submarine cable	17 câble sous-marin	17 Unterwasserkabel	17 onderwater kabel
18 submarine pipe line	18 canalisation sous-marine	18 Rohrleitung unter Wasser	18 onderwater pijpleiding
Coastguard	**Garde Côtière**	**Küstenwacht**	**Kustwachtpost**
1 watch tower	1 vigie (Vig.)	1 Wache (W.), Wachtturm (W-Tm.)	1 uitkijk, wachtpost (KW)
2 life-boat station (L.B.S.)	2 bateau de sauvetage (B. de sauv.)	2 Rettungsbootstation (R-S.)	2 reddingsboot
3 pilot station	3 station de pilotage	3 Lotsenstelle (L-S.)	3 loodsstation
4 storm-signal station	4 station de signaux de tempête	4 Sturmsignalstelle (Strm-S.)	4 stormseinstation (SS)

DANSK	ITALIANO	ESPAÑOL	PORTUGUÊS
Havne	**Porti e rade**	**Puertos, radas**	**Portos**
1 lystbådehavn	1 porticciolo per yachts	1 dársena de yates	1 doca de recreio
2 havnekontor	2 Capitaneria di porto	2 Comandancia de Marina	2 Capitania
3 toldbod	3 ufficio della dogana	3 aduana (Ad.)	3 Alfândega
4 forbudt omrade	4 area interdetta	4 zona prohibida ($Z^{a \cdot}$ proh.)	4 zona proíbida
5 duc d'albe	5 briccola	5 noray	5 duque de alba
6 fortøjningsring	6 anello d'ormeggio	6 amarradero	6 cabeço
7 landingstrappe	7 scaletta di sbarco	7 escala de desembarque	7 escada de desembarque
8 bassin, dok	8 bacino, darsena	8 dique	8 doca
9 kølhalingsplads	9 scalo di carenaggio	9 dique de peine, carenero	9 grade de marés
10 ophalerbedding	10 scalo d'alaggio	10 varadero	10 plano inclinado, rampa
11 bølgebryder	11 frangionde	11 rompeolas	11 quebra-mar
12 mole	12 molo	12 muelle	12 molhe
13 **Ankerplads**	13 **Ancoraggio**	13 **Fondeadero**	13 **Fundeadouro**
14 ankring forbudt	14 divieto d'ancoraggio	14 fondeadero prohibido ($Fond^{o \cdot}$ proh.)	14 fundeadouro proíbido
15 grænse for ankerplads	15 limite d'ancoraggio	15 límite de fondeadero	15 limite de fundeadouro
16 losseplads	16 zona di scarico	16 vertedero ($Vert^{o \cdot}$)	16 zona para descarga de dragados ou entulhos
17 undersøisk kabel	17 cavo sottomarino	17 cable submarino	17 cabo submarino
18 undersøisk rørledning	18 oleodotto sottomarino	18 canalización submarina, tuberia	18 conduta submarina
Kystvagt	**Guardia costiera**	**Guardacostas**	**Guarda costeiro**
1 vagttårn	1 torre guardiana, d'avvistamento	1 vigía	1 posto de vigia
2 redningsbåd-station (RS.)	2 stazione dei batelli di salvataggio	2 estación de salvamento	2 estação de salva-vidas
3 lodsstation (Lods)	3 stazione dei piloti	3 caseta de prácticos	3 estação de pilôtos
4 stormvarselstation (St V)	4 stazione segnali di tempesta	4 estación de semáforo de señales de temporal	4 posto de sinais de mau tempo

ENGLISH	FRANÇAIS	DEUTSCH	NEDERLANDS
Tidal streams	**Courants de marée**	**Gezeitenströme**	**Getijstromen**
1 flood stream	1 courant de flot, de flux	1 Flutstrom	1 vloedstroom
2 ebb stream	2 courant de jusant	2 Ebbstrom	2 ebstroom
3 slack water	3 marée étale	3 Stauwasser	3 dood tij
4 turn of the tide	4 renverse de courant	4 Kentern des Stromes	4 de kentering
5 rate	5 vitesse	5 Geschwindigkeit	5 snelheid
6 knot	6 nœud	6 Knoten	6 knopen
7 set	7 porter	7 setzen	7 zetten
8 current	8 courant	8 Strom	8 stroom
9 fair tide	9 courant favorable ou portant	9 mitlaufender Strom	9 stroom mee
10 foul tide	10 courant contraire ou debout	10 Gegenstrom	10 tegenstroom
Tide	**Marée**	**Gezeiten**	**Getij**
1 high water (H.W.)	1 pleine mer	1 Hochwasser (H.W.)	1 hoogwater (HW)
2 low water (L.W.)	2 basse mer	2 Niedrigwasser (N.W.)	2 laagwater (LW)
3 flood (Fl.)	3 marée montante	3 Flut	3 vloed
4 ebb	4 marée descendante	4 Ebbe	4 eb
5 stand	5 étale	5 Stillstand	5 stilwater
6 range	6 amplitude	6 Tidenhub	6 verval
7 spring tide (Sp.)	7 vive eau, grande marée	7 Springtide	7 springtij
8 neap tide (Np.)	8 morte eau	8 Nipptide	8 doodtij
9 sea level	9 niveau	9 Wasserstand	9 waterstand
10 mean	10 moyen	10 mittlere	10 gemiddeld

Chart Datum: British fathoms charts are based on low water ordinary spring tides; metric charts on Lowest Astronomical Tide

Zéro des cartes: exprimé sur les cartes françaises au niveau des plus basses mers.

Kartennull: Ebene des mittleren Springniedrigwassers

Reductievlak: kaartpeil voor Nederland is het vlak van gemiddeld laag laagwaterspring

DANSK	ITALIANO	ESPAÑOL	PORTUGUÊS
Tidevand	**Correnti di marea**	**Corrientes de marea**	**Correntes de maré**
1 flod	1 corrente di flusso	1 corriente de creciente	1 corrente de enchente
2 ebbe	2 corrente di riflusso	2 corriente de vaciante	2 corrente de vasante
3 slæk vand	3 stanca	3 repunte	3 águas paradas
4 tidevands-skifte	4 cambio della marea	4 cambio de marea	4 mudança de maré
5 fart	5 velocità della corrente	5 velocidad	5 força da corrente
6 knob	6 nodo	6 nudo	6 nó
7 sætte	7 direzione di une corrente	7 dirección	7 direcção
8 strøm	8 corrente non di marea	8 corriente	8 corrente
9 god tidevand	9 corrente favorevole	9 corriente favorable	9 maré favorável
10 dårlig tidevand	10 corrente contraria	10 corriente contraria	10 maré desfavorável
Tidevand	**Marea**	**Marea**	**Maré**
1 højvande	1 alta marea (A.M.)	1 pleamar	1 preia-mar (P.M.)
2 lavvande	2 bassa marea (B.M.)	2 bajamar	2 baixa-mar (B.M.)
3 flod	3 flusso	3 entrante	3 enchente
4 ebbe	4 riflusso	4 vaciante	4 vasante
5 stand	5 marea ferma	5 margen	5 estofa da maré
6 hub	6 ampiezza della marea	6 repunte	6 amplitude de maré
7 springtid	7 marea sizigiale	7 marea viva, zizigias	7 águas-vivas (sizígia)
8 niptid	8 marea alle quadrature	8 aguas muertas	8 águas-mortas (quadratura)
9 vandstand	9 livello del mare	9 nivel del mar	9 nível do mar
10 middel	10 medio	10 media	10 média

Kortets niveau: middel vandstand inden for Skagen; i øvrigt er vandstanden anført på søkortene

Livello di riferimento scandagli (L.R.S.) per le carte italiane è il livello medio delle basse maree sizigiali

Bajamar escorada: en las cartas españolas, las sondas estan referidas a la maxima bajamar.

Zero hidrográfico: referido ao maior baixamar de águas vivas em cartas Portuguesas

ENGLISH	FRANÇAIS	DEUTSCH	NEDERLANDS
Coastal navigation	**Navigation côtière**	**Küstennavigation**	**Zeevaartkunde, Kleine vaart**
1 North pole	1 nord	1 Nordpol	1 noord pool
2 bearing	2 relèvement	2 Peilung	2 peiling
3 course	3 cap, route	3 Kurs	3 koers
4 true	4 vrai	4 rechtweisend	4 rechtwijzende, ware
5 magnetic	5 magnétique	5 mißweisend	5 magnetische
6 compass course	6 cap au compas	6 Kompaßkurs	6 kompaskoers
7 variation	7 déclinaison	7 Mißweisung	7 variatie
8 deviation	8 déviation	8 Deviation, Ablenkung	8 deviatie
9 leeway	9 dérive	9 Abdrift	9 drift, wraak
10 allowance for current	10 tenir compte du courant	10 Stromvorhalt	10 correctie voor de stroom
11 course through the water	11 route au compas	11 Weg durchs Wasser	11 koers door het water
12 course made good	12 route sur le fond	12 Weg über Grund	12 koers over de grond
13 distance sailed	13 chemin parcouru	13 gesegelte Distanz	13 afgelegde afstand
14 to plot	14 tracer	14 absetzen, eintragen	14 uitzetten
15 position	15 position	15 Schiffsort, Standort	15 standplaats
16 to take a bearing	16 prendre ou effectuer un relèvement	16 peilen, eine Peilung nehmen	16 een peiling nemen
17 cross bearings	17 relèvements croisés	17 Kreuzpeilung	17 kruispeiling
18 position line	18 droite de relèvement	18 Standlinie	18 positielijn
19 transferred position line	19 droite de relèvement déplacée	19 versetzte Standlinie	19 verzeilde positie lijn
20 running fix	20 relèvements successifs d'un même amer	20 Doppelpeilung, Versegelungspeilung	20 kruispeiling met verzeiling
21 four-point bearing	21 relèvement à 4 quarts	21 Vierstrichpeilung	21 vierstreek-peiling
22 doubling the angle on the bow	22 doubler l'angle	22 Verdoppelung der Seitenpeilung	22 dubbelstreek-peiling
23 dead reckoning	23 navigation à l'estime	23 Koppelung, Gissung	23 gegist bestek
24 estimated position	24 point estimé	24 gegißtes Besteck	24 gegiste standplaats
25 distance off	25 distance de . . .	25 Abstand von . . .	25 atstand tot . . .
26 seaward	26 vers le large	26 seewärts	26 buiten

DANSK	ITALIANO	ESPAÑOL	PORTUGUÊS
Kystnavigation	**Navigazione costiera**	**Navegación costera**	**Navegação costeira**
1 nordpol	1 polo nord	1 polo norte	1 polo norte
2 pejling	2 rilevamento	2 marcación, demora	2 azimute
3 kurs	3 rotta	3 rumbo	3 rumo
4 sand	4 vero	4 verdadero	4 verdadeiro
5 magnetisk	5 magnetico	5 magnético	5 magnético
6 kompaskurs	6 prora bussola	6 rumbo de aguja	6 rumo agulha
7 misvisning	7 declinazione	7 variación	7 declinação
8 deviation	8 deviazione	8 desvio	8 desvio
9 afdrift	9 scarroccio	9 deriva	9 abatimento
10 strøm-beregning	10 tener conto della corrente	10 error por corriente	10 desconto para corrente
11 kurs gennem vandet	11 rotta di superfice	11 rumbo	11 rumo em relação à água
12 beholdende kurs	12 rotta vera	12 rumbo verdadero	12 rumo em relação ao fundo
13 udsejlet distance	13 distanza percorsa	13 distancia navegada	13 distância navegada
14 udlægge kurs	14 tracciare, plottare	14 situarse en la carta	14 marcar na carta
15 position	15 posizione	15 situación	15 o ponto
16 tage en pejling	16 prendere un rilevamento	16 tomar una marcación	16 marcar
17 krydspejling	17 punto nave con rilevamenti	17 situación por dos marcaciones	17 marcar por dois azimutes
18 stedlinie	18 linea di posizione	18 línea de marcación	18 linha de posição
19 overført stedlinie	19 linea di posizione trasportato	19 marcación trasladada	19 linha de posição transportada
20 stedsbestemmelse	20 punto nave con rilevamenti successivi	20 situación por dos marcaciones a un mismo punto	20 marcar, navegar e tornar a marcar
21 fire-stregs pejling	21 45° e traverso	21 situación por marcación a 45°	21 marcação as quatro quartas
22 stedsbestemmelse ved to pejlinger, hvoraf den ene er dobbelt så stor som den anden	22 raddoppiamento del rilevamento polare	22 distancia a la costa por angulas especiales	22 marcação pelo ângulo duplo
23 bestik	23 navigazione stimata	23 estima	23 navegação estimada
24 gisset plads	24 punto stimato	24 situación por estima	24 posição estimada
25 afstand ud for . . .	25 distanza al . . .	25 distancia a . . .	25 distância a . . .
26 mod søsiden	26 al largo	26 hacia la mar, mar adentro	26 do lado do mar

ENGLISH	FRANÇAIS	DEUTSCH	NEDERLANDS
Sailing instructions	**Instructions nautiques**	**Segelanweisungen**	**Zeilaanwijzingen**
1 lighted channel	1 chenal éclairé	1 befeuertes Fahrwasser	1 verlicht vaarwater
2 buoyed channel	2 chenal balisé	2 ausgetonntes Fahrwasser	2 betond vaarwater
3 dredged channel	3 chenal dragué	3 gebaggerte Fahrrinne	3 gebaggerd vaarwater
4 navigable channel	4 chenal navigable	4 Fahrrinne	4 bevaarbaar vaarwater
5 leading line	5 alignement	5 Leitlinie	5 geleidelijn
6 in line	6 aligné	6 in Linie	6 ineen
7 transit line	7 passe, alignement	7 Deckpeilung	7 peilingslijn
8 open two breadths	8 ouvert à deux largeurs	8 offen halten	8 twee breedten open houden
9 pass not less than one cable off . . .	9 passer au moins à une encâblure de . . .	9 mindestens eine Kabellänge Abstand halten	9 tenminste een kabellengte buiten blijven
10 leave to port	10 laisser à bâbord	10 an Backbord halten	10 aan bakboord houden
11 round an object	11 contourner un amer	11 einen Gegenstand runden	11 ronden
12 least depth	12 profondeur minimum	12 Mindestiefe, geringste Tiefe	12 minste diepte
13 subject to change	13 irrégulier, mobile, changeant	13 Veränderungen unterworfen	13 aan verandering onderhevig, veranderlijk
14 off-lying dangers extend 3 miles	14 dangers s'étendant sur 3 milles au large	14 Gefahren, die 3 Seemeilen vor der Küste liegen	14 voor de kust liggend gevaren reiken 3 mijlen in zee
15 breaking seas on bar	15 la mer déferle ou brise sur la barre	15 auf der Barre brechende Seen	15 branding op drempel
16 make an offing	16 prendre le large	16 freien Seeraum gewinnen	16 vrij van de wal varen
17 lee shore	17 côte sous le vent	17 Legerwall, Leeküste	17 lage wal
18 windward shore	18 côte au vent	18 Luvküste	18 hoge wal
19 flood tide sets across entrance	19 le courant de flot porte en travers de l'entrée	19 Flutstrom setzt quer zur Hafeneinfahrt	19 vloedstroom trekt dwars over havenmond
20 tide race during flood	20 remous violents par courant de flot	20 Stromschnellen bei Flut n	20 stroomkabbeling met vloed
21 north-going current	21 le courant porte au nord	21 nach Norden setzender Strom	21 noordgaande stroom
22 water level may be reduced	22 abaissement de niveau possible par vent de . . .	22 Wasserstand kann geringer sein	22 lagere waterstanden zijn mogelijk

DANSK	ITALIANO	ESPAÑOL	PORTUGUÊS
Sejl-instruktion	**Norme per la navigazione**	**Derrotero**	**Instruções para navegação**
1 farvand afmærket med fyr	1 canale illuminato	1 canal abalizado con luces	1 canal farolado
2 afmærket farvand	2 canale segnalato da boe	2 canal balizado	2 canal balizado
3 uddybet farvand	3 canale dragato	3 canal dragado	3 canal dragado
4 farvandet kan besejles	4 canale navigabile	4 canal navegable	4 canal navegável
5 ledelinie	5 allineamento	5 enfilación	5 enfiamento
6 i linien	6 in allineamento	6 en línea	6 enfiado
7 stedlinie med to fyr overet	7 passaggio, transito	7 enfilación por el través	7 alinhado
8 at åbne to bredder	8 aprire due larghezze	8 ——	8 aberto por duas bocaduras
9 gå ikke tættere end I kabellængde	9 passare a non meno di 1/10 di miglio da . . .	9 pasar a más de un cable	9 não passar a menos de 1/10 milha
10 holde bagbord over	10 lasciare a sinistra	10 dejar a babor	10 deixar a bombordo
11 at runde en genstand	11 scansare un oggetto	11 bojear	11 rondar um obstáculo
12 mindste dybde	12 minimo fondale	12 calado minimo	12 altura minima de água
13 ændringer forbeholdt	13 soggetto a variazione	13 sujete a cambiar	13 sujeito a variação
14 udliggende fare strækker sig over 3 sømil	14 pericoli al largo che si estendono per 3 mg.	14 peligro hasta 3 millas	14 linha de resguardo de perigo a três milhas
15 søen brækker på barren	15 il mare frange sulla diga	15 rompientes en la barra	15 com mar a arrebentar na barra
16 stå til søs	16 andare al largo, prendere il largo	16 en altamar, franquia	16 amarar
17 lægerval, lækyst	17 costa di sottovento	17 costa de sotavento	17 terra a sotavento
18 luvkyst	18 costa di sopravento	18 costa de barlovento	18 terra a barlavento
19 flodstrømmen sætter tværs havneindløbet	19 la corrente di flusso è diretto di traverso all'entrada	19 la creciente tira atravesada a la entrada	19 corrente transversal à entrada durante a enchente
20 urolig sø under flodtid	20 frangenti di marea durante il flusso	20 correnton durante la crecida	20 estoque de água durante a enchente
21 nordgående strøm	21 corrente di nord	21 corriente sur	21 corrente em direcção ao norte
22 måske reduceres vandstanden	22 ii livello del mare può essere inferiore	22 la sonda puede disminuir	22 nível de água pode ser reduzido

127

ENGLISH	FRANÇAIS	DEUTSCH	NEDERLANDS
Inland waterways	**Eaux intérieures**	**Binnengewässer**	**Binnenwater**
1 canal	1 canal	1 Kanal	1 kanaal
2 lock	2 écluse, sas	2 Schleuse	2 sluis
3 length	3 longueur, de long	3 Länge	3 lengte
4 breadth	4 largeur, de large	4 Breite	4 breedte
5 depth	5 profondeur	5 Tiefe	5 diepte
6 to lock in	6 entrer dans le sas	6 einschleusen	6 schutten
7 to lock out	7 sortir de l'écluse	7 ausschleusen	7 schutten
8 lock dues	8 droits de sas	8 Schleusengebühr	8 sluisgeld
9 opening times	9 heures d'ouverture	9 Betriebszeiten	9 openingstijden
10 bridge dues	10 droits de pont	10 Brückenzoll	10 bruggegeld
11 movable bridge	11 pont mobile	11 bewegliche Brücke	11 beweegbare brug
12 lifting bridge	12 pont basculant	12 Hubbrücke	12 hefbrug
13 swing bridge	13 pont tournant	13 Drehbrücke	13 draaibrug
14 fixed bridge	14 pont fixe	14 feste Brücke	14 vaste brug
15 span	15 écartement, travée, largeur	15 Durchfahrtsweite	15 vak
16 height, headroom	16 tirant d'air	16 Durchfahrtshöhe	16 doorvaarthoogte
17 upstream	17 amont	17 stromauf, flußaufwärts	17 bovenstroomzijde, boven
18 downstream	18 aval	18 stromab, flußabwärts	18 benedenstroomzijde, onder
19 ferry	19 bac, ferry	19 Fähre	19 veer
20 high tension cable	20 câble à haute tension	20 Hochspannungskabel	20 hoogspanningskabel
21 mooring place	21 point d'accostage	21 Festmacheplatz	21 meerplaats
22 mooring forbidden	22 accostage interdit	22 anlegen verboten	22 verboden aan te leggen
23 to quant, punt	23 conduire à la gaffe, à la perche	23 staken	23 bomen

DANSK	ITALIANO	ESPAÑOL	PORTUGUÊS
Indenlandske vandveye	**Navigazione interna**	**Canales**	**Vias fluviais**
1 kanal	1 canale	1 canal	1 canal
2 sluse	2 chiusa	2 compuerta, esclusa	2 eclusa
3 længde	3 lunghezza	3 longitud	3 comprimento
4 bredde	4 larghezza	4 ancho, anchura	4 largura
5 dybde	5 profondità	5 fondo, profundidad	5 profundidade
6 at sluse ind	6 entrare in una chiusa	6 entrar en la esclusa	6 entrar na eclusa, docar
7 at sluse ud	7 uscire da una chiusa	7 salir de la esclusa	7 sair da eclusa ou doca
8 sluseafgift	8 diritti di chiusa	8 derecho de esclusa	8 taxa de docagem
9 åbningstid	9 orario di apertura	9 tiempo de apertura	9 hora de abrir
10 bro-afgift	10 diritti di ponte	10 tarifa de puente	10 taxa de passagem numa ponte
11 løfte-, svingbro	11 ponte mobile	11 puente móvil	11 ponte movediça
12 bro til at løfte	12 ponte levatoio	12 puente levadizo	12 ponte levadiça
13 svingbro	13 ponte girevole	13 puente giratorio	13 ponte giratória
14 fast bro	14 ponte fisso	14 puente fijo	14 ponte fixa
15 spændvidde	15 luce	15 anchura del puente	15 vão
16 højde, fri højde	16 altezza libera di passaggio	16 altura	16 altura
17 ovenfor	17 a monte	17 aguas arriba	17 montante
18 nedenfor	18 a valle	18 aguas abajo	18 jusante
19 færge	19 traghetto	19 transbordador	19 ferry boat, barco da travessia
20 højspændingskabel	20 cavo elettrico ad alta tensione	20 cable de alta tensión	20 cabo de alta tensão
21 fortøjningsplads	21 posto d'ormeggio	21 amarradero	21 ponte de atracação
22 fortøjning forbudt	22 ormeggio, ancoraggio proibito	22 amarradero prohibido	22 proíbido atracar
23 at stage	23 spingere una barca con la pertica	23 fincar	23 zingar

LAS ZONAS DE RESPONSABILIDAD
METEOROLOGICA DE ESPAÑA

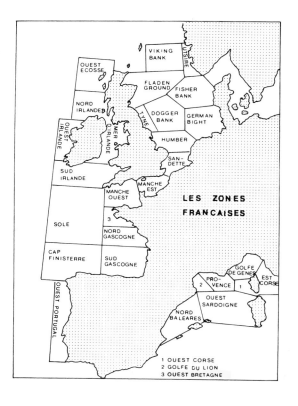

LES ZONES FRANCAISES

1 OUEST CORSE
2 GOLFE DU LION
3 OUEST BRETAGNE

ENGLISH	FRANÇAIS	DEUTSCH	NEDERLANDS
Meteorology	**Météorologie**	**Meteorologie**	**Meteorologie**
1 weather forecast	1 prévisions météo	1 Wettervorhersage	1 weersvoorspelling
2 weather report	2 bulletin du temps	2 Wetterbericht	2 weerbericht
3 area	3 région, parages	3 Gebiet	3 gebied
4 aneroid barometer	4 baromètre anéroïde	4 Aneroidbarometer	4 aneroidebarometer
5 barograph	5 barographe	5 Barograph	5 barograaf
6 rise/fall	6 monter/baisser	6 steigen/fallen	6 rijzen/vallen
7 steady	7 stable	7 gleichbleibend	7 vast
8 thermometer	8 thermomètre	8 Thermometer	8 thermometer
9 temperature	9 température	9 Temperatur	9 temperatuur
10 rise/drop	10 hausse/chute	10 Zunahme/Sturz	10 stijging/daling
11 anemometer	11 anémomètre	11 Windmesser, Anemometer	11 windmeter
12 velocity	12 vitesse	12 Geschwindigkeit	12 snelheid

DANSK	ITALIANO	ESPAÑOL	PORTUGUÊS
Meteorologi	**Meteorologia**	**Meteorología**	**Meteorologia**
1 vejrudsigt	1 previsioni meteo	1 previsión metereólogica	1 previsão de tempo
2 vejrmelding	2 bolletino meteo	2 boletín metereólogico	2 boletim meteorológico
3 område	3 regione, zona	3 región	3 área, zona
4 aneroid barometer	4 barometro aneroide	4 barómetro aneroide	4 barómetro aneroide
5 barograf	5 barografo	5 barógrafo	5 barógrafo
6 stige/falde	6 salire/discendere	6 subir/bajar	6 subindo/descendo
7 uforandret	7 costante	7 fijo, constante	7 constante
8 termometer	8 termometro	8 termómetro	8 termómetro
9 temperatur	9 temperatura	9 temperatura	9 temperatura
10 stige/falde	10 salita/discesa	10 subida/caida	10 subida/descida
11 vindmåler	11 anemometro	11 anemómetro	11 anemómetro
12 hastighed	12 velocità	12 velocidad	12 velocidade

ENGLISH

1 low-pressure area
2 depression, low
3 trough
4 high-pressure area
5 anticyclone, high
6 ridge
7 wedge
8 front, cold, warm

9 occlusion
10 fill up
11 deepen
12 stationary
13 quickly
14 slowly
15 spreading
16 settled
17 changeable

18 clearing up
19 fine

Sky
1 clear sky
2 cloudy
3 overcast
4 high cloud
5 low cloud

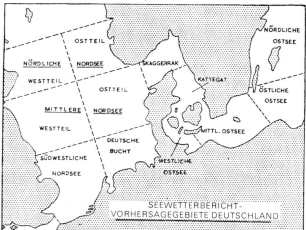

FRANÇAIS

1 zone de basse pression
2 dépression, bas
3 creux
4 zone de haute pression
5 anticyclone, haut
6 crête
7 coin
8 front froid, chaud
9 occlusion
10 se combler
11 se creuser
12 stationnaire
13 rapidement
14 lentement
15 s'étalant s'étendant
16 temps établi
17 variable
18 éclaircies
19 beau temps

Ciel
1 pur, clair, dégagé
2 nuageux
3 couvert
4 nuages hauts, élevés
5 nuages bas

DEUTSCH

1 Tiefdruckgebiet

2 Depression, Tief
3 Trog, Ausläufer
4 Hochdruckgebiet

5 Hoch
6 Rücken
7 Keil
8 Front, kalt, warm
9 Okklusion
10 auffüllen
11 sich vertiefen
12 stationär
13 schnell, rasch
14 langsam
15 sich ausbreitend
16 beständig
17 wechselhaft
18 aufklarend
19 heiter, schön

Himmel
1 wolkenlos, klarer Himmel
2 bewölkt, wolkig
3 bedeckt
4 hohe Wolken
5 niedrige Wolken

NEDERLANDS	DANSK	ITALIANO	ESPAÑOL	PORTUGUES
1 lagedrukgebied	1 lavtryks-område	1 area di bassa pressione	1 zona de baja presión	1 área de baixa pressão
2 depressie	2 lavtryk	2 depressione	2 depresión	2 depressão, baixa
3 dal	3 udløber af lavtryk	3 saccatura di bassa pressione	3 vaguada	3 linha de baixa pressão
4 hogedrukgebied	4 højtryks område	4 area di alta pressione	4 zona de alta presión	4 área de alta pressão
5 hogedrukgebied	5 anticyklon, høj	5 anticiclone	5 anticiclón, alta	5 anticiclone, alta
6 rug	6 ryg	6 cresta	6 dorsal, cresta	6 crista
7 wig	7 kile	7 cuneo	7 cuna	7 cunha
8 front, koud, warm	8 front, kold, varm	8 fronte, freddo, caldo	8 frente, frío, cálido	8 frente, fria, quente
9 occlusie	9 okulation	9 occlusione	9 oclusión	9 oclusão
10 opvullen	10 udfylde	10 colmarsi	10 debilitamiento	10 encher
11 dieper worden	11 uddybe	11 approfondirsi	11 intensificación	11 agravar
12 stationair	12 stationær	12 stazionario	12 estacionario	12 estacionária
13 snel	13 hurtig	13 rapidamente	13 rápidamente	13 rápidamente
14 langzaam	14 langsom	14 lentamente	14 lentamente	14 lentamente
15 uitbreidend	15 spredende	15 allargantesi, che si sparge	15 extendiendo	15 alastrando
16 vast	16 stadig vejr	16 stabile	16 sostenido, asentado	16 estável
17 veranderlijk	17 omskiftelig	17 variabile	17 variable	17 variável, instável
18 opklarend	18 klarer op	18 miglioramento	18 clarear, escampar	18 limpando
19 helder	19 fint	19 bello	19 tranquilo, despejado	19 bom tempo

Lucht	Himmel	Cielo	Cielo	Céu
1 onbewolkt	1 klar himmel	1 cielo chiaro, sereno	1 claro, despejado	1 céu limpo
2 bewolkt	2 skyet	2 nuvoloso	2 nubloso	2 nublado
3 betrokken	3 overtrukket	3 coperto	3 cubierto	3 coberto
4 hoge wolken	4 høje skyer	4 nubi alte	4 nubes altas	4 núvem alta
5 lage wolken	5 lave skyer	5 nubi basse	5 nubes bajas	5 núvem baixa

ENGLISH		FRANÇAIS		Knots	Metres/ Second	DEUTSCH		NEDERLANDS		SVENSK	
Beaufort Scale		**Echelle de Beaufort**				**Windstärke nach Beaufort**		**Windschaal van Beaufort**		**Beauforts skala**	
calm	0	calme		0– 1	0– 0,2	Windstille	0	stil	0	stilte	
light air	1	très légère brise		1– 3	0,3– 1,5	leiser Zug	1	flauw en stil	1	näsan stilte	
light breeze	2	légère brise		4– 6	1,6– 3,3	leichte Brise	2	flauwe koelte	2	lätt bris	
gentle breeze	3	petite brise		7–10	3,4– 5,4	schwache Brise	3	lichte koelte	3	god bris	
moderate breeze	4	jolie brise		11–16	5,5– 7,9	mäßige Brise	4	matige koelte	4	frisk bris	
fresh breeze	5	bonne brise		17–21	8 –10,7	frische Brise	5	frisse bries	5	styf bris	
strong beeze	6	vent frais		22–27	10,8–13,8	starker Wind	6	stijve bries	6	hård bris	
near gale	7	grand frais		28–33	13,9–17,1	steifer Wind	7	harde wind	7	styv kuling	
gale	8	coup de vent		34–40	17,2–20,7	stürmischer Wind	8	stormachtig	8	hard kuling	
strong gale	9	fort coup de vent		41–47	20,8–24,4	Sturm	9	storm	9	halv storm	
storm	10	tempête		48–55	24,5–28,4	schwerer Sturm	10	zware storm	10	storm	
violent storm	11	violente tempête		56–63	28,5–32,6	orkanartiger Sturm	11	zeer zware storm	11	svar storm	
hurricane	12	ouragan		64 <	32,7 <	Orkan	12	orkaan	12	orkan	

BRITISH SYSTEM OF STORM CONES

(Force 8 and over)

By day

▲ **N.W. and N.E. quadrants**

▼ **S.W. and S.E. Quadrants**

By night

r.*
r.*r.*

w.*w.*
w.*

CONTINENTAL SYSTEM OF STORM CONES ETC.

France, Deutschland, Nederland, Danmark
Italia, España, Portugal, Belgique

STORM CONES (Force 8<)

By day		**By night**
▼	S.W. Quadrant	w.* w.*
▲	N.W. Quadrant	r.* r.*
▼ ▼	S.E. Quadrant	w.* r.*
▲ ▲	N.E. Quadrant	r.* w.*

France, Belgique, Deutschland, Nederland,
Danmark, Portugal

Mauvais temps ⎫
Windwarnung ⎬ Force 6–7
Harde wind ⎭

By night
*w
*g

Gale expected to veer:

N → E → S → W → N

Gale expected to back:

N → W → S → E → N

By day
●

DANSK Beauforts skala		ITALIANO Scala Beaufort	Knots	Metres/Second	ESPAÑOL Escala de Beaufort		PORTUGUÊS Escala Beaufort		NORSK Beaufort skala
stille	0	calma	0– 1	0 – 0,2	calma	0	calma	0	stille
svag luftning	1	bava di vento	1– 3	0,3– 1,5	ventolina	1	aragem	1	flau vind
svag brise	2	brezza leggera	4– 6	1,6– 3,3	flojito	2	vento fraco	2	svak vind
let brise	3	brezza tesa	7–10	3,4– 5,4	flojo	3	vento bonançoso	3	lett bris
iævn brise	4	vento moderato	11–16	5,5– 7,9	bonancible	4	vento moderado	4	laber bris
frisk brise	5	vento teso	17–21	8 –10,7	fresquito	5	vento frêsco	5	frisk bris
blæst, kuling	6	vento fresco	22–27	10,8–13,8	fresco	6	vento muito frêsco	6	liten kuling
stiv blæst,—kuling	7	vento forte	28–33	13,9–17,1	frescachón	7	vento forte	7	stiv kuling
hård blæst	8	burrasca	34–40	17,2–20,7	duro	8	vento muito forte	8	sterk kuling
storm	9	burrasca forte	41–47	20,8–24,4	muy duro	9	vento tempestuoso	9	liten storm
stærk storm	10	tempesta	48–55	24,5–28,4	temporal	10	temporal	10	full storm
orkanagtig storm	11	tempesta violenta	56–63	28,5–32,6	borrasca	11	temporal desfeito	11	sterk storm
orkan	12	uragano	64 <	32,7 <	huracán	12	furacão	12	orkan

w. =	r. =	By day	By night	Gale warning	Storm warning	Cone	Quadrant
white	red	By day	By night	Gale warning	Storm warning	Cone	Quadrant
blanc	rouge	De jour	De nuit	Avis de coup de vent	Avis de tempête	Cône	Secteur
weiß	rot	tags	nachts	Windwarnung	Sturmwarnung	Kegel	Quadrant
wit	rood	Overdag	's nachts	Windwaarschuwing	Stormwaarschuwing	Kegel	Kwadrant
hvid	rød	Om dagen	Om natten	Stormvarsel	Stormvarsel	Kegle	Kvadrant
bianco	rosso	Di giorno	DI notte	Avviso di burrasca	Avviso di tempesta	Cono	Quadrante
blanco	rojo	De dia	De noche	Aviso de mal tiempo	Aviso de temporal	Cono	Cuadrante
branco	vermelha	Durante o dia	Durante o noite	Aviso de vento forte	Aviso de temporal	Cone	Quadrante

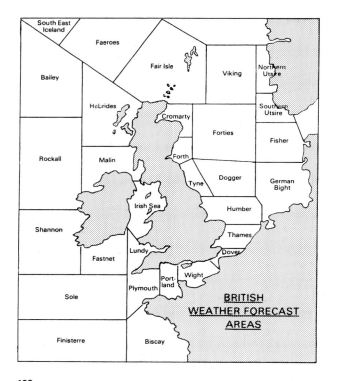

BRITISH WEATHER FORECAST AREAS

ENGLISH
Visibility
1 good
2 moderate
3 poor
4 haze
5 mist
6 fog

DEUTSCH
Sichtweite
1 gut
2 mittel
3 schlecht
4 Dunst
5 feuchter Dunst, diesig
6 Nebel

ITALIANO
Visibilità
1 buona
2 discreta
3 cattiva
4 foschia
5 caligine
6 nebbia

FRANÇAIS
Visibilité
1 bonne
2 médiocre, réduite
3 mauvaise
4 brume de beau temps, ou brume sèche
5 brume légère ou mouillée
6 brouillard

NEDERLANDS
Zicht
1 ruim
2 matig
3 slecht
4 nevel
5 nevel
6 mist

ESPAÑOL
Visibilidad
1 buena
2 regular
3 mala
4 calima
5 neblina
6 niebla

DANSK
Sigtbarhed
1 god
2 moderat
3 ringe, dårlig
4 dis tåge
5 let tåge
6 tåge

PORTUGUÊS
Visibilidade
1 bôa
2 moderada
3 fraca, má
4 cerração
5 neblina
6 nevoeiro

ENGLISH	FRANÇAIS	DEUTSCH	NEDERLANDS
Wind	**Vent**	**Wind**	**Wind**
1 lull	1 accalmie, bonace	1 vorübergehendes Abflauen	1 luwte
2 drop, abate	2 tomber, diminuer de force	2 nachlassen	2 afnemen
3 decreasing, moderating	3 décroissant	3 abnehmend	3 afnemend
4 increasing, freshening	4 fraîchissant	4 zunehmend, auffrischend	4 toenemend
5 gust	5 rafale	5 Windstoß	5 windvlaag
6 squall	6 grain	6 Bö	6 bui
7 sea breeze	7 brise de mer	7 Seebrise	7 zeebries
8 land breeze	8 brise de terre	8 ablandige Brise, Landbrise	8 landbries
9 prevailing wind	9 vent dominant	9 vorherrschender Wind	9 heersende wind
10 trade winds	10 vents alizés	10 Passatwinde	10 passaatwinden
11 veer	11 virer au . . . (dans le sens des aiguilles d'une montre)	11 rechtsdrehen, ausschießen	11 ruimen
12 back	12 adonner (dans le sens contraire aux aiguilles d'une montre	12 zurückdrehen, krimpen	12 krimpen

DANSK	ITALIANO	ESPAÑOL	PORTUGUÊS
Vind	**Vento**	**Viento**	**Vento**
1 ophold	1 bonaccia	1 encalmado	1 sota, calma temporária
2 vinden lægger sig	2 caduta, attenuazione	2 disminuir	2 acalmar
3 aftagende	3 che cala, che diminuisce	3 disminuyendo	3 decrescendo de intensidade
4 tiltagende	4 in aumento, che aumenta	4 aumentando	4 aumentando
5 vindstød	5 raffica	5 racha	5 rajada
6 byge	6 groppo	6 turbonada	6 borrasca
7 søvind	7 brezza di mare	7 brisa de mar, virazón	7 brisa do mar
8 landbrise,	8 brezza di terra	8 terral	8 brisa da terra
9 fremherskende	9 vento predominante	9 viento dominante	9 ventos predominantes
10 passat-vinden	10 alisei	10 vientos alisios	10 ventos alíseos
11 vinden drejer til højre	11 girare del vento in senso orario	11 rola con las manillas del reloj	11 no sentido dos ponteiros de relógio
12 vinden drejer til venstre	12 girare del vento in senso antiorario	12 rola contra las manillas del reloj	12 de sentido retrógrado

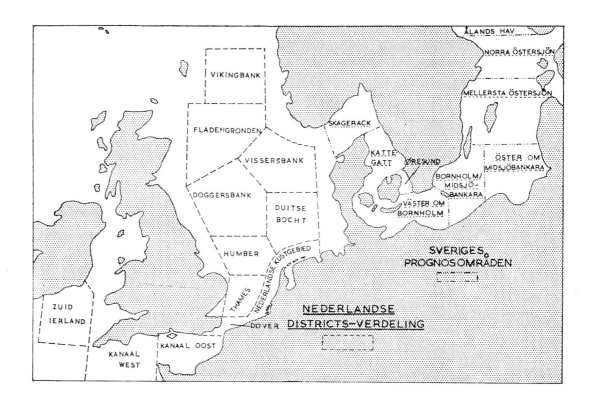

VIKINGBANK

FLADENGRONDEN

VISSERSBANK

DOGGERSBANK

DUITSE BOCHT

HUMBER

NEDERLANDSE KUSTGEBIED

THAMES

ZUID IERLAND

DOVER

KANAAL WEST

KANAAL OOST

SKAGERACK

KATTE GATT

ØRESUND

VÄSTER OM BORNHOLM

BORNHOLM/ MIDSJÖ- BANKARA

ÅLANDS HAV

NORRA ÖSTERSJÖN

MELLERSTA ÖSTERSJÖN

ÖSTER OM MIDSJÖBANKARA

SVERIGES PROGNOSOMRÅDEN

NEDERLANDSE DISTRICTS-VERDELING

ENGLISH
Sea
1 calm
2 ripples
3 waves
4 rough sea
5 swell
6 crest
7 trough
8 breaking seas
9 head sea
10 following sea
11 choppy
12 short
13 steep

FRANÇAIS
Mer
1 plate, calme
2 vaguelettes, rides
3 vagues, ondes, lames
4 grosse mer, mer agitée
5 houle
6 crête
7 creux
8 lames déferlantes
9 mer debout
10 mer arrière ou suiveuse
11 croisée ou hachée; clapot
12 lames courtes
13 mer creuse

DEUTSCH
See
1 glatt, ruhig
2 gekräuselt
3 Wellen, Seen
4 grobe See
5 Dünung
6 Wellenkamm
7 Wellental
8 brechende Seen
9 See von vorn
10 achterliche See
11 kabbelig
12 kurz
13 steil

NEDERLANDS
Zee
1 vlak
2 rimpels
3 golven
4 ruwe zee
5 deining
6 kam, golftop
7 trog
8 brekende golven
9 tegenzee
10 meelopende zee
11 kort en steil
12 kort
13 steil

DANSK
Søen
1 stille
2 krusning
3 bølger
4 grov sø
5 dønning
6 bølgetop
7 bølgedal
8 brydende sø
9 stik i stævn
10 medløbende sø
11 krap
12 kort
13 stejl

ITALIANO
Mare
1 calmo
2 ondulato, increspato
3 onde
4 mare molto agitato
5 mare morto o lungo
6 cresta
7 gola, solco
8 frangenti
9 mare in prora
10 mare in poppa
11 maretta
12 mare corto
13 onde alte

ESPAÑOL
Mar
1 calma
2 mar rizada
3 olas
4 picada
5 mar de leva,—de fondo
6 cresta
7 seno
8 rompientes
9 mar de proa
10 mar de popa
11 marejadilla
12 mar corta
13 mar gruesa

PORTUGUÊS
Mar
1 calmo, plano
2 ondinhas
3 ondas
4 mar bravo
5 ondulação, mar de vaga
6 crista da onda
7 cava da onda
8 arrebentação
9 mar de proa
10 mar de pôpa
11 mareta
12 mar de vaga curta
13 mar cavado

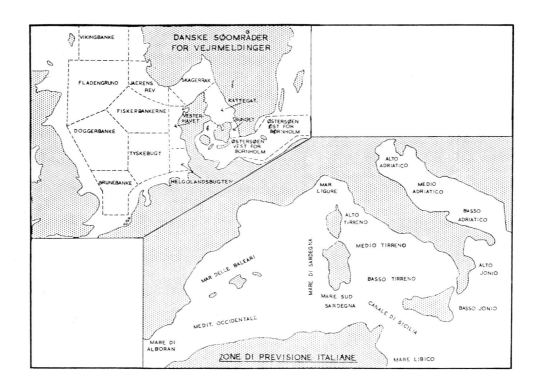

DANSKE SØOMRÅDER
FOR VEJRMELDINGER

VIKINGBANKE

FLADENGRUND   JAERENS   SKAGERRAK
                REV
                                    KATTEGAT
        FISKERBANKERNE   VESTER-
                              HAVET   SUNDET   ØSTERSØEN
                                                  ØST FOR
DOGGERBANKE   BORNHOLM

                                        ØSTERSØEN
                          TYSKEBUGT   VEST FOR
                                        BORNHOLM

BRUNEBANKE   HELGOLANDSBUGTEN

                                            ALTO
                                          ADRIATICO

                              MAR   MEDIO
                            LIGURE   ADRIATICO

                              ALTO   BASSO
                            TIRRENO   ADRIATICO

                    MARE DI SARDEGNA   MEDIO TIRRENO
            MAR DELLE BALEARI   ALTO
                                                            JONIO
                                BASSO TIRRENO

                            MARE SUD
                            SARDEGNA   CANALE DI SICILIA   BASSO JONIO

        MEDIT. OCCIDENTALE

    MARE DI
    ALBORAN   ZONE DI PREVISIONE ITALIANE   MARE LIBICO

ENGLISH
1 wet
2 dry
3 rain
4 sleet
5 snow
6 hail
7 drizzle
8 shower
9 thunderstorm

FRANÇAIS
1 humide
2 sec
3 pluie
4 neige fondue
5 neige
6 grêle
7 bruine
8 averse
9 orage

DEUTSCH
1 naß
2 trocken
3 Regen
4 Schneeregen
5 Schnee
6 Hagel
7 Sprühregen
8 Schauer
9 Gewitter

NEDERLANDS
1 nat
2 droog
3 regen
4 natte sneeuw
5 sneeuw
6 hagel
7 motregen
8 stortbui
9 onweer

DANSK
1 våd
2 tør
3 regn
4 slud
5 sne
6 hagl
7 støvregn
8 byge
9 tordenvejr

ITALIANO
1 umido
2 secco
3 pioggia
4 pioggia ghiacciata
5 neve
6 grandine
7 pioviggine
8 rovescio, acquazzone
9 temporale

ESPAÑOL
1 húmedo
2 seco
3 lluvia
4 aguanieve
5 nieve
6 granizada
7 llovizna
8 aguacero
9 tempestad, borrasca

PORTUGUÊS
1 húmido
2 sêco
3 chuva
4 geáda miúda
5 neve
6 saraiva, chuva
   de pedra
7 chuvisco
8 aguaceiro
9 trovoada

ENGLISH	FRANÇAIS	DEUTSCH	NEDERLANDS
Racing	**En course**	**Wettsegeln**	**Wedstrijdzeilen**
1 race	1 régate	1 Regatta	1 wedstrijd
2 race committee	2 comité de course	2 Wettfahrtleitung	2 wedstrijd comité
3 entry form	3 bulletin d'inscription	3 Meldeformular	3 inschrijfbiljet
4 entrance fee	4 droit d'inscription	4 Meldegeld	4 inschrijfgeld
5 closing date	5 date de clôture	5 Meldeschlußtermin	5 sluitings datum
Sailing instructions	**Instructions de course**	**Segelanweisungen**	**Wedstrijdbepalingen**
1 committee vessel	1 bateau du comité de course	1 Boot der Wettfahrtleitung	1 opname-vaartuig
2 starting line	2 ligne de départ	2 Startlinie	2 lijn van afvaart
3 inner, outer limit	3 marque intérieure, marque extérieure	3 innere, äussere Begrenzung	3 binnen merkteken, buiten merkteken
4 course signal	4 signal de parcours	4 Bahnsignal	4 wedstrijdsein
5 to round a mark	5 contourner une marque	5 Bahnmarke runden	5 merkteken ronden
6 leave to port	6 laisser à bâbord	6 an Backbord passieren	6 aan bakboord houden
7 leave to starboard	7 laisser à tribord	7 an Steuerbord passieren	7 aan stuurboord houden
8 twice round	8 deux tours	8 zwei Runden	8 twee ronden
9 mark of the course	9 marque de parcours	9 Bahnmarke	9 merkteken van de baan
10 finishing line	10 ligne d'arrivée	10 Ziellinie	10 lijn van aankomst
Signals and guns	**Signaux et coups de canon**	**Signale und Kanonenschüsse**	**Seinen en schoten**
1 warning signal	1 signal d'attention	1 Ankündigungssignal	1 waarschuwingssein
2 preparatory signal	2 signal d'avertissement	2 Vorbereitungssignal	2 voorbereidingssein
3 starting signal	3 signal de départ	3 Startsignal	3 startsein
4 general recall	4 signal de rappel général	4 allgemeiner Rückruf	4 algemeen terugroepsein
5 postpone	5 retarder	5 verschieben	5 uitstellen
6 abandon	6 abandonner	6 abbrechen	6 afbreken
7 shorten course	7 réduire le parcours	7 Bahnabkürzung,- verkürzung	7 afkorten van de baan
8 cancellation	8 annulation	8 Annullierung	8 afgelasting
9 time limit	9 limite de temps	9 Zeitbegrenzung	9 tijdslimiet

DANSK

Kapsejlads
1 kapsejlads
2 kapsejladskomite
3 anmeldelses blanket
4 indskud
5 sidste dag for anmeldelse

Sejladsbestemmelser
1 dommerskib
2 startlinie
3 startliniens luv et læ
  begrænsningsmærke
4 banesignalerne
5 runde et mærke
6 holde om bagbord
7 holde om styrbord
8 to gange rundt
9 banemærke
10 mållinie

Dommerskibets signaler
1 varselsignal
2 klarsignal
3 startsignal
4 signal til omstart
5 udsætte
6 opgive
7 afkorte banen
8 aflyse
9 tidsbegrænsning

ITALIANO

In regata
1 regata
2 comitato, giuria
3 modulo di iscrizione
4 tassa di iscrizione
5 data di chiusura delle
  iscrizioni

Istruzioni di regata
1 battello della giuria
2 linea di partenza
3 limite interno ed esterno

4 segnale di percorso
5 girare una boa
6 lasciare a sinistra
7 lasciare a dritta
8 doppio giro
9 boa del percorso
10 traguardo, linea d'arrivo

Segnali e cannoncini
1 segnale di avviso
2 segnale preparatorio
3 segnale di partenza
4 richiamo generale
5 differire
6 interrompere
7 ridurre il percorso
8 soppressione
9 tempo massimo, tempo limite

ESPAÑOL

En regata
1 regata
2 comité de regatas
3 modelo de inscripción
4 derecho de inscripción
5 termino de la inscripción

Instrucciones de regata
1 bote del jurado
2 línea de salida
3 baliza interior, exterior

4 señal de recorrido
5 montar la baliza
6 montar por babor
7 montar por estribor
8 dos vueltas
9 balizaje de la regata
10 línea de llegada

Señales y disparos
1 señal de atención
2 señal de preparación
3 señal de salida
4 llamada general
5 aplazar
6 suspender
7 acortar el recorrido
8 anulación
9 límite de tiempo

PORTUGUÊS

Regatas
1 regata
2 juri de regatas
3 boletim de inscrição
4 preco de inscrição
5 data de fecho de inscrição

Instruções de regata
1 barco de juri
2 linha de largada
3 limites interiores e
  exteriores
4 sinal de percurso
5 rondar a baliza
6 deixar a bombordo
7 deixar a estibordo
8 duas voltas
9 baliza, marca do percurso
10 linha de chegada

Sinais e disparos
1 sinal de aviso
2 sinal de preparação
3 sinal de largada
4 chamada geral
5 adiar
6 abandonar
7 reduzir o percurso
8 anulamento
9 limite de tempo

ENGLISH Under I.Y.R.U. rules	FRANÇAIS Sous les règlements de l'I.Y.R.U.	DEUTSCH Nach den Regeln der I.Y.R.U.	NEDERLANDS Onder het reglement der I.Y.R.U.
1 starboard tack yacht	1 yacht tribord amures	1 Backbordbugyacht, Steuerbordhalsenyacht	1 jacht over bakboordsboeg
2 port tack yacht	2 yacht bâbord amures		2 jacht over stuurboordsboeg
3 windward yacht	3 yacht au vent	2 Steuerbordbugyacht, Backbordhalsenyacht	3 loefwaarts jacht
4 leeward yacht	4 yacht sous le vent		4 lijwaarts jacht
5 clear ahead/astern	5 libre devant/derrière	3 Luvyacht	5 vrij voor/achter
6 overlap	6 engagement	4 Leeyacht	6 boord aan boord
7 on the same tack	7 sur le même bord	5 klar voraus/achteraus	7 over dezelfde boeg
8 on opposite tacks	8 sur des bords opposés	6 Überlappung	8 over verschillende boegen
9 to keep clear	9 s'écarter	7 auf gleichem Bug	9 vrij blijven
10 to alter course	10 modifier la route	8 auf verschiedenem Bug	10 koers veranderen, wijzigen
11 proper course	11 route normale	9 frei halten, ausweichen	11 juiste koers
12 above/below a proper course	12 plus près que/abattre de la route normale	10 Kurs ändern	12 hoger dan/lager dan de juiste koers zeilen
13 two overall lengths	13 deux longueurs	11 richtiger Kurs	13 twee scheepslengten
14 right to luff	14 droit de lofer	12 über/unter einem richtigen Kurs segeln	14 recht om te loeven
15 mast abeam	15 mât par le travers		15 mast dwars
16 obstruction	16 obstacle	13 zwei Bootslängen	16 hindernis
17 hail for room to tack, call for water	17 demander de l'eau pour virer de bord	14 Luvrecht	17 aanroepen voor ruimte om overstag te gaan
18 give a yacht room	18 laisser place à un yacht	15 Mast querab	18 ruimte geven
19 touch a mark	19 aborder une marque, toucher la bouée	16 Hindernis	19 raken van een merkteken
20 fair sailing	20 navigation correcte	17 Anruf um Raum zum Wenden	20 eerlijk of sportief varen
21 misleading	21 manœuvres irrégulières	18 Raum geben	21 misleiding
22 balking	22 manœuvres trompeuses	19 Berührung einer Bahnmarke	22 hinderen
23 means of propulsion	23 moyens de propulsion	20 faires Segeln	23 middelen van voortbeweging
24 onus	24 charge	21 täuschen	24 bewijslast
25 right of way yacht	25 yacht prioritaire	22 behindern	25 recht van de weg hebbend jacht
		23 Fortbewegungsmittel	
		24 Beweislast	
		25 Wegerecht-Yacht	

DANSK

Efter I.Y.R.U.'s regler
1 styrbords halse båd
2 bagbords halse båd
3 luv båd
4 læ båd
5 klar foran/agter
6 overlap
7 samme halse
8 modsat halse
9 holde klar af
10 ændre kurs
11 rigtig kurs
12 højere/lavere end rigtig kurs
13 to overalt-længder
14 ret til at luffe
15 mast tværs
16 hindring
17 prajning for plads til at vende
18 give en båd plads
19 berøring af et mærke
20 fair sejlads
21 vildlede
22 narre
23 fremdrivningsmidler
24 bevisbyrde
25 båd med retten til vejen

ITALIANO

In base al regolamento I.Y.R.U.
1 yacht con mure a dritta
2 yacht con mure a sinistra
3 yacht al vento
4 yacht sottovento
5 libero dalla prua/poppa
6 ingaggiamento
7 sulle stesse mure
8 su mure differenti
9 tenersi fuori
10 modificare la rotta
11 giusta rotta
12 oltre/sotto la giusta rotta
13 due lunghezze fuori tutto
14 diritto di orzare
15 albero al traverso
16 ostacolo
17 richiedere acqua per virare
18 dare acqua ad uno yacht
19 toccare una boa
20 corretto navigare
21 inganno
22 impedimento
23 mezzi di propulsione
24 onere
25 yacht con diritto di rotta

ESPAÑOL

Bajo el reglamento de la I.Y.R.U.
1 yate amurado a estribor
2 yate amurado a babor
3 yate de barlovento
4 yate de sotavento
5 claramente por proa/popa
6 compromiso
7 en la misma amurada
8 a distantas amuras
9 mantenerse separado
10 alterar el rumbo
11 rumbo correcto
12 más ceñido que/más arribado que el rumbo a la proxima baliza
13 dos esloras
14 derecho a orzar
15 palo al través
16 obstáculo
17 voces para pedir agua para virar
18 ceder espacio
19 abordar a una baliza
20 deportividad
21 maniobra equivoca
22 confundir
23 medios de propulsión
24 prueba
25 yate con derecho de paso

PORTUGUÊS

Sob as regras da I.Y.R.U.
1 barco com amuras a estibordo
2 barco com amuras a bombordo
3 barco a barlavento
4 barco a sotavento
5 livre por ante a vante/a ré
6 sobreladeamento
7 amurados pelo mesmo bordo
8 amurados por bordos diferentes
9 afastar-se do caminho
10 alterar o rumo
11 rumo próprio
12 a barlavento/a sotavento do rumo próprio
13 dois comprimentos
14 direito a orçar
15 pelo través do mastro
16 obstáculo
17 pedir espaço para virar
18 dar espaço a um iate
19 tocar na balisa
20 correr honestamente
21 que engana
22 obstruir a passagem a outros
23 meios de propulsão
24 obrigação, onus
25 iate com direito a rumo

ENGLISH	FRANÇAIS	DEUTSCH	NEDERLANDS
To make a protest	**Déposer une protestation**	**Protestieren**	**Een protest indienen**
1 to fly a protest flag	1 montrer un pavillon de protestation	1 eine Protestflagge zeigen	1 een protest vlag tonen
2 to hear a protest	2 examiner une protestation	2 Anhören eines Protestes	2 een protest behandelen
3 retire	3 abandonner	3 aufgeben	3 opgeven
4 disqualification	4 disqualification	4 Disqualifikation, Ausschluß	4 uitsluiting, diskwalificatie
5 collision	5 abordage	5 Kollision, Berührung	5 aanvaring
6 infringe the rules	6 enfreindre le règlement	6 Regelverstoß	6 overtreding van de reglementen
7 to sign a declaration form	7 signer une déclaration	7 Verklarung unterzeichnen	7 een verklaring tekenen
8 appeal	8 appel	8 Berufung	8 hoger beroep
Classes	**Classes**	**Klassen**	**Klassen**
1 International	1 Internationale	1 internationale	1 Internationale
2 National	2 Nationale	2 nationale	2 Nationale
3 Restricted	3 à restrictions	3 beschränkte Klasse	3 Beperkte
4 One Design	4 Monotype	4 Einheitsklasse	4 Eenheidsklasse
5 Handicap	5 Handicap	5 Ausgleichsklasse	5 Handicapklasse
6 rating	6 jauge, rating	6 Rennwert	6 wedstrijdmaat
7 corrected time	7 temps compensé	7 berechnete Zeit	7 berekende tijd
Tactics	**Tactique**	**Taktik**	**Taktiek**
1 cover	1 faire exactement les mêmes manæuvres que . . .	1 genau die gleichen Manöver machen wie . . .	1 afdekken
2 blanket, take a boat's wind	2 masquer, déventer	2 abdecken	2 de wind uit de zeilen nemen
3 safe leeward position	3 position favorable sous le vent	3 sichere Leestellung	3 zekere lij positie
4 backwind a boat	4 perturber	4 Wind stören	4 een boot vuile wind geven
5 false tack	5 faux virement de bord	5 Scheinwende	5 schijnwending
6 double tack	6 double virement de bord	6 Doppelwende	6 tweemaal het achter elkaar door de wind gaan
7 split tacks	7 choisir le bord opposé	7 auf den entgegengesetzten Bug gehen	7 verschillende boegen
8 luff head to wind	8 lofer jusqu'au vent debout	8 bis in den Wind luven	8 oploeven met de kop op de wind

DANSK
Protestere
1 sætte protestflag
2 afhøring af en protest
3 udgå
4 diskvalifikation
5 kollision
6 overtræde reglerne
7 underskrive en deklaration
8 appellere

Klasser
1 International
2 National
3 Restricted
4 Entype
5 Handicap
6 kapsejladsmål
7 rettet tid

Taktik
1 dække
2 tage vinden fra et fartøj
3 sikker læstilling
4 at give en båd bagluft
5 narrevending
6 dobbelt vending
7 at gå hver på sin bov
8 at luffe op i vinden

ITALIANO
Inoltrare una protesta
1 alzare la bandiera di protesta
2 esaminare una protesta
3 ritirarsi
4 squalifica
5 collisione
6 infrangere il regolamento
7 sottoscrivere una dichiarazione
8 appello

Classi
1 Internazionale
2 Nazionale
3 a restrizione
4 Monotipo
5 a formula
6 stazza
7 tempo corretto

Tattiche
1 coprire
2 togliere il vento ad una barca
3 posizione di privilegio di sottovento
4 sottoventare una barca
5 falsa virata
6 doppia virata
7 virare mentre l'altro yacht rimane sulle stesse mure
8 orzare fino ad avere la prua al vento

ESPAÑOL
Hacer una protesta
1 izar señal de protesta
2 tratar de una protesta
3 retirarse de una regata
4 descalificación
5 abordaje
6 infringir las reglas
7 firmar la declaración
8 apelación

Clases
1 Internacional
2 Nacional
3 De fórmula
4 Monotipo
5 Handicap
6 arqueo
7 tiempo compensado

Tácticas
1 cubrir
2 desventar, quitar el viento
3 posición segura a sotavento
4 desventar desde sotavento
5 virar en falso
6 virada doble
7 hacer la virada contraria
8 orzarle hasta aproarlo

PORTUGUÊS
Protestar
1 içar a bandeira de protesto
2 ouvir um protesto
3 desistir
4 desclassificação
5 abalroamento
6 infringir as regras
7 assinar a declaração de ter respeitado as regras
8 recorrer

Classes
1 Internacional
2 Nacional
3 Restrito
4 Monotipo
5 De Abôno, De Cruzeiro
6 abôno, rating
7 tempo corregido

Táticas
1 cobrir
2 pôr na sombra, tirar o vento
3 posição favorável a sotavento
4 colocar outro barco na sombra
5 manobra de virar fingida
6 virar e tornar a virar
7 manter amuras apostas
8 orçar até aproar ao vento

ENGLISH	FRANÇAIS	DEUTSCH	NEDERLANDS
First aid box	**Pharmacie de bord**	**Bordapotheke**	**Eerste hulp doos**
1 wound dressing	1 pansement stérilisé	1 Notverband	1 noodverband
2 to dress a wound	2 faire un bandage, poser un pansement	2 einen Verband anlegen	2 een wond verbinden
3 cotton wool	3 ouate, coton hydrophile	3 Watte	3 watten
4 sticking plaster	4 pansement adhésif, sparadrap	4 Heftplaster	4 kleefpleister
5 bandage	5 bandage	5 Binde, Verband	5 verband
6 elastic bandage	6 bandage élastique	6 elastische Binde	6 elastisch verband
7 scissors	7 ciseaux	7 Schere	7 schaar
8 safety pin	8 épingle de sûreté	8 Sicherheitsnadel	8 veiligheidsspeld
9 tweezers	9 pince à échardes	9 Pinzette	9 pincet
10 thermometer	10 thermomètre	10 Thermometer	10 thermometer
11 antiseptic cream	11 onguent antiseptique	11 antiseptische Salbe	11 antiseptische zalf
12 penicillin ointment	12 onguent à la pénicilline	12 Penicillin-Salbe	12 penicilline zalf
13 disinfectant	13 désinfectant	13 Desinfektionsmittel	13 desinfecterend middel
14 Optrex	14 lotion oculaire	14 Borwasser	14 boorwater
15 aspirin tablets	15 aspirine	15 Aspirin	15 aspirine
16 sleeping pills	16 somnifère, sédatif	16 Schlaftabletten	16 slaapmiddel
17 laxative	17 laxatif, purgatif	17 Abführmittel	17 laxeermiddel
18 anti-seasick pills	18 remède contre le mal de mer	18 Medikament gegen Seekrankheit	18 pillen tegen zeeziekte
19 suppositories	19 suppositoires	19 Zäpfchen	19 zetpillen
Please can you direct me to . . .?	S'il vous plaît, où puis-je trouver . . .?	Bitte zeigen Sie mir den Weg . . .	Als 't-U-blieft, kunt U me de weg wijzen naar . . .
1 the doctor	1 un médecin	1 zum Arzt	1 de dokter
2 the hospital	2 l'hôpital	2 zum Krankenhaus	2 het ziekenhuis
3 the dentist	3 un dentiste	3 zum Zahnarzt	3 de tandarts
4 the chemist	4 un pharmacien	4 zur Apotheke	4 een drogisterij, apotheek

148

DANSK
Førstehjælpkasse

1 sårforbinding, forbinds-
   pakke
2 at forbinde et sår
3 vat
4 hæfteplaster
5 forbinding
6 elastikbind, idealbind
7 saks
8 sikkerhedsnåle
9 pincet
10 termometer
11 antiseptisk cream
12 penicillin cream
13 desinfektionsmiddel
14 borvand, badevand
   til øjet
15 aspirin-tabletter
16 sovepiller
17 afføringsmidler
18 søsyge-tabletter
19 stikpiller

Hvor er der . . .?
1 læge
2 hospital
3 tandlæge
4 apotek

ITALIANO
Cassetta del pronto soccorso

1 pacchetto di medicazione

2 medicare una ferita
3 cotone idrofilo
4 cerotto
5 benda
6 benda elastica
7 forbici
8 spillo di sicurezza
9 pinze
10 termometro
11 pomata antisettica
12 pomata alla penicillina
13 disinfettante
14 collirio
15 compresse di aspirina
16 pillole per dormire,
   sonnifero
17 lassativo
18 pillole contro il mal di
   mare
19 supposte

Per piacere potete indicarmi
   . . .?
1 dov'è un dottore
2 dov'è l'ospedale
3 dov'è il dentista
4 dov'è il farmacista

ESPAÑOL
Botiquin

1 gasa

2 curar una herida
3 algodón hydrófilo
4 esparadrapo
5 venda
6 venda de elástico
7 tijeras
8 imperdibles
9 pinzas
10 termómetro
11 pomada de sulfamidas
12 pomada de penicilina
13 desinfectante
14 Optrex
15 pastillas de aspirina
16 píldoras somníferas
17 laxante
18 píldoras contra el mareo
19 supositorios

¿Por favor puede Vd
   guiarme . . .?
1 al médico
2 al hospital
3 al dentista
4 al farmacéutico

PORTUGUÊS
Caixa de medicamentos para socorro

1 penso

2 tratar uma ferida
3 algodão
4 adesivo
5 ligadura
6 ligadura elástica
7 tesoura
8 alfinetes de dama
9 pinças
10 termómetro
11 pomada antiséptica
12 pomada de penicilina
13 desinfectante
14 Optrex
15 aspirina, comprimidos de
   aspirina
16 comprimidos para dormir
17 laxativo
18 comp. para não enjoar
19 supositórios

Faz favor indica-me
1 um médico
2 um hospital
3 um dentista
4 uma farmácia

ENGLISH	FRANÇAIS	DEUTSCH	NEDERLANDS
Accident and illness	**Accidents et maladies**	**Unfälle und Krankheiten**	**Ongelukken en ziekte**
1 hæmorrhage	1 hémorragie	1 Blutung	1 bloeding
2 internal hæmorrhage	2 hémorragie interne	2 innere Blutung	2 inwendige bloeding
3 burn, scald	3 brûlure	3 Brandwunde, Verbrennung	3 brandwond, brandblaar
4 shock	4 traumatisme, choc	4 Schock	4 shock
5 fracture	5 fracture	5 Fraktur, Bruch	5 breuk
6 compound fracture	6 fracture compliquée	6 komplizierter Bruch	6 gecompliceerde breuk
7 swelling	7 enflure, hypertrophie	7 Schwellung	7 zwelling
8 bruise	8 contusion	8 Prellung	8 kneuzing, blauwe plek
9 drown, drowning	9 se noyer, noyade	9 Ertrinken	9 verdrinking
10 artificial respiration	10 respiration artificielle	10 künstliche Beatmung	10 kunstmatige ademhaling
11 carbon monoxide poisoning	11 asphyxie ou empoisonne-ment par l'oxyde de carbone	11 Kohlenmonoxidvergiftung	11 kolendamp vergiftiging
12 suffocation	12 asphyxie	12 Erstickung	12 verstikking
13 poisoning	13 empoisonnement	13 Vergiftung	13 vergiftiging
14 sunstroke	14 coup de soleil	14 Sonnenstich	14 zonnesteek
15 heatstroke	15 coup de chaleur	15 Hitzschlag	15 ——
16 sunburn	16 brûlure par le soleil	16 Sonnenbrand	16 zonnebrand
17 unconscious	17 évanoui, inconscient, comateux	17 ohnmächtig, bewußtlos	17 bewusteloos
18 electric shock	18 décharge électrique	18 elektrischer Schlag	18 elektrische schok
19 pulse	19 pouls	19 Puls	19 pols
20 high temperature, fever	20 fièvre	20 Fieber	20 een hoge temperatuur
21 pain	21 douleur	21 Schmerz	21 pijn
22 toothache	22 rage de dents	22 Zahnschmerzen	22 tandpijn
23 abscess	23 abcès	23 Abszeß	23 abces, zweer
24 infection	24 infection	24 Infektion	24 infectie
25 paralysis	25 paralysie	25 Lähmung	25 verlamming
26 rash	26 éruption	26 Hautausschlag	26 huiduitslag
27 stomach upset	27 digestion dérangée	27 Bauchbeschwerden, Magenbeschwerden	27 last van de maag, buik

DANSK	ITALIANO	ESPAÑOL	PORTUGUÊS
Ulykke og sygdom	**Infortunio e malattia**	**Acidentes y enfermedad**	**Acidentes e doenças**
1 blødning	1 emorragia	1 hemorragia	1 hemorragia
2 indvendig blødning	2 emorragia interna	2 hemorragia interna	2 hemorragia externa
3 brandsår	3 ustione, scottatura	3 quemadura, escaldado	3 queimadura, escaldadura
4 chok	4 shock	4 shock	4 choque
5 brud	5 frattura	5 fractura	5 fractura
6 kompliceret brud	6 frattura composta	6 fractura conminuta	6 fractura múltipla
7 svulme, hæve	7 gonfiore	7 hinchazón, hinchado	7 inchação
8 kvæstet, forslået	8 contusione	8 cardenal, chichón	8 contusão
9 drukne	9 annegare	9 ahogarse	9 afogar-se
10 kunstigt åndedræt	10 respirazione artificiale	10 respiración artificial	10 respiração artificial
11 kulilte-forgiftning	11 avvelenamento da monossido di carbonio	11 envenenamiento por óxido de carbono	11 intoxicação por gaz de óxido de carbono
12 kvælning	12 soffocazione	12 asfixia	12 sufocação
13 forgiftning	13 avvelenamento	13 envenenamiento	13 envenenamento
14 solstik	14 colpo di sole	14 insolación	14 insolação
15 hedeslag	15 colpo di calore	15 insolación	15 insolação devido ao calôr
16 solbrændt	16 scottatura da sole	16 quemadura del sol	16 queimadura de sol
17 bevidstløs	17 inconscienza	17 sin conocimiento	17 sem sentidos
18 elektrisk chock	18 shock elettrico	18 descarga eléctrica	18 choque eléctrico
19 puls	19 polso	19 pulso	19 pulso
20 feber, høj temperatur	20 febbre, temperatura alta	20 fiebre alta	20 temperatura alta, febre
21 smerte	21 dolore	21 dolor	21 dôr
22 tandpine	22 dolore di denti	22 dolor de muelas	22 dôr dos dentes
23 byld	23 ascesso	23 abceso, flemón	23 abcesso
24 infektion	24 infezione	24 infección	24 infecção
25 lammelse	25 paralisi	25 parálisis	25 paralisia
26 udslæt	26 sfogo, eruzione	26 urticaria	26 erupção de sangue
27 mavepine	27 stomaco in disordine	27 mal de estómago	27 cólicas

ENGLISH	FRANÇAIS	DEUTSCH	NEDERLANDS
On shore	**A terre**	**An Land**	**Aan land**
1 Please direct me to . . .	1 S'il vous plaît, voulez-vous m'indiquer . . .?	1 Bitte zeigen Sie mir den Weg nach . . .	1 Als't-U-blieft, kunt U mij de weg wijzen naar . . .
2 Where can I get . . .?	2 Où puis-je obtenir . . .?	2 Wo kann ich . . . bekommen?	2 Waar kan ik . . . verkrijgen?
3 How far is it to . . .?	3 Est-ce loin?	3 Wie weit ist es nach?	3 Hoe ver is het naar . . .?
4 left	4 à gauche	4 links	4 links
5 right	5 à droite	5 rechts	5 rechts
6 straight on	6 tout droit	6 geradeaus	6 recht door
7 How much does that cost?	7 Combien?	7 Was kostet es?	7 Hoeveel kost het?
8 Please give me 2 lbs	8 S'il vous plaît, voulez-vous me donner un kilo de . . .	8 Bitte geben Sie mir ein Kilo . . .	8 Kan ik als't-U-blieft een kilo hebben
9 garage	9 le garage	9 die Garage	9 de garage
10 bus	10 l'autobus	10 der Bus	10 de bus
11 tram	11 le tram	11 die Straßenbahn	11 de tram
12 bank	12 la banque	12 die Bank	12 de bank
13 railway station	13 la gare	13 der Bahnhof	13 het station
14 post office	14 la poste	14 das Postamt	14 het postkantoor
15 stamps	15 des timbres	15 die Briefmarken	15 de postzegels
16 ironmonger	16 la quinçaillerie	16 der Eisenwarenhändler	16 de ijzerwarenwinkel
17 dairy	17 la laiterie	17 das Milchgeschäft	17 de melkwinkel
18 milk	18 du lait	18 die Milch	18 de melk
19 butter	19 le beurre	19 die Butter	19 de boter
20 cheese	20 le fromage	20 der Käse	20 de kaas
21 eggs	21 des œufs	21 die Eier	21 de eieren
22 newspapers	22 les journaux	22 die Zeitungen	22 de kranten
23 beer	23 la bière	23 das Bier	23 het bier
24 wine	24 le vin	24 der Wein	24 de wijn
25 drinking water	25 l'eau potable	25 das Trinkwasser	25 het drinkwater

DANSK	ITALIANO	ESPAÑOL	PORTUGUÊS
I land	**A terra**	**En tierra**	**Em terra**
1 Hvor er der en . . .?	1 Per piacere potate indicarmi dov'è il . . .?	1 ¿Por favor puede Vd. guiarme à . . .?	1 Faz favor indica-me . . .?
2 Hvor kan jeg få . . .?	2 Dove posso procurarmi . . .?	2 ¿Dónde puedo conseguir . . .?	2 Aonde posso comprar . . .?
3 Hvor langt er der til . . .?	3 Quanto è distante . . .?	3 ¿Qué distancia hay a . . .?	3 Qual a distância até . . .?
4 venstre	4 sinistra	4 izquierda	4 esquerda
5 højre	5 destra	5 derecha	5 direita
6 lige ud	6 dritto cosi	6 derecho	6 sempre em frente
7 Hvad koster det?	7 quanto costa?	7 ¿Cuanto cuesta?	7 quanto custa
8 Vær så venlig at give mig et kilo	8 Per piacere mi dia un chilo di . . .	8 Por favor deme un kilo de . . .	8 Faz favor dá-me um quilo . . .
9 garage	9 il garage, l'autorimessa	9 garage	9 a garagem
10 omnibus	10 l'autobus	10 autobús	10 o autocarro
11 sporvogn	11 il treno	11 tranvía	11 o eléctrico
12 banken	12 la banca	12 banco	12 o banco
13 jernbanestation	13 la stazione ferrovia	13 estación de ferrocarril	13 a estação de combóios
14 postkontor	14 l'ufficio postale	14 correo	14 o correio
15 frimærker	15 i francobolli	15 sellos	15 os sêlos
16 isenkræmmer	16 il fabbro ferraio	16 ferretería	16 a loja de ferragens
17 mejeri	17 la latteria	17 lechería	17 a leitaria
18 mælk	18 il latte	18 leche	18 o leite
19 smør	19 il burro	19 mantequilla	19 a manteiga
20 ost	20 il formaggio	20 queso	20 o queijo
21 æg	21 le uova	21 huevos	21 os ovos
22 aviser	22 i giornali	22 periódicos	22 o jornal
23 øl	23 la birra	23 cerveza	23 a cerveja
24 vin	24 il vino	24 vino	24 o vinho
25 drikkevand	25 l'acqua potabile	25 agua potable	25 a água para beber

ENGLISH	FRANÇAIS	DEUTSCH	NEDERLANDS
On shore	**A terre**	**An Land**	**Aan land**
1 the butcher	1 le boucher	1 der Schlachter, Metzger	1 de slager
2 pork	2 le porc	2 das Schweinefleisch	2 het varkensvlees
3 ham	3 le jambon	3 der Schinken	3 de ham
4 bacon	4 le lard fumé	4 der Speck	4 de bacon, het ontbijtspek
5 veal	5 le veau	5 das Kalbfleisch	5 het kalfsvlees
6 lamb	6 l'agneau	6 das Lammfleisch	6 het lam
7 mutton	7 le mouton	7 das Hammelfleisch	7 het schapenvlees
8 chicken	8 poulet, coq, poularde	8 das Hühnchen	8 de kip
9 beef	9 le bœuf	9 das Rindfleisch	9 het rundvlees
10 the grocer	10 l'épicier	10 der Lebensmittelhändler	10 de kruidenier
11 tea	11 le thé	11 der Tee	11 de thee
12 coffee	12 le café	12 der Kaffee	12 de koffie
13 lard, fat	13 le saindoux	13 das Schmalz, Fett	13 het vet
14 oil	14 l'huile	14 das Öl	14 de olie
15 sugar	15 le sucre	15 der Zucker	15 de suiker
16 flour	16 la farine	16 das Mehl	16 de bloem, het meel
17 rice	17 le riz	17 der Reis	17 de rijst
18 jam	18 la confiture	18 die Marmelade	18 de jam
19 honey	19 le miel	19 der Honig	19 de honing
20 baker	20 le boulanger	20 der Bäcker	20 de bakker
21 bread	21 le pain	21 das Brot	21 het brood
22 greengrocer	22 le marchand de légumes	22 der Gemüsehändler	22 de groentewinkel
23 fruit	23 les fruits	23 das Obst	23 het fruit
24 vegetables	24 les légumes	24 das Gemüse	24 de groenten
25 fishmonger	25 le marchand de poisson	25 der Fischhändler	25 de vishandel
26 fish	26 le poisson	26 der Fisch	26 de vis
27 biscuits	27 les biscuits	27 die Kekse, das Gebäck	27 de koekjes, biscuitjes
28 vinegar	28 le vinaigre	28 der Essig	28 de azijn
29 detergent	29 le détergent	29 das Waschmittel	29 het wasmiddel

DANSK	ITALIANO	ESPAÑOL	PORTUGUÊS
I land	**A terra**	**En tierra**	**Em terra**
1 slagter	1 il macellaio	1 carnicero	1 o talho
2 svinekød	2 la carne di maiale	2 carne de cerdo	2 a carne de porco
3 skinke	3 il prosciutto	3 jamón	3 o fiambre
4 bacon	4 il lardo affumicato	4 tocino	4 o toucinho inglês
6 lammekød	5 la carne di vitello	5 carne de ternera	5 a carne de vitela
5 kalvekød	6 l'agnello	6 carne de cordero	6 a carne de borrêgo
7 bedekød	7 il montone	7 carne de cordero	7 a carne de carneiro
8 kylling	8 il pollo	8 pollo	8 a galinha, o frango
9 oksekød	9 il manzo	9 carne de vaca	9 a carne de vaca
10 købmand, urtekræmmer	10 il salumiere, il droghiere	10 tendero de comestibles	10 a mercearia
11 te	11 il té	11 té	11 o chá
12 kaffe	12 il caffè	12 café	12 o café
13 fedt	13 lo strutto, il lardo	13 manteca	13 a banha
14 spise-olie	14 l'olio	14 aceite	14 o azeite, óleo
15 sukker	15 lo zucchero	15 azúcar	15 o açúcar
16 mel	16 la farina	16 harina	16 a farinha
17 ris	17 il riso	17 arroz	17 o arroz
18 syltetøj	18 la marmellata	18 mermelada	18 o dôce, a compota
19 honning	19 il miele	19 miel	19 o mel
20 bager	20 il fornaio	20 panadero	20 a padaria
21 brød	21 il pane	21 pan	21 o pão
22 grønthandler	22 il verduraio	22 verdulero	22 a frutaria
23 frugt	23 la frutta	23 frutas	23 a fruta
24 grøntsager	24 le verdure	24 legumbres, verduras	24 os legumes, as hortaliças
25 fiskehandler	25 il pescivendolo	25 pescadería	25 a peixeira
26 fisk	26 il pesce	26 pescado	26 o peixe
27 tvebak-kiks	27 i biscotti	27 galletas	27 as bolachas, os biscoitos
28 eddike	28 l'aceto	28 vinagre	28 o vinagre
29 rensemiddel, sabe	29 il detergente	29 detergente	29 o detergente

METRES—FEET

Metres	Feet or Metres	Feet
0,31	1	3,28
0,61	2	6,56
0,91	3	9,84
1,22	4	13,12
1,52	5	16,40
1,83	6	19,69
2,13	7	22,97
2,44	8	26,25
2,74	9	29,53
3,05	10	32,81
6,10	20	65,62
9,14	30	98,42
12,19	40	131,23
15,24	50	164,04
30,48	100	328,09

1 metre = 3,280845 feet
1 foot = 0,3047995 metres

CENTIMETRES—INCHES

Cm	In or Cm	In
2,54	1	0,39
5,08	2	0,79
7,62	3	1,18
10,16	4	1,57
12,70	5	1,97
15,24	6	2,36
17,78	7	2,76
20,32	8	3,15
22,86	9	3,54
25,40	10	3,94
50,80	20	7,87
76,20	30	11,81
101,60	40	15,75
127,00	50	19,69
254,00	100	39,37

1 inch = 2,539996 centimetres
1 centimetre = 0,3937014 inches

KILOGRAMMES—POUNDS

Kg	Lb or Kg	Lb
0,45	1	2,20
0,91	2	4,41
1,36	3	6,61
1,81	4	8,82
2,27	5	11,02
2,72	6	13,23
3,18	7	15,43
3,63	8	17,64
4,08	9	19,84
4,54	10	22,05
9,07	20	44,09
13,61	30	66,14
18,14	40	88,19
22,68	50	110,23
45,36	100	220,46

1 kilogramme = 2,20462 lb
1 lb = 0,45359 kilogrammes

BRITISH MEASURES

12 inches = 1 foot: 3 feet = 1 yard
6 feet — 1 fathom
100 fathoms — 1 cable
6080 feet = 10 cables = 1 nautical mile
1852 metres — 1 nautical mile
1760 yards = 5280 feet = 1 statute mile

16 oz (ounces) — 1 lb
14 lb (pounds) — 1 stone
112 lb — 1 cwt
20 cwt (hundredweight) 1 ton

2 pints = 1 quart: 4 quarts = 1 gallon

CUBIC CAPACITY

1 cu. inch	16,387 c.c.
1 cu. foot 1728 cu. in	0,028 c.m.
1 cu. yard (27 cu. ft)	0,765 c.m.
1 cu. centimetre	0,061 cu. in
1 cu. decimetre	61,023 cu. in
1 cu. metre (1000 c.dm.)	35,315 cu. ft
1 cu. metre	1,31 cu. yd

N.B.—The comma has been used throughout in place of the decimal point, because this is the Continental method.

LB/IN^2 — KG/CM^2

Lb/in^2	Kg/cm^2	Lb/in^2	Kg/cm^2
10	0,703	32	2,250
12	0,844	34	2,390
14	0,984	36	2,531
16	1,125	40	2,812
18	1,266	45	3,164
20	1,406	50	3,515
22	1,547	60	4,218
24	1,687	70	4,921
26	1,828	80	5,625
28	1,969	90	6,328
30	2,109	100	7,031

TEMPERATURE			LITRES—IMPERIAL GALLONS		
Celsius	Fahrenheit	Litres	Litres or Gals	Gals	
−30	−22	4,55	1	0,22	
−20	−4	9,09	2	0,44	
−10	+14	13,64	3	0,66	
−5	+23	18,18	4	0,88	
0	+32	22,73	5	1,10	
+5	+41	27,28	6	1,32	
+10	+50	31,82	7	1,54	
+20	+68	36,37	8	1,76	
+30	+86	40,91	9	1,98	
+36,9	+98,4	45,46	10	2,20	
+37,2	+99	90,92	20	4,40	
+38,8	+100	136,38	30	6,60	
+38,3	+101	181,84	40	8,80	
+38,9	+102	227,30	50	11,10	
+39,4	+103	340,95	75	16,50	
+40	+104	454,60	100	22,00	
+41,1	+106	909,18	200	44,00	
+50	+122	2272,98	500	110,00	
+60	+140	4545,96	1000	220,00	
+70	+158				
+80	+176		1,42 dcls = $\frac{1}{4}$ pint		
+90	+194		2,48 dcls = $\frac{1}{2}$ pint		
+100	+212		5,68 dcls = 1 pint		
			5,68 dcls = $\frac{1}{8}$ gallon		

METRES²—FEET²

Metres²		Feet²
0,09	1	10,76
0,93	10	107,64
1,86	20	215,28
2,79	30	322,92
3,72	40	430,56
4,65	50	538,19
5,57	60	645,83
6,50	70	753,47
7,43	80	861,11
8,36	90	968,75
9,29	100	1076,39

KILOMETRES—STATUTE MILES

Kms		Miles
1,61	1	0,62
8,05	5	3,11
12,87	8	4,97
16	10	6
32	20	12
48	30	19
64	40	25
80	50	31
121	75	47
161	100	62
402	250	155
805	500	311

METRES—FATHOMS

Metres	Fathoms	Feet
0,91	$\frac{1}{2}$	3
1,83	1	6
3,66	2	12
5,49	3	18
7,32	4	24
9,14	5	30
18,29	10	60
36,58	20	120
54,86	30	180

ROPE

In England rope is measured by its circumference. On the Continent rope is measured by its diameter. A formula to convert these dimensions is:

$$\frac{\text{Circumference}}{\text{in inches}} = \frac{\text{Diameter in mm}}{8}$$

N.B.—The comma has been used throughout in place of the decimal point because this is the Continental method.

ENGLISH
International Code of Signals

D Keep clear of me, I am manœuvring with difficulty
E I am altering my course to starboard
F I am disabled. Communicate with me
G I require a pilot
H I have a pilot on board
I I am altering my course to port

L You should stop your vessel instantly
O Man overboard
Q My vessel is healthy and I request free pratique

S My engines are going astern

U You are running into danger
V I require assistance
W I require medical assistance

FRANÇAIS
Code des Signaux Internationaux

D Je manœuvre difficilement

E Je viens sur tribord

F Je suis désemparé

G Je demande un pilote
H J'ai un pilote à bord
I Je viens sur bâbord

L Stoppez immédiatement

O Un homme à la mer
Q Mon navire n'a pas de malades à bord et je demande la libre-pratique

S Je bats en arrière

U Vous courez un danger
V J'ai besoin de secours
W J'ai besoin d'un médecin

DEUTSCH
Internationale Signalbuch

D Halten Sie frei von mir. Ich manövriere unter Schwierigkeiten
E Ich ändere meinen Kurs nach Steuerbord
F Ich bin manövrierunfähig; treten Sie mit mir in Verbindung
G Ich benötige einen Lotsen
H Ich habe einen Lotsen an Bord
I Ich ändere meinen Kurs nach Backbord
L Bringen Sie ihr Fahrzeug sofort zum Stehen
O Mann über Bord
Q An Bord ist alles 'gesund' und ich bitte um freie Verkehrserlaubnis
S Meine Maschine geht rückwärts
U Sie begeben sich in Gefahr
V Ich benötige Hilfe
W Ich benötige ärztliche Hilfe

NEDERLANDS
Internationale Seinkode

D Houdt vrij van mij. Ik kan moeilijk manœvreren
E Ik verander koers naar stuurboord
F Ik ben ontredderd. Stelt u met mij in verbinding
G Ik verlang een loods
H Ik heb een loods aan boord
I Ik verander koers naar bakboord

L Gij moet uw schip onmiddelijk tot stilstand brengen
O Man over boord
Q Mijn schip is gezond. Ik verzoek practica

S Ik sla achteruit

U Gij stuurt een gevaarlijke koers
V Ik heb hulp nodig
W Ik heb medische hulp nodig

DANSK
International Signalkode

D Hold klar af mig, jeg har vanskelighed ved at manøvrere

E Jeg drejer til styrbord
F Jeg er ikke manøvredygtig: sæt Dem i forbindelse med mig
G Jeg ønsker lods
H Jeg har lods ombord
I Jeg drejer til bagbord
L Stands farten øjeblikkelig

O Mand overbord
Q Mit skib er smittefrit, og jeg anmoder om fri praktika

S Min maskine bakke

U De stævner mod fare

V Jeg behøver hjælp
W Jeg ønsker lægehjælp

ITALIANO
Codice Internazionale dei Segnali

D Mantenetevi largo da me. Sto manovrando con difficoltà

E Sto accostando a dritta
F Sono inabilitato. Comunicate con me
G Ho bisogno del pilota
H Ho il pilota a bordo
I Sto accostando a sinistra
L Fermate immediatamente la vostra nave

O Uomo in mare
Q Le condizioni di salute a bordo sono buone e chiedo libera pratica

S Le mie macchine vanno indietro

U State dirigendo verso un pericolo
V Ho bisogno di aiuto
W Ho bisogno di assistenza sanitaria

ESPAÑOL
Código Internacional de Señales

D Manténgase separado de mí; estoy maniobrando con dificultad

E Estoy cayendo a estribor
F Estoy inutilizado. Comunique conmigo
G Necesito práctico
H Tengo práctico a bordo
I Estoy cayendo a babor
L Pare usted su buque inmediatamente

O ¡Hombre al agua!
Q Mi buque está 'sano' y pido libre plática

S Mis máquinas van atrás

U Gobierna usted hacia un peligro
V Necesito auxilio
W Necesito asistencia médica

PORTUGUÊS
Código Internacional de Sinais

D Conserve-se afastado de mim. Estou manobrando com dificuldade

E Estou guinando para estibordo
F Estou com avaria. Comunique comigo
G Preciso de Pilôto
H Tenho um Pilôto a bordo
I Estou guinando para bombordo
L Pare o seu navio imediatamente

O Homem ao mar
Q O estado sanitário do meu navio é bom. Peço livre prática

S As minhas máquinas estão andando a ré
U Você vai sobre um perigo

V Preciso de socorro
W Peço assistência mêdica

ENGLISH	FRANÇAIS		DEUTSCH	NEDERLANDS	DANSK		ITALIANO	ESPAÑOL	PORTUGUÊS
one	un	1	eins	een	en	1	uno	uno	um
two	deux	2	zwei	twee	to	2	due	dos	dois
three	trois	3	drei	drie	tre	3	tre	tres	três
four	quatre	4	vier	vier	fire	4	quattro	cuatro	quatro
five	cinq	5	fünf	vijf	fem	5	cinque	cinco	cinco
six	six	6	sechs	zes	seks	6	sei	seis	seis
seven	sept	7	sieben	zeven	syv	7	sette	siete	sete
eight	huit	8	acht	acht	otte	8	otto	ocho	oito
nine	neuf	9	neun	negen	ni	9	nove	nueve	nove
ten	dix	10	zehn	tien	ti	10	dieci	diez	dez
eleven	onze	11	elf	elf	elleve	11	undici	once	onze
twelve	douze	12	zwölf	twaalf	tolv	12	dodici	doce	doze
thirteen	treize	13	dreizehn	dertien	tretten	13	tredici	trece	treze
fourteen	quatorze	14	vierzehn	veertien	fjorten	14	quattordici	catorce	catorze
fifteen	quinze	15	fünfzehn	vijftien	femten	15	quindici	quince	quinze
sixteen	seize	16	sechzehn	zestien	seksten	16	sedici	dieciséis	dezaseis
seventeen	dix-sept	17	siebzehn	zeventien	sytten	17	diciassette	diecisiete	dezasete
eighteen	dix-huit	18	achtzehn	achttien	atten	18	diciotto	dieciocho	dezoito
nineteen	dix-neuf	19	neunzehn	negentien	nitten	19	diciannove	diecinueve	dezanove
twenty	vingt	20	zwanzig	twintig	tyve	20	venti	veinte	vinte
thirty	trente	30	dreißig	dertig	tredive	30	trenta	treinta	trinta
forty	quarante	40	vierzig	veertig	fyrre	40	quaranta	cuaranta	quarenta
fifty	cinquante	50	fünfzig	vijftig	halvtreds	50	cinquanta	cincuenta	cinquenta
sixty	soixante	60	sechzig	zestig	tres	60	sessanta	sesenta	sessenta
seventy	soixante-dix	70	siebzig	zeventig	halvfjerds	70	settanta	setenta	setenta
eighty	quatre-vingt	80	achtzig	tachtig	firs	80	ottanta	ochenta	oitenta
ninety	quatre-vingt-dix	90	neunzig	negentig	halvfems	90	novanta	noventa	noventa
one hundred	cent	100	einhundert	honderd	hundrede	100	ciento	cien	cem
thousand	mille	1000	tausend	duizend	tusind	1000	mille	mil	mil